Framing Empire

Framing Empire

Postcolonial Adaptations of Victorian Literature in Hollywood

Jerod Ra'Del Hollyfield

EDINBURGH
University Press

Edinburgh University Press is one of the leading university presses in the UK. We publish academic books and journals in our selected subject areas across the humanities and social sciences, combining cutting-edge scholarship with high editorial and production values to produce academic works of lasting importance. For more information visit our website: edinburghuniversitypress.com

Edinburgh University Press Ltd
The Tun – Holyrood Road
12 (2f) Jackson's Entry
Edinburgh EH8 8PJ

First published in hardback by Edinburgh University Press 2018

Typeset in 11/13 Monotype Ehrhardt by
Servis Filmsetting Ltd, Stockport, Cheshire

A CIP record for this book is available from the British Library

ISBN 978 1 4744 2994 8 (hardback)
ISBN 978 1 4744 2995 5 (paperback)
ISBN 978 1 4744 2996 2 (webready PDF)
ISBN 978 1 4744 2997 9 (epub)

Contents

Figures

Acknowledgements

I owe a great deal to those who have directly and indirectly offered their support, guidance and suggestions during the gestation of this project. I began my career as a graduate student with a vague idea of studying the relationship between postcolonial studies, film and the Victorian novel. Over the course of the next seven years, a series of insightful and inspiring academics trained me to articulate my inchoate thoughts. As both a mentor and friend, Professor Pallavi Rastogi at Louisiana State University (LSU) served as my dissertation director and advisor, helping me shape portions of this project. Professor Rastogi gave me opportunities to teach courses during my postdoctoral year to upper-division students; I trial-ballooned my notes on several of the adaptations under discussion in this book (that were not part of my graduate work) in these teaching sessions. My other mentors at LSU, including Professors Sharon Weltman, Carl Freedman and the late Jack May, also shared their wealth of knowledge and were essential to guiding my intellectual development toward the interdisciplinary approach central to this project. I would also like to thank Professors Chris Holmlund, Charles Maland, Misty Anderson and Urmila Seshagiri at the University of Tennessee-Knoxville, who continue to provide advice, friendship and support though I have been out of their classrooms for over a decade.

This book would not have been possible without the interest of the editorial staff at Edinburgh University Press, especially Gillian Leslie, who encouraged me to submit my proposal and offered helpful feedback at every juncture. So did Richard Strachan, who navigated the sundry paperwork and logistics with the patience required of working with a first-time academic monograph writer. Copyeditor Jill Laidlaw also made innumerable contributions to this final iteration of the book with suggestions that increased the precision of its language and an eye for detail that caught issues that no one else noticed, including its author.

I also owe endless gratitude to Ryan Pait and Sarah De George, my graduate research assistants, who took on a host of sometimes rote (and often brutally boring) tasks with an unwavering energy and positive attitudes despite ending up down many a rabbit hole. My colleague, Professor Dawn Hall, was also instrumental in suggesting I take this project to Edinburgh. I must additionally give credit to the faculty at Georgia Southern University who host the annual British Commonwealth and Postcolonial Studies conference in Savannah, Georgia, especially Professors Joe Pellegrino, Dustin Anderson and Gautam Kundu. I have presented work from nearly every chapter of this book at these meetings, which has fostered vital conversation from some of the best scholars in the field and has greatly shaped the content.

I thank my good fortune for Melinda Darby Phipps, who came into my life just as the deadline for this project loomed and sacrificed numerous evenings and weekends to voluntary proofreading, formatting and pep-talking that I never asked for and often didn't deserve, considering my months-long academic quarantine. Years after the release of this book, I will remember her dedication to a project for which she never signed up. Finally, to my parents, Jerry and Cynthia Hollyfield, I owe the greatest debt. They have seen me draft version after version of this idea since suggesting I pursue graduate study and encouraged me to remain vigilant until it reached this final form. You gave me the space to develop my perspectives and supported my education and intellectual growth unconditionally, which I can never repay.

INTRODUCTION

Accented Slants, Hollywood Genres – an Interfidelity Approach to Adaptation Theory

In the wake of British decolonisation, Hollywood has seen an influx of filmmakers from former colonised territories forging successful Hollywood careers after achieving notoriety in their homelands, including Peter Weir, Mira Nair, Gavin Hood, Shekhar Kapur, Gillian Armstrong, George Miller, Baz Luhrmann, Craig Gillespie, Jane Campion, Taika Waititi, John Woo, and Kar Wai Wong. Considering the preoccupations with the postcolonial concerns of their homelands in career cementing films such as Australian Weir's meditation on urban aboriginals in *The Last Wave* (1977) and Hood's Oscar-winning account of South African gangs, *Tsotsi* (2005), such postcolonial filmmakers who made the transition to Hollywood find themselves in a unique position, not only to address the lingering influence of European colonialism on their nations of origin but also to negotiate transnational corporate imperialism through their participation in and often subversive use of Hollywood filmmaking. For such filmmakers, maintaining their political sensibilities during the transition from national cinema to Hollywood allowed them to extend their postcolonial critique to an international scale.

However, while such filmmakers have retained their auteur status in Hollywood, several have opted to undertake film adaptations of British texts over the past two decades, frequently choosing the Victorian literature of Britain's imperial century as their sources as a way to integrate the perspectives of their homelands into works that stereotype or ignore the presence of the colonised in a manner similar to a wide array of postcolonial texts such as Jean Rhys's *Wide Sargasso Sea* (1966), Tayeb Salih's *Season of Migration to the North* (1966), J. M. Coetzee's *Foe* (1986), and Peter Carey's *Jack Maggs* (1997) that, in the words of Salman Rushdie, 'write back' to the imperial centre.[1] In addition, such postcolonial filmmakers rewrite and reappropriate Empire literature within an industry that represents the cultural arm of the transnational corporation central to contemporary imperialism. As a result, these adaptations deserve scrutiny as useful texts in understanding how post-colonial nations contend with the legacy of colonialism while firmly rooted in the imperial tendencies of global capitalism.

This project discusses how postcolonial filmmakers adapting Victorian novels for Hollywood studios contend with the legacies of British colonialism while addressing Hollywood's cultural and economic influence in the globalised world. I seek to highlight the importance of such adaptations to the fields of postcolonial, film and Victorian studies. In addition, I hope to fill the gaps in previous critical work on the relationship between postcolonial studies and film adaptations of Victorian novels largely because, aside from brief mentions in texts such as Linda Hutcheon's *A Theory of Adaptation* (2006) and Sandra Ponzanesi's *The Postcolonial Culture Industry* (2014), such adaptations have either been relatively ignored by the academic community or, in the case of films like Campion's *The Portrait of a Lady* (1996) and Danny Boyle's *Slumdog Millionaire* (2008) not considered Victorian adaptations at all.

While contemporary trends in international film financing have challenged Hollywood's status as a prolific, solitary production entity, the industry has always maintained an international scope even during the peak of studio system filmmaking. Founded primarily by Eastern European Jewish immigrants and sustaining itself with the work of immigrant filmmakers from Fritz Lang, Alfred Hitchcock, and Billy Wilder to Roman Polanski, Paul Verhoeven, and Guillermo del Toro, Hollywood is an industry built on diaspora, historically acting as a shelter for artists seeking to escape tumultuous political situations, be they World War II, the Cold War or the various civil wars of the late 20th century. As the imperial power structure has shifted from European nations dominating native populations to multinational conglomerates shaping the globalised economy, filmmakers from former colonies have employed the film medium to respond. Since film surpassed literature as the dominant form of mass artistic communication in the middle of the 20th century, the imperialist critiques of postcolonial writers such as Chinua Achebe and Rushdie have in many cases shifted to the multiplex. However, while artists from colonised nations who desire to meditate on their own native cultures in their work used to face only the paradox of critiquing an empire through its own language, filmmakers desiring similar critiques in the contemporary economic climate must now also face what Martin Scorsese calls 'acting as a smuggler' for their own ideologies to finance multimillion-dollar projects.[2] As a result of this shift toward neocolonial multinational influence, attempts to write back must now traverse the barriers of media, history and corporate culture to reach their intended audience.

Yet, in a global economy fueled by what Ellen Meiksins Wood deems 'surplus imperialism' in which the 'economic imperatives of "the market" do much of the imperial work' in lieu of 'extra-economic powers' such as national militaries and territorial empires, the concepts of diaspora and the imperial centre become much more complicated.[3] When the United Nations Educational, Scientific, and Cultural Organization released the results of its study on national film production in May 2009, it revealed a slippage in industrial prominence for a Hollywood already undergoing dramatic economic shifts because of recession, devalued currency, mergers, and the beginnings of the streaming revolution that would disrupt the industry in the next decade. Though long ago surpassed by India and its Bollywood film industry in the sheer number of films produced each year, the American film industry found itself usurped by Nigeria's burgeoning film industry, Nollywood, for the first time. In the study that surveyed film production in 99 countries during 2006, UNESCO found that Bollywood produced 1,091 feature-length films to Nollywood's 872 productions. Maintaining a distant third with 485 features, the US's numbers were much closer to those of Japan (417 productions) and China (330 productions) than the two nations that now maintain the greatest production presences in the international film industry.[4]

Although demonstrating what appears to be a weakening of the American film industry's status as a centre for film production, the UNESCO study also reveals the enduring privileged status of Hollywood cinema in the international culture industry. Hollywood films continued to dominate the global box-office and English remained the most frequently used language in the industry to maximise international distribution potential, exhibiting that while postcolonial national film industries of countries like India and Nigeria may be growing, they remain controlled by the lingering, albeit less direct, influence of Hollywood.[5] A more indicative example of Hollywood's ubiquitous international presence than sheer statistical data is apparent in how the Bollywood and Nollywood film industries that have surpassed Hollywood in production remain defined by Western media and organisations such as the United Nations as permutations of 'Hollywood'. Despite their relative autonomy, they remain rooted within the framework of a dominant cultural force. As Edward W. Said writes:

> Whereas a century ago European culture was associated with a white man's presence, indeed with his directly domineering (and hence resistible) physical presence, we now have in addition an international media presence that insinuates itself, frequently at a level below conscious awareness, over a fantastically wide range. The phrase 'cultural imperialism' . . . loses some of its meaning when applied to the presence of television serials like *Dynasty* or *Dallas* in, say France or Japan, but becomes pertinent again when viewed in a global perspective.[6]

Said's characterisation of American media certainly positions Hollywood's international presence as a mechanism of cultural imperialism. However, it also exposes how the definitions of Indian and Nigerian cinema as Bollywood and Nollywood respectively have affected the structure of national film industries so deeply that even their content and business models mirror that of their namesake. Seeking to challenge the global dominance of Hollywood, Bollywood cinema is produced to appeal to both domestic and international audiences, more focused on presenting musical spectacle and heteronormative romantic fantasies that re-enforce the values of traditional family structures.[7] Likewise, though utilising independent film practices such as digital video and alternative screening in homes, Nollywood cinema has largely borrowed its content from politically innocuous soap operas and the work of the Yoruba travelling theatre in an effort for multi-demographic appeal and international popularity.[8] Though some Nollywood films such as Kingsley Ogoro's *Osuofia in London* (2003) and its 2004 sequel (*Osuofia in London 2*) have begun contending with the legacies of colonialism, diaspora and military rule, they remain broad comedies with mass appeal.

As a result of their similarities with the Hollywood film industry's goal of international dissemination, both Bollywood and Nollywood echo Michael Hardt and Antonio Negri's discussion of the culture industry infrastructure that produces the conditions and terms of government for Empire – the globalised imperial force of transnational corporations that have replaced nation-based colonial endeavours. As Hardt and Negri write:

> . . . there is already under way a massive centralization of control through the (de facto or de jure) unification of the major elements of the information and communication power structure: Hollywood, Microsoft, IBM, AT&T, and so forth. The new communication technologies, which hold out the promise of a new democracy and a new social equality, have in fact created new lines of inequality and exclusion, both within the dominant countries and especially outside them.[9]

With national film industries such as Bollywood and Nollywood operating under similar mechanisms as Hollywood, the potential not only for Empire's commodification of national cultures but also for the culture industry to curtail dissent from media artists comes to fruition under the aegis of cultural fusion and globalised perspectives. Such efforts at control often manifest themselves in the international coproductions that have become increasingly prominent: Paramount Pictures and Reliance BIG Entertainment's historically unprecedented 2010 declaration for more Bollywood productions in Los Angeles, Nollywood actress Omoni Oboli turning down a role in a Hollywood project that called for multiple nude scenes, American filmmaker Paul Schrader signing a contract to direct a Bollywood action film, and – perhaps most famously – New Zealand-based filmmaker Peter Jackson using his *The Lord of The Rings Trilogy*'s on-location shooting in his homeland to revitalise the nation's film industry to such an extent it developed an official Ministry of *The Lord of the Rings* to address the production's effects on tourism and the local economy.[10] Such instances occasionally cause controversy, such as the whitewashing debate centred around Matt Damon's starring role in Zhang Yimou's Chinese-American coproduction and box-office failure *The Great Wall* (2016) or the additional scenes added exclusively to the Chinese release of Marvel's *Iron Man 3* (2013) – a partnership between Disney and DMG Entertainment.[11] However, considering that over 57% of ticket sales for Hollywood films come from the international box-office, even the national culture of the American blockbuster is not immune from the effects of Hardt and Negri's Empire as studios have become far more concerned with appealing to diverse global audiences, shifts that, in the words of Kirk Goldsberry, 'directly affect the look and feel of our precious summer blockbusters . . . Once upon a time, Hollywood studios catered strictly to American tastes. And in a way, they still do – after all, what's more American than unbridled global capitalism?'[12]

Arguing that the narrative and stylistic conventions that Hollywood developed in the early twentieth century were an attempt to break away from British influences and create a distinctly American cultural form, this project discusses how Hollywood has assumed a contradictory identity – originally functioning as a form of resistance but transitioning into an imperial force in line with the unbridled global capitalism Goldsberry discusses. In articulating an 'interfidelity' theory of adaptation, I bridge fidelity criticism, postcolonial studies, and contrapuntal readings of source texts with studies of political economy in order to position Hollywood cinema as a location of past and present imperialisms. What results is a method of adaptation based on the relationships between literary texts that also demonstrates a shared foundation among the postcolonial adaptations featured in this study. Establishing my theoretical framework, I structure the rest of the book as an application of the interfidelity model to a series of postcolonial film adaptations of Victorian literature made within distinct national and colonial contexts.

DETERMINING AN INTERFIDELITY APPROACH TO POSTCOLONIAL FILM ADAPTATION

Adaptations of Victorian literature have remained a staple in Hollywood and other national film industries since the advent of cinema, especially after, as Thomas Leitch writes, 'the aesthetic of the dialogue-driven synch-sound film merged more closely with that of the nineteenth-century English novel.'[13] Even as tentpole franchises and reboots began overtaking multiplexes in the mid-2000s, the films in what Dudley Andrew deems the 'cine-literary blockbuster' genre continue to best reflect the self-image of 'Global Hollywood.'[14] However, despite these clear parallels between the colonial discourse of the Victorian novel and the cultural prowess of Hollywood's product, viewing Hollywood adaptations as postcolonial has remained rare barring discussions of overtly political films such as Jack Gold's *Man Friday* (1975) and Patricia Rozema's *Mansfield Park* (1999).[15]

One could, in part, attribute this critical oversight to a confusion over what constitutes postcolonial cinema, an umbrella category that, when taking ideology, artistic collaboration, financing, shooting locations, and thematic concerns into consideration could include films as disparate as Sydney Pollack's *Out of Africa* (1985), *Tsotsi*, James Cameron's *Avatar* (2009), Baz Luhrmann's *William Shakespeare's Romeo + Juliet* (1996), *Osuofia in London*, George Miller's *Mad Max: Fury Road* (2015), Gurinder Chadha's *Bend It Like Beckham* (2002), Michael Showalter's *The Big Sick* (2017) and the entire oeuvre of Merchant Ivory Productions. Such an unwieldy definition has led postcolonial critics such as Sandra Ponzanesi to proclaim the impossibility of the category, especially in comparison to postcolonial literature. As Ponzanesi writes, 'What makes a film postcolonial is rather its engagement with the paradigm shift that involves opening up critical boundaries, both of film genres, schools and traditions, and of geographical locations.'[16] Additionally, the intersections of the Victorian and postcolonial in film have likely escaped scholarly attention due in part to the ongoing discussions concerning the purpose and status of adaptation within film studies. Over the past two decades, adaptation theory has sought to extricate itself from the confines of fidelity criticism's model of pitting literary text against film, an approach that Brian McFarlane views as dependent 'on a notion of the text as having and rendering up to the (intelligent) reader a single, correct 'meaning' which the filmmaker has either adhered to or in some sense violated or tampered with.'[17]

Perceiving fidelity criticism as limited beyond evaluation purposes, critics embraced the theoretical framework of contemporary film theory, with its focus on applying the structuralism of Barthes and Saussure and the Althusserian-Lacanian paradigm to uncover the overarching ideology of cinema. Contemporary film theory's effect on adaptation studies has led to numerous and detailed breakdowns of source texts and adaptations. Yet, through its focus on the relationship between ideological formation and cinema, such a model of adaptation theory neglects critical reading of individual texts' content beyond explaining their structures, a weakness that complicates its effectiveness in analysing adaptation as a form of resistance so vital to its study in a postcolonial context. As Noël Carroll writes:

> I deny that structures of representation, at the level of abstraction discussed by contemporary film theorists, are essentially ideological. In my view, the ideological operation of films resides, roughly speaking, in their content and its rhetorical inflection rather than in their use, *simpliciter*, of cinematography, narration, and what is called classical editing.[18]

While approaching adaptation from the perspectives of structuralism and the Althusserian-Lacanian paradigm is helpful in navigating post- and neocolonial contexts, as Carroll indicates, too broad a focus on cinematic ideology as a whole overlooks the adaptation strategies postcolonial writers and filmmakers deploy as forms of resistance and subversion in individual texts. These strategies are not only vital to understanding postcolonial identity and opposing imperial forces but also are reliant on an iteration of the much-maligned fidelity criticism that, in the words of Fredric Jameson, serves as a scarecrow that is a reminder to

> Keep faith with some Lacanian gap or rift within this equally split subject that is the object of adaptation studies; it stages a well-nigh Derridean vigilance to the multiple forms difference takes in the object of such studies and insists on fidelity to the difference rather than to this or that ideology of the original.[19]

With global capitalism evolving as an international force as a result of media advances such as digitisation and the Internet, adaptation theory has also focused increased attention on the adaptation industry amid its anti-fidelity crusade in an attempt to extend adaptation studies beyond the realm of literature and film. In advocating an 'Industry-centric adaptation model', Simone Murray writes

> . . . rather than seeing production-focused analysis as merely a corrective to existing critical imbalances and this an end, the current project flags how conceptualizing the industrial subculture of adaptation provides new understanding of why texts take shape the way they do and how they influence and respond to audience evaluation.[20]

Through the industry-centric model, adaptation theory seeks an understanding of adaptation in the age of global capital; how transnational media corporations position novels such as Michael Crichton's *Jurassic Park* (1990) or Stephenie Meyer's *Twilight* (2005) in an endless cycle of adaptation through various media, including films, television commercials, video games, Internet content, film novelisations, theme-park rides, and, in the case of the former, soft reboots steeped in nostalgia that reinvigorate a franchise and its earning potential.[21] Similar to contemporary film theory, the industry-centric model aids in understanding the mechanisms of corporate imperialism through its focus on the commodification and dissemination of textual properties. However, it fails to account for the fissures that erupt in the adaptation process – the moments when writers and filmmakers can subvert the structure and imbue the adaptation with their own political perspectives – as a result of its attention to market forces rather than the content of individual texts and the various iterations integral to the industry-centric model.

Though useful in grappling with the complexities of adaptation, previous models of adaptation theory all demonstrate deficiencies in addressing the politics inherent in adaptation, highlighting the necessity of an approach that examines the process as a fundamental tool in interrogating past and present imperial ideologies. As Leitch writes, 'The whole process of film adaptation offers an obvious practical demonstration of the necessity of rewriting that many commentators have ignored because of their devotion to literature.'[22] This necessity to rewrite innate to adaptation is fundamental to discussions of how postcolonial writers and filmmakers 'write back' to the imperial forces that subjugate them. Taking up Carroll's call to 'generate small-scale theories, watching out of the corner of our eye to see if their results can be gathered into larger theoretical constructions', I propose an approach to adaptation that focuses on the various interactions between individual literature and film texts in a postcolonial context and accents the potential of adaptation to disrupt imperial power structures and negotiate a voice for its subjects, which I call the interfidelity approach to postcolonial film adaptation.[23]

Rather than oppose the numerous advancements that previous adaptation theories have made over the past fifty years, the interfidelity approach bridges the field's rich history of criticism with a politically relevant analysis informed by postcolonial theory. With its focus on analysing the relationships between specific texts, fidelity criticism serves as a strong foundation for the interfidelity approach, illustrating Casie Hermansson's contention that,

> Just as announcing the 'death of the author', *pace* Roland Barthes – while freeing – proved premature and in many ways costly to literary studies, so too claiming the 'death of the source', while it undoubtedly catalyzed adaptation studies, now needs to reckon with what has been lost in the process.[24]

Within the context of interfidelity, what has been lost with the demonisation of fidelity criticism is a cohesive approach to postcolonial film studies that hinges on textual difference, politicised omissions and inclusive rewriting. As its name implies, interfidelity also owes a debt to Linda Hutcheon, whose groundbreaking work on intertextuality as an adaptation approach for 'opening up a text's possible meanings to intertextual echoing' has significant implications for a postcolonial outlook focused on negotiating colonial legacies and contemporary concerns.[25] Likewise, contemporary film theory and the industry-centric adaptation model prove helpful in engaging with the ideological structure of cinema and its relationship to forms of imperialism – as long as they are addressed in conjunction with individual texts. Like the 'in' of the term, the influence of past adaptation theories wedges itself into interfidelity, able to move fluidly through both individual texts and an overarching discussion of the medium.

In addition to the legacies of other forms of adaptation theory, the interfidelity approach engages with the contributions of film scholars outside the realm of adaptation. Focusing on individual texts, interfidelity criticism owes much to the auteur theory and Andrew Sarris' contention that critics who subscribe to the auteur theory view film in a holistic manner. As Sarris writes, 'The auteur critic is obsessed with the wholeness of art and artist . . . The parts, however entertaining individually, must cohere meaningfully. This meaningful coherence is more likely when the director dominates the proceedings with skill and purpose.'[26] Though film is clearly a collaborative art, the positionality of the director is essential to understanding the politics behind individual adaptations, especially in the case of directors from postcolonial nations hired by Hollywood after the international success of films made in their native countries. The approach is also heavily influenced by Robin Wood's advocation of films that expose and interrogate the fascist tendencies inherent in cinema's structure: 'Many films *merely* reproduce, and thereby, reinforce, but there are also many – the interesting ones, the complex ones, the distinguished ones – that, in reproducing the social and psychic structures of our culture, also subject them to criticism.'[27] As adaptation theorists concerned with the ideology of cinema demonstrate, filmmaking's structure acts as a controlling force. Yet, the adaptation process is especially adept at producing films that criticise said structure while writing back.

In dealing with the realm of postcolonial literature and cinema, interfidelity theory appropriates approaches and terms from film criticism with an international scope as well as postcolonial theory. When referring to Hollywood cinema, the theory applies Carroll's concept of 'Hollywood International' – films made in Hollywood and other national film industries that are meant for global dissemination.[28] Given Hollywood's international reach, the theory also operates under a modified definition of what Hamid Naficy refers to as 'accented cinema', films by diasporic filmmakers that, 'Are in dialogue with the home and host societies and their respective national cinemas, as well as with audiences, many of whom are similarly transnational, whose desires, aspirations and fears they express.'[29] While helpful in discussing postcolonial cinema, the term must be modified as many of the filmmakers that Naficy deems accented, such as Mira Nair, Canadian director Atom Egoyan, and Iranian-American indie gadfly Caveh Zahedi, have become frequent, albeit semi-independent, presences in Hollywood.

While postcolonial theorists such as Said categorise Hollywood as an agent of cultural imperialism, Hollywood cinema occupies a contradictory position as a medium for writing back to the imperial centre and a hegemonic force that absorbs filmmakers from national cinema movements into the order of global capital. However, by viewing Hollywood adaptations made by postcolonial filmmakers within the context of Homi K. Bhabha's work on hybridity and mimicry, the disjunctions and potential for subversion become evident. As Rochelle Hurst writes in the edited collection *In/Fidelity: Essays on Film Adaptation*, 'An adaptation is a hybrid, an amalgam of media – at once a cinematised novel *and* a literary film, confusing, bridging, and rejecting the alleged discordance between page and screen, both insisting upon and occupying the overlap', a clear, if unintentional, parallel to these fundamental concepts of postcolonial studies.[30] Given Hollywood's dominant role in international culture, my project also employs Gayatri Chakravorty Spivak's discussions of subaltern agency as a basis for interrogating the effectiveness of the films I discuss in both resisting imperial forces and speaking for the subjugated. The educational opportunities and class backgrounds of postcolonial filmmakers working in Hollywood also make addressing Spivak's questions essential to the overall effectiveness of my project. As a theoretical approach, interfidelity also purposefully draws on its marital connotation to foreground colonialism's intertwined strategies of, according to Oyèrónké Oyěwùmí, 'inferiorization' of natives and women 'embedded in the colonial situation'.[31] In recalling the mechanisms of colonial control in the age of global capital, interfidelity extends the opposition to patriarchal imperial structures to the adaptation process, cultivating a hybrid form of resistance from film theory and postcolonial studies applicable to the contemporary politics formed from an amalgamation of colonialism and more recent imperial contexts.

Elaborating on Said's claims concerning the cultural imperialism of international media entities, my definition of contemporary imperial forces is largely informed by Hardt and Negri's work in *Empire* (2000), *Multitude: War and Democracy in the Age of Empire* (2004), and *Commonwealth* (2009). However, my project applies a working definition of Empire that mediates between Hardt and Negri's corporation-centric view and theorists such as Wood and David Harvey who emphasise the continuing role of the individual nation state in global domination. Reconciling such conflicting theoretical perspectives allows me to highlight Hollywood's contradictory status as both a national industry and global cultural force. Directly applying Hollywood's dissemination power within the globalised economy to Guy Debord's discussions of celebrity and spectacle's roles in achieving ideological totality is also useful in differentiating between Hollywood cinema and Hardt and Negri's definition, which lumps cinema, television news, print, and advertising under the moniker 'media.' My project also discusses how Hollywood's increased globalisation and coproduction activity relate to the political and economic ramifications of the rise of what Robert O. Keohane refers to as the 'international regimes' of the globalised world, which 'facilitate the smooth operation of decentralized international political systems' and 'become increasingly useful for governments that wish to solve common problems and pursue complementary purposes.'[32]

Despite interfidelity's application of adaptation studies to the shifting economics of the globalised film industry, it remains an approach that relates only to a specific set of adaptations within international cinema. While such postcolonial film adaptations certainly use the film medium to write back to Empire by integrating their respective national perspectives into the literature of their colonisers and to address the current imperial powers of global corporations, their opposition does not fully represent efforts by filmmakers to resist. The filmmakers under consideration here hail from developed nations with strong national film industries and a history of international coproduction. In the cases of directors such as Peter Jackson, Patrick Lussier and Jane Campion, international media corporations have fostered filmmaking in their native countries through shooting on location to curtail the higher production costs and tax burdens associated with filming in the US. Similarly, filmmakers who originated from Bollywood and other Indian national film industries benefit from an influx of foreign production revenues that supplement the income of a country that is recognised as home to the second most profitable national film industry in the world. With the exceptions of these Bollywood-associated filmmakers such as Nair and Kapur, the filmmakers I have chosen all hail from settler colonial nations that maintain financial ties with Europe. As a result, their native countries have stronger and more cohesive film industries than nations such as Iran, Brazil, Venezuela, Uganda and Afghanistan, where tumultuous political situations and current global military conflicts greatly hinder the ability to finance and market films for global distribution. While numerous works from these nations address postcolonial and neocolonial relationships and receive some semblance of worldwide distribution, they remain relatively severed from international film industry economics.

INTERFIDELITY THEORY: CATEGORIZATION AND APPLICATION

With its focus on both the content and industrial context of individual films, the interfidelity approach hinges on identifying the various ways that postcolonial literature and film relate to the adaptation process. A Nigerian filmmaker adapting a Victorian novel can use the adaptation process to imbue the colonised's perspective into a cultural product of the British Empire. However, a starkly different political context exists for a British filmmaker adapting an international bestseller by a Nigerian author. In addition, the conditions that the film industry imposes on a given adaptation can radically affect the politics of the process. For postcolonial filmmakers who either work in Hollywood or make independent films for international distribution, an adaptation of colonial literature must contend with the former colonising presence and address the implications of Empire's control that Hollywood embodies. In *The Postcolonial Culture Industry*, Ponzanesi includes a taxonomy of strategies that attempts to showcase the plurality and frequency of postcolonial adaptations, dividing them into five categories.

1. Adaptation of empire or colonial novels with a critical edge such as David Lean's *A Passage to India* (1984) or *Out of Africa*.
2. Adaptation of classics with a view toward including a feminist postcolonial lens such as Gurinder Chadha's *Bride and Prejudice* (2004) and Mira Nair's *Vanity Fair* (2004), which I will discuss at length in Chapter 4.
3. Adaptation of postcolonial literature transposed to film by the western culture industry, the most famous of which may be Anthony Minghella's adaptation of Michael Ondaatje's novel *The English Patient* (1996).
4. Adaptation of postcolonial novels by postcolonial filmmakers, including Nair's *The Namesake* (2007) based on Jhumpa Lahiri's novel and Deepa Mehta's adaptation of Salman Rushdie's *Midnight's Children* (2012).
5. Bollywood remakes of Hollywood films.[33]

Although Ponzanesi's list is a helpful starting point for understanding film adaptation through a postcolonial lens, it also raises several questions about postcolonial resistance in a world of global capital. The list does not make a distinction between theatrical and television adaptations, eschewing a discussion of how broadcast affects the content and structure of the adaptation process. In addition, such a classification system does not consider how various film financing structures affect the political context of the production. A BBC Films-funded adaptation of a Victorian novel helmed by an Australian filmmaker may contain a postcolonial critique, yet the same film financed by a mini-major Hollywood studio provides the filmmaker with an opportunity to both address Australia's postcolonial identity and Hollywood's longstanding influence over the nation's domestic film culture. Most importantly,

Ponzanesi's list does not make a distinction between 'classics' and the literature of the Victorian era that represents the pinnacle of Britain's colonial power and, with the global dissemination of the works of writers such as Charles Dickens and Rudyard Kipling, the artistic height of its colonial discourse. While the aforementioned types of projects have the potential for fruitful postcolonial critique, those filmmakers from formerly colonised nations who undertake adaptations of Victorian literature with Hollywood financing occupy a unique position from which to address multiple forms of imperialism, writing back and into the present moment. The following categorisation is not meant to counter Ponzanesi's work or be an all-inclusive outline of the various relationships that occur in postcolonial film adaptations. Instead, it is a move toward an examination of the complex relationships between postcolonial theory and film adaptation through an explicit focus on Hollywood and its global influence that concern the interfidelity approach.

CATEGORY I: HOLLYWOOD ADAPTATION OF VICTORIAN LITERATURE

Largely the products of the Hollywood studio system and post-World War II British companies such as the Rank Organisation, the adaptations in this category are marked by a reinforcement of nationalism, a fairly uninterrogated depiction of imperial cultural forces, and an appeal to both British and American audiences. In most cases, American or European directors oversee the production and aim to create adaptations that are faithful to the content and themes of the source material. However, the effects of World War II and the US's newly acquired superpower status often inform these films. David Lean's *Great Expectations* (1946) serves as the quintessential work of this category because of its strict adherence to Pip's development and Lean's attempts to recreate through *mise-en-scène* a sense of nostalgia for Victorian-era England. However, the film also streamlines Dickens narrative by excising characters such as Orlick, Wopsle and Trabb's boy, who are denied Pip's opportunity, allowing the film to elide the sociopolitical failures of the era so important to Dickens while accentuating Pip's class mobility. Lean's abandonment of Dickens' politics is most apparent in the film's choice to opt for Dickens' less ambiguous ending and amplify its optimism. Shifting the setting from the ruined Satis House to an intact version of the mansion, the film features Pip ripping rotting curtains from the windows to let light in – a scene not in Dickens' novel – while imploring Estella to leave its confines. As the united couple exits the gates of Satis House, the film's title rolls, an ending that reinforces Pip, according to McFarlane, as 'an apt hero for post-World War II Britain' whose tearing down of the curtains serves as 'a metaphoric letting in of light on British life at large after the rigours of the war'.[34] Though as well-executed and sumptuous as any Lean film, *Great Expectations* depicts a Victorian England freed from the class politics of its source material, a sanitised historical portrait that reveres a society built on the profits of imperialism during the anxiety of the British Empire's fall.

While Lean's *Great Expectations* serves as a unifying text for a flailing empire, the numerous Hollywood studio system adaptations of British literature in this category, such as George Cukor's *David Copperfield* (1935), William Wyler's *Wuthering Heights* (1939) and George Stevens' *Gunga Din* (1939), appropriate the texts of empire to translate their nationalism into an American context while demonstrating the scope of Hollywood studio filmmaking. *Gunga Din* and other Hollywood entries in the canon of Empire cinema will be discussed at length in Chapter 1.

CATEGORY II: HOLLYWOOD ADAPTATION OF POSTCOLONIAL LITERATURE

As the critical and commercial success of *The English Patient* and, as I later discuss in Chapter 8, Danny Boyle's *Slumdog Millionaire* indicate, Hollywood's adaptation of postcolonial texts without regard to the source material's politics has increased in prominence and frequency as international film industries and cultures have become united through the forces of transnational corporate Empire. Films in this category either dilute or erase the postcolonial critique of source texts, exploiting perspectives not often represented in Hollywood film. Though they initially may be funded by European companies or international coproductions, their distribution by Hollywood studios and extensive Academy Award campaigns often amplify their global cultural influence and associations with the American film industry.

CATEGORY III: INDIE ADAPTATION OF VICTORIAN LITERATURE

These films adapt the literature of empire as a method of writing back to the colonising force largely by integrating and calling attention to absent perspectives in the source texts. However, they are typically produced outside of the Hollywood system, largely through government grants and film boards. While they often receive distribution from Hollywood mini-majors and boutique distributors, the adaptations employ experimental techniques and local allusions that make them difficult to market to mass audiences. As a result, they conform more to 'European-Model Art Cinemas' meant for success at international films festivals such as Cannes and Sundance.[35] Many also fall into the category of 'indies', which is, according to Michael Z. Newman, 'a form of niche media, a reaction against conglomerate gigantism and at the very same time, considering its mini-major producer-distributors, a symptom of it.'[36] One such example is Canadian filmmaker Guy Maddin's *Dracula: Pages from a Virgin's Diary* (2002), an adaptation of Bram Stoker's 1897 novel *Dracula*, that accents its source text's anxieties with race and miscegenation, probing the ideas of Britishness integral to the nation's colonial endeavours and extending its lingering presence to Canada's multiculturalism. Maddin's casting of Asian-Canadian dancer Wei Qiang Zhang as Dracula cements the film's political motivations, allowing it to engage with debates concerning Canada's largest minority group. While Maddin adheres faithfully to Stoker's novel, he executes the project as a silent-film interpretation of the Royal Winnipeg Ballet performing the narrative, which incorporates earlier iconic depictions of vampires such as F. W. Murnau's *Nosferatu* (1922). Yet, this choice also calls attention to the exclusion of Dracula's own perspective from Stoker's novel, which depicts the foreign Count through newspaper articles and the journal entries of its British characters. Through his silent film aesthetic, Maddin denies Dracula and, by extension, his Canadian cast a voice, accenting the marginal status of colonised groups in a project that appealed to American distributors and ultimately led Maddin to work with MGM and IFC Films on his $3.4 million follow up, *The Saddest Music in the World* (2003), starring Isabella Rossellini.[37] This book will further discuss this category as it relates to Dickens, a veritable subgenre of Victorian adaptations, in its analysis of South African filmmaker Tim Greene's *Boy Called Twist*, which was an 'official selection' of the 2005 Cannes Film Festival.

CATEGORY IV: ACCENTED HOLLYWOOD ADAPTATION OF POSTCOLONIAL LITERATURE

Over the past two decades, postcolonial filmmakers such as Australian Peter Weir, South African Gavin Hood and Pakistani Shekhar Kapur have received international critical and commercial success with films made in their native countries, allowing them to transition to Hollywood. The adaptations in this category result from established directors from postcolonial nations using their Hollywood clout to adapt works of literature from their homelands with larger budgets and mini-major studio distribution, resulting in films that increase the profile of postcolonial literary texts. In his adaptation of Patrick McCabe's 1998 novel *Breakfast on Pluto* (2005), Irish filmmaker Neil Jordan revisits the use of transgendered characters that made his 1992 film *The Crying Game* a career-making commercial success and Academy Award winner for Best

Original Screenplay in a project distributed by Sony Pictures Classics. Like *The Crying Game*, McCabe uses a trans motif within the framework of Irish Republican Army conflicts to emphasise the liminal identity of his homeland. As Patrick 'Pussy' Braden navigates London and her Irish town of Tyreelin in the novel, her first-person narration is littered with references to Hollywood studio comedies from Doris Day vehicles to *Breakfast at Tiffany's*. While the film preserves both Braden's adoration of Hollywood and the anticolonial politics of McCabe (who coauthored the screenplay with Jordan), the adaptation process permits Jordan to execute the film in the style of the Technicolor comedies to which Braden alludes. As a result, a stark contrast erupts between the film's lavish costumes, pop-music interludes, and slapstick humour and the visceral IRA bombings and police raids central to the narrative. Through his juxtaposition of Hollywood comedy convention and gritty realism, Jordan interrogates the representational authority of traditional narrative structures, criticising conventions while using Hollywood's dissemination power to extend McCabe's narrative reach.

CATEGORY V: ACCENTED HOLLYWOOD ADAPTATION OF VICTORIAN LITERATURE

In creating the adaptations of Victorian literature within Hollywood central to this project, postcolonial filmmakers must cultivate a way to write back to their former colonisers while addressing the imperial structures of filmmaking in the age of Empire. Unable to adopt radical techniques because of a necessary adherence to Hollywood's industrial demands, methods of resistance in these films are often subtly embedded into the narrative and stylistic traits of the adaptation, allowing a greater potential for subversion. To fully understand how adaptations in the category contend with colonialism and Empire, one must examine in greater detail how filmmakers use both narrative and cinematic style in individual instances to call attention to the fissures in what are typically marketed as prestige adaptations or event films. Considering these caveats to the interfidelity approach, a case study of a particular film situated directly between Victorian adaptation and Hollywood spectacle may be of use to further probe the limits and potential of interfidelity before undertaking the analytical work of which the rest of this study consists. Through the following discussion of Peter Jackson's Conrad-inspired 2005 remake of the Hollywood classic *King Kong*, I hope not only to demonstrate how the interfidelity approach works but also to highlight its applicability to a text that blurs the lines between adaptation, remake and postcolonial cinema.

THE INTERFIDELITY APPROACH AND PETER JACKSON'S *KING KONG*

When Universal Studios released Jackson's remake of the 1933 film *King Kong* during the 2005 holiday movie season, it achieved a melding of positive critical and commercial response not seen in the American film industry since the release of Jackson's final installment of J. R. R. Tolkien's *The Lord of Rings* trilogy two years previously. In a marketplace crowded with blockbuster family films such as *Harry Potter and the Goblet of Fire* and *The Chronicles of Narnia: The Lion, The Witch and The Wardrobe* and prestige pictures such as *Syriana* and *Munich*, Jackson's *King Kong* possessed the integral elements required for it to endure both the holiday box-office and awards season: a recognisable brand, a PG-13 rating, a director following up his first Academy Award win, a cast featuring Academy Award nominee Naomi Watts, Academy Award winner Adrien Brody, and popular comedian Jack Black, and a marketing campaign that simultaneously ran Kellogg's cereal promotions and 'for your consideration' ads in *Variety*. For Jackson, who honed his filmmaking skills making low-budget horror films such as *Bad Taste* (1987) and *Dead-Alive* (1992) using his mother's oven to bake prosthetics, the *King Kong* remake represented an ascension to Hollywood power player usually reserved for American directors like Steven Spielberg and Tim Burton. With a Best Director Academy Award for *The Lord of the Rings: Return of the King* (2003) and the $3 billion international box-office revenue from Tolkien's trilogy, Jackson persuaded Universal Studios to undertake the $200 million remake of his favorite childhood film with minimal studio interference.

Revered as one of the classic films of the Golden Age of Hollywood and made during the waning of the British Empire's global influence, the narrative of Merian C. Cooper's original *King Kong* (1933) bears strong postcolonial undercurrents that Jackson refines in his remake. The story of opportunistic filmmaker Carl Denham's journey to an uncharted island ruled by an enormous gorilla, *King Kong* serves as an example of imperial power's tendencies to conquer and subjugate foreign cultures, both in its production and narrative. Beginning his film career as a documentarian in Ethiopia, Cooper crafted his public image and promotional material in the style of James 'Biggles' Bigglesworth and other late-Victorian adventure heroes, a persona that extended to his projects, including the 1929 American adaptation of A. E. W. Mason's *The Four Feathers*.[38] Similar to Cooper, Denham (Robert Armstrong) is not content passively observing; he undertakes a more grandiose plan for Kong by capturing the gorilla, transporting him to New York City, branding him the 'Eighth Wonder of the World,' and reducing the beast to a life bound by chains as he reenacts his capture for the city's socialites. Though Kong rebels against his captor by breaking free and commencing a rampage through New York, his reign as king comes to an

Figure I.1 Jimmy the cabin boy's copy of *Heart of Darkness* in Jackson's *King Kong*.

end when military planes cause him to fall to his death from the Empire State Building, a victim of the Western World's economic and military prowess.

Jackson's remake leaves the original film's plot intact, only altering the basic narrative structure by including scenes that were either too expensive or technically unfilmable during the original film's production. Yet, Jackson clarifies Cooper's original engagement with colonialism by integrating the literary work Peter Childs holds above all others as the central text of postcolonial discourse, Joseph Conrad's 1899 novella *Heart of* Darkness, into his narrative.[39] The remake adds two new characters to the plot: Hayes (Evan Parke), an African-American officer on the ship, and Jimmy the Cabin Boy (Jamie Bell), a rogue, white adolescent Hayes tries to civilise by critiquing his behaviour and stressing the importance of education, a directive Jimmy follows by reading a copy of *Heart of Darkness* he filched from the New York Public Library (Figure I.1). As the ship reaches Kong's Skull Island in the film, Jimmy delves further into Conrad's novella, allowing Jackson to draw parallels between Marlow's descent into the horrors of colonialism in the novella and the ship's passengers' journey into the darkness of Skull Island, from which only a handful survive. According to Clifford T. Manlove, Jackson's inclusion of Conrad is a way to explicitly develop 'the link between filmmaking and the cinematic gaze in European colonization of Africa' despite falling victim to the same 'blank space' mentality of which Achebe accused Conrad.[40] However, Manlove treats Jackson's use of Conrad as allusion, underestimating its intertextual interplay with the novella and Cooper's version. Through his integration of Conrad's narrative, Jackson creates an amalgam of modern and postmodern discourse on the nature of Empire in the contemporary world (Figure I.2).

While the colonisers in Conrad's novella attempt to alternatively conquer and civilise the black natives of lands they control, Jackson's characters reverse roles, positioning the African-American Hayes as the model of civil-

Figure I.2 Jimmy (Jamie Bell) tells Hayes (Evan Parke) about being educated by Conrad's novella.

ity attempting to reform the unruly Jimmy who, as Hayes tells playwright Jack Driscoll (Adrien Brody), 'means no harm' and 'was wilder than half the animals' on the ship when he first found the boy stowed away. Establishing the dynamic between Hayes and Jimmy in the first half hour, Jackson spends the remainder of the film juxtaposing it with Kong's subjugation at the hands of Denham (Jack Black). Yet, the film's depiction of Skull Island's native tribes is one-dimensional – not out of place in a 1930s Hollywood production. As a result, Jackson's film articulates a layered, often problematic, criticism of colonialism.[41] Using Hayes and Jimmy's relationship and integrating *Heart of Darkness* to 'write back' to the empires that colonised New Zealand and Conrad's Belgian Congo, Jackson enters the postcolonial era despite maintaining the same structures of representation for his 'native' characters as British colonial discourse.

However, through the relationships between Kong/Denham and Hayes/Jimmy, Jackson also writes toward a contemporary version of Empire manifested in the global corporate powers that own companies such as the film's financer, Universal Studios. If, as Manlove contends, Jackson's remake metaphorically meditates on the connections between filmmaking and colonialism, then the director's production decisions are the inverse of Denham's designs to bring Kong's spectacle to New York. Adopting a similar strategy as he did on *The Lord of the Rings* and *The Hobbit* (2012–14) franchises, Jackson filmed the remake entirely in and around Auckland and Wellington, New Zealand, production choices that strengthen the international profile of the country's film industry and self-reflexively comment on the film's colonial undercurrents.[42] Likewise, despite the fact that all the central characters in the film are American, Jackson cast English actor Bell as Jimmy, Jamaican-born Evan Parke as Hayes, and Australian Naomi Watts as the film's female lead, Ann Darrow, upending a traditional colonial hierarchy via casting and leaving his actors to perform the roles of American colonists in one of Hollywood's most iconic narratives. Nations such as New Zealand may have developed distinct national cultures in the wake of decolonisation but, given Hollywood's outsized influence over them, they remain under the control of a refashioned Denham treating them as commodities that serve as primary attractions for an elite few.

Elaborating on these intersections between film adaptation, Victorian literature, and postcolonial cinema, the remainder of this book demonstrates how the interfidelity approach to adaptation is useful in understanding Hollywood's evolution from national film industry to the foundation of global cinema in the contemporary world. The book is organised into three sections. Tracing the postcolonial roots of studio-era Hollywood, section one shows how early success at Americanising Britain's Cinema of Empire in epics such as *Gunga Din* resulted in settler colonial filmmakers like Canada's genre director Patrick Lussier (*Dracula 2000*) and New Zealander/Australian art-house icon Jane Campion (*The Portrait of a Lady*) subverting genre conventions in their adaptations to position America as heir to imperialism. Section two focuses on adaptations made by Indian filmmakers working in Hollywood – Mira Nair's *Vanity Fair* and Shekhar Kapur's *The Four Feathers* – films that integrate perspectives absent from their Victorian source texts while addressing Orientalist stereotypes that persist in the globalised world. The final section considers three adaptations of works by quintessential Victorian author Charles Dickens: Mexican filmmaker Alfonso Cuarón's *Great Expectations*, South African Tim Greene's *Boy Called Twist*, and UK director Danny Boyle's *Oliver Twist*-inspired *Slumdog Millionaire*. Through examining these disparate versions of Dickens narratives, this section interrogates adaptation's effectiveness as a framework to engage with current political conflicts and highlights the limits of postcolonial resistance as Hollywood and other transnational entities exert an ever-increasing economic and cultural influence over individual nations

CHAPTER I

An American Kipling: Colonial Discourse, Settler Culture and the Hollywood Studio System in George Stevens' *Gunga Din*

Focusing on Hollywood's early attempts at Victorian literature adaptations, this chapter examines George Stevens' 1939 version of Kipling's poem 'Gunga Din,' emphasising how the film's loose resemblance to its source material demonstrates a break in the American valorisation of British culture. *Gunga Din* completely dismantles Kipling's poem, recreating it as an example of a uniquely American form: the seamless studio system product that led to Hollywood's international dominance in cultural production. Yet, while the politics of the adaptation resemble textual strategies of resistance prevalent in settler colonial cultures, the film's retention of colonial literature's representation of Kipling's 'natives' addresses an America beginning to assert a distinct national culture while positioning itself as a future imperial power.

As 1939 drew to a close, the golden age of Hollywood had just experienced a twelve-month period that saw the release of the 'best of American cinema' staples *Gone with the Wind*, *The Wizard of Oz*, *Mr. Smith Goes to Washington*, *Stagecoach*, *Of Mice and Men*, *Wuthering Heights*, and *Goodbye, Mr. Chips*. However, despite the spate of critically and commercially successful films released during what film historians have deemed Hollywood's 'Golden Year,' one of the year's biggest box-office draws was a genre picture that, although acclaimed for its entertainment value and sheer scope, has never quite earned the prominence in cinema history as its much-touted competitors: George Stevens' *Gunga Din*.[1] Loosely adapted from Rudyard Kipling's ballad of the same name, *Gunga Din* has seen its reputation as one of the finest epics of the studio era damaged over the intervening decades as a result of allegations of condescending and one-dimensional depictions of its Indian characters.[2]

Though *Gunga Din* has not achieved the same stature in the history of American cinema as its 'Golden Year' counterparts, the film's popularity upon its release is indicative of the cultural anxieties gripping America during the time period stemming from the death rattle of Manifest Destiny and the traumas of the Great Depression – anxieties that led to the reinvigorated popularity of the western and what Robert B. Ray calls the 'disguised western' during the studio era. According to Ray:

> As a form, the western served as one of the principal displacement mechanisms in a culture obsessed with the inevitable encroachments on its gradually diminishing space. By portraying the advancing society's abiding dependence on the frontier's most representative figure – the individualistic, outlaw hero – the pure western reassured its audience about the permanent availability of both sets of values . . . Thus many of Classic Hollywood's genre movies, like many of the most important American novels, were thinly camouflaged westerns.[3]

If, as Ray contends, the function of westerns both real and disguised during the Classical Hollywood era was to cope with anxiety over the disappearance of America's diminishing space, then *Gunga Din*'s appropriation of western conventions into the realm of the British imperial project provides a framework for the opening of an unclaimed cultural frontier: the British colonial epic.[4] For Ray, the disguised western acts as an elastic category that encompasses a wide range of films featuring reluctant heroes from Michael Curtiz's James Cagney gangster film *Angels with Dirty Faces* (1938), to Stevens' Astaire–Rogers musical *Swing Time* (1936), to nearly every Clark Gable film, including *Gone with the Wind*. However, despite the broadness of Ray's genre categorisations, a film such as *Gunga Din* refuses to conform to the conventions of either the real or disguised western. Following the adventures of maverick British Army sergeants Cutter (Cary Grant), MacChesney (Victor McLaglen) and Ballantine (Douglas Fairbanks, Jr) through India's landscape as they seek treasure, contend with Ballantine's upcoming marriage, and combat a Thugee cult led by the Guru (Eduardo Ciannelli) with the aid of their Indian water bearer Gunga Din (Sam Jaffe), the film exhibits many of the conventions that critics such as Thomas Schatz see as hallmarks of the western: a concern with restoring 'rites of order' to a frontier landscape, a juxtaposition between domesticity and the frontier, a group of reluctant, individualistic heroes, and a prosocial sidekick who shares the heroes' moral sensibilities.[5]

Yet, the film's India setting – which shared the shooting location of Lone Pine, California, with many of the period's westerns – and focus on the British complicate *Gunga Din*'s associations with either genre; different enough from John Ford productions to escape the designation of western, but too thinly disguised to be anything but.[6] While critics such as Jeffrey Richards characterise *Gunga Din* and other Hollywood films set in the British colonies as a 'Cinema of Empire' that serves to endow the faceless builders of the British Empire by 'clothing them in the flesh and features of the great stars', they neglect to discuss the motivational impulses that led an industry responsible for cultivating its own genres to imitate and engage with narratives that were the hallmark of Victorian literature.[7] Throughout the 1930s, London Film Productions released a series of 'Empire films' that were critically and commercially successful in Britain and America, including Robert Flaherty and Zoltan Korda's Kipling adaptation *Elephant Boy* (1937), Herbert Wilcox's biopics *Victoria the Great* (1937) and *Sixty Glorious Years* (1938), and Korda's 'Imperial Trilogy' of *Sanders of the River* (1935), *The Drum* (1938), and *The Four Feathers* (1939). Considering that America had not only dominated the international film industry since World War I after lagging behind England and France for decades but also relied on a host of outsourced European talent from Charlie Chaplin and Alfred Hitchcock to *Gunga Din*'s own Cary Grant, Hollywood could not afford to overlook the international popularity of the 'Cinema of Empire'.[8] As a result, studios embarked on a series of their own imperial epics during the late 1930s, releasing films such as Henry Hathaway's *Lives of a Bengal Dancer* (1935), John Ford's Kipling adaptation *Wee Willie Winkie* (1937), and *Gunga Din* in addition to the screwball comedies, westerns and melodramas that made up the majority of the releases that culminated with the industry's 'Golden Year' – a business model that merged Hollywood genres and Victorian texts while opening the cultural frontier through absorption of a competing industry's own stylistic and narrative conventions.

Though one could dismiss Hollywood's intervention into the production of the imperial epic as cooption from a less powerful, albeit still formidable, competitor, an inherent political dimension exists in the creation of Hollywood's Cinema of Empire. Such a conflict between Hollywood and Victorian narrative convention illustrates the often contentious relationship between colonial powers and settler colonies such as the US, especially considering the ascension of American cinema within the global film industry. Discussing colonial relationships through the metaphor of infection, Lorenzo Veracini makes a distinction between colonialism's viral form and the bacterial traits of the settler colony. According to Veracini:

> Thus, viruses and bacteria, like colonial and settler colonial forms, often coexist and mutually support each other, even though at times they can inhibit their respective operations. Besides, it is often a matter of scale, and all the settler colonies were established and flourished within a globalising context fundamentally shaped by colonial relations. When they oppose each other, bacteria struggling against bacteriophage viruses defend themselves by producing enzymes that destroy alien DNA. It is a process that targets what is foreign and identifies what has successfully indigenised—the equivalent of a settler declaration of independence preceded by a party of settlers running amok dressed as natives.[9]

While Veracini's simile succinctly differentiates between the politics of colonial and settler colonial ideologies, it is also helpful in understanding a cultural product such as *Gunga Din*. As a colonial narrative told through Hollywood genres, the film retains elements of British culture while attempting to articulate them within the conventions of storytelling modes that became standard for a global film industry disproportionately controlled by the US. However, in its integration of colonial discourse, the film also displays its inability to fully separate itself from colonial dichotomies.

Seizing upon the popularity of Empire narratives, an industry based in a settler nation addressed the cultural attributes of its former coloniser. At the same time, it integrated its own perspectives and anxieties into a final product that was a hybrid of colonial narrative and American western while preserving both forms' foundational reliance on ethnic otherness. Yet, unlike other instances of 'writing back' such as those of Rhys and Carey, the American imperial epics stemmed from source texts that were minor works by major figures of Empire literature (Kipling's *The Jungle Book* and 'Gunga Din') or works by the period's relatively obscure authors. When Hollywood did adapt the classic texts of Empire literature, the resulting films were either prestige adaptations relatively faithful to their source texts (George Cukor's *David Copperfield* [1935] and William Wyler's *Wuthering Heights* [1939]), adaptations entrusted to British filmmakers (Victor Saville's *Kim* [1950]), or loose adaptations that displaced the narrative from an American-British context (Jacques Tourneur's *I Walked with a Zombie* [1943] – a *Jane Eyre*-influenced Val Lewton horror film about Canadians in the West Indies).[10]

While Hollywood could use such adaptations to demonstrate its mastery of literary adaptation and technological prowess by recreating Victorian England on a studio lot, it could do little more than imitate. Only in Hollywood's imperial adventure epics could the industry pit its own modes of storytelling against the traditions of its former coloniser in a manner customary of what Peter Limbrick deems 'settler cinemas' that 'embody in their transnational, conflictual practices the uneasy unequal status of the settler colonial societies and empires that produce and are produced by them.'[11]

However, in melding empire literature and the Hollywood epic, films such as *Gunga Din* faced the problem of representing their 'native' characters, which *Gunga Din* failed to adequately address if its banning in India, Japan and Malaya is any indication.[12] Through integrating American cultural attributes into their source texts, Hollywood's imperial adventure epics were faced with a fragmentation of identity that they could not reconcile. These problems of representation extend further than general accusations of Orientalism. Hollywood convention dictated not only a certain audience identification with stars such as Grant and Errol Flynn (if one overlooks their nations of origin) but also a narrowly defined savage/noble savage dichotomy for the Indian characters borrowed from the western. At the same time, American identity was equally split between the rugged individualism of the films' leading men and the colonised Indian figures who became antagonists when they rebelled against the encroaching Empire. Despite its negotiation of the relationship between its own ideology and that of its former coloniser, the Hollywood imperial epic could not contain the ruptures caused by its settler colonial foundations, a failure apparent in *Gunga Din*'s ambivalent depictions of its Americanised English heroes and anticolonial Indian Thugees.

THE IMPERIAL SCREWBALL WESTERN

Given that RKO Radio Pictures was the most financially unstable of the five major studios, its decision to employ the notorious perfectionist George Stevens to direct Grant, Fairbanks and hundreds of extras on intricate interior sets for an adaptation of an 85-line poem seems a risky endeavour.[13] Yet, under Stevens' control as director and producer, the most expensive production in the studio's history was designed to prove that a studio known primarily for screwball comedies, musicals and Cooper's *King Kong* could make a significant epic film and position the genres it executed so well into a prestigious package by attaching Kipling's name.[14] Heralded as one of the great English writers by, according to David Gilmour, the 'solid and conservative Victorian men of letters', including Thomas Hardy and J. M. Barrie, Kipling added an air of importance to *Gunga Din* that elevated its status beyond a western taking place in colonial India.[15] While the studio courted Kipling's estate for the rights to the poem, Stevens relished working on a project adapted from the work of an author he said was always 'right at my elbow' and 'more important to me than the assistant director' when making a film – an admiration that made him bristle when those in Hollywood not involved with the project dismissed it as little more than another cowboys and Indians tale.[16]

The resulting conflicts between RKO's desire for prestige and need to recoup such a large investment positions the film at a significant point in the history of Hollywood film adaptations. Rather than attempt to make a Kipling adaptation that captured, in the words of William B. Dillingham, the 'complex and magisterial achievement of his extensive body of work with its wide range of subject matter and its almost infinite variety of themes', RKO settled on a film that superficially engaged narrative and biographical aspects of Kipling's oeuvre while relying primarily on proven genre conventions.[17] Though it borrows its title and a character from an entry in Kipling's *Barrack-Room Ballads* (1892) as well as its focus on three British soldiers from Kipling's story collection *Soldiers Three* (1888), the narrative has little resemblance to either text, which is solely the invention of the film's writing team.[18] Instead, it makes the highly unconventional choice of including the character Rudyard Kipling (Reginald Sheffield) as a journalist who accompanies the unit during the film's climatic battle and, inspired by Gunga Din's death, writes the poem on the battlefield, an addition that angered the Kipling estate and was excised from many prints of the film after its initial theatrical run.[19]

Considering the film's highly unorthodox, tacked-on approach to adaptation, one could view the tensions between Hollywood style and source-text fidelity as little more than another example of profit overshadowing artistic integrity. Yet, the prominence of both Hollywood and America in the aftermath of World War I also had a profound effect on *Gunga Din*'s relationship to Kipling. As Frederic Cople Jaher and Blair B. Kling write:

> By the late 1930s, Hollywood was ready to look more critically at British hegemony. America had become a superpower; Britain, weakened in World War I, was already in decline. The modification of Hollywood's British Indian epic was imminent. Participants in the production of *Gunga Din* could feel it.[20]

Though Jaher and Kling carefully construct the historical context of *Gunga Din*'s production and highlight the ambivalence inherent in the passing of the torch between superpowers, they opt not to focus on how the film's source text and use of genre reflect the period. In relying on Kipling's literary reputation while simultaneously pushing his influence to the margins in favour of Hollywood convention, the film captures the moment when American forms began to encroach upon the prestige of British culture while proposing a solution for a nation in which open space was in decline.

Throughout *Gunga Din*, Stevens' primary strategy to address American attitudes toward Britain occurs through narrative and stylistic play between American and British cultural tropes. As the film opens, Stevens fades to a close-up of the base of a statue of Queen Victoria with the inscription 'Victoria Regina Imperatrix' (the Queen's monogram after she became Empress of India) in the foreground of the shot. As the camera zooms out to reveal the entirety of the statue and cuts to a close-up of a parade of flags, a voiceover of Kipling's ballad begins:

> Now in Injia's sunny clime
> Where I used to spend my time
> A-servin' of 'Er Majesty the Queen,
> Of all them blackfaced crew
> The finest man I knew
> Was our regimental bhisti . . .[21]

Figure 1.1 The shift from Queen Victoria to the RKO Pictures logo.

The voiceover abruptly goes silent midway through line 12, replaced by the opening chords of the film's score as the title card 'RKO Radio Pictures Presents Gunga Din' appears superimposed over a large gong (Figure 1.1). Such a shift echoes Judith Plotz's comments on the exuberant appetite in America for edited collections of Kipling's work during the early 20th century. As Plotz writes:

> The pattern that emerges is that of a *translatio regni*, the vision and ethic of an imperial dominion that is passing from Britain to a youthfully buoyant and curious America. These collections of works by Kipling selected by Americans for Americans build up this vision of a global role, once sustained by a now-wearied Britain . . . but now devolving on the hard, masculine, united, technologically savvy young American republic, the Elephant's child of the nations.[22]

While the combination of the inscription, the statue's image and Kipling's verse serve to ground the film in a distinctly Victorian place and time, the cut to the RKO title card marks a shift from the attributes of British culture to the grammar of Hollywood cinema – a version of Kipling edited by Americans for Americans. In addition, the choice to mute the voiceover narration of the poem and allow the title card to announce the identity of 'our regimental bhisti' indicates the establishment of new narrative forms in which to package Victorian tales of adventure. Taking up the mantle from the ballad, the sequence indicates a break from British traditions, conveying to its audience the power of Hollywood to make canonical texts of Empire literature seem fresh, epic and adventurous.

Although the contrast of the statue and title card accents the differences between Kipling and Hollywood's modes of storytelling, the film's selective inclusion of the poem's opening stanza strengthens the narrative prowess of Hollywood convention by stripping away the complexities of Kipling's work. A writer who has often been misread as depicting a poetic, timeless and essential version of India, Kipling had a multifaceted relationship with the nation, as both a figure complicit in Empire's endeavours and, as Said positions him in *Culture and Imperialism*, an Anglo-Indian with a hybrid identity.[23] As a result, Kipling's writing is founded on ambivalent and contradictory depictions of both Britain and India. As John McBratney writes:

> Kipling, more than any British imperial writer, inaugurated the pervasive image of the twentieth-century British Empire as a kind of highly self-conscious drama . . . Kipling, who devoted himself to securing that government's permanence, may have most truly succeeded in pointing up its extravagant dumb show.[24]

An example of the complexities of this 'dumb show' plays out in the opening lines of 'Gunga Din', which were cut from the recitation of the film adaptation's opening:

> You may talk o' gin and beer
> When you're quartered safe out 'ere,
> An' you're sent to penny-fights an' Aldershot it;
> But when it comes to slaughter
> You will do your work on water,
> An' you'll lick the bloomin' boots of 'im that's got it.[25]

Here, Kipling deftly addresses the self-consciousness innate in the military operations at the foundation of the imperial project. The British Army was well trained by 'penny fight' operations at Aldershot, yet wildly unprepared for service in India. The speaker of the poem claims to have had experience in India worthy of boot licking, but unspools his story to an audience from the safe quarters of a training base. The army is organised as a hierarchy of soldiers in training and those 'that's got it', but implicitly acknowledges the danger and untamable aspects of the crown jewel of the British Empire. However, Stevens' film neatly sacrifices the complexities of these contradictions by only including the lines of the stanza that, when taken out of context, depict India as merely a 'sunny clime' with a host of brave natives eager to be a part of the Empire's 'blackfaced crew', a choice that allows the film adaptation to revel in the atmosphere of imperial adventure while leaving ample room to assert its own ideology.

After establishing the conflict between this British tradition and Hollywood spectacle in the title sequence, Stevens extends the tension to his characterisation of the film's British soldiers. Though *Gunga Din* relied heavily on actors Jaher and Kling refer to as the 'British Colony' living in Beverly Hills for at least two-thirds of its cast, including Grant and McLaglen, Stevens gives the three soldiers at the centre of the film personalities innate to Hollywood westerns and far removed from the behaviour of the film's other British characters.[26] As the opening sequence begins, a member of a Thugee cult smashes a telegraph wire while his cohorts dig a row of graves. Stevens then cuts to a small group of British soldiers on horseback as they encounter a Thugee posing as a local. Rigidly mannered and perfectly groomed, the group is massacred in their sleep by the Thugees, who use the opportunity to exterminate the rest of the British at the outpost of Tantrapur. Discovering that the telegraph wires have gone dead, Colonel Weed (Montagu Love) and Major Mitchell (Lumsden Hare) appear unable to deal with the situation, responding with little more than an 'I don't like this'. The two commanding officers immediately approach Sgt. Higginbotham (Robert Coote) – a character so buttoned-up and stiff that the film's British military consultants deemed him an offense to the army – and order him to find Cutter, MacChesney and Ballantine to investigate.[27]

While Stevens' depiction of the film's British authority figures as pretentious and inept borders on satire, it furthers his critique of the British establishment by pitting the personalities of his three leads against those of their colleagues. In response to the command of his superior officers, Higginbotham tells Weed and Mitchell that the trio, 'has gone on some mysterious mission', which the film later reveals is a treasure hunt spurred by a fake map Cutter bought from a private in a Scottish regiment. The film introduces its stars via Higginbotham walking into an epic street brawl instigated by the trio. In response to Higginbotham's calls, MacChesney throws an opponent through a window and Ballantine follows suit. When Higginbotham sees Cutter dangling the private who sold him the map out the window, he orders him to 'Take his hands off that man'. Cutter obliges by dropping the private while flashing Grant's trademark smirk.Though all of the characters Stevens introduces in the film's first ten minutes belong to the same military regiment, only the soldiers three embody the combination of anti-authority spirit and physical prowess indicative of the American action hero archetype fundamental to the Hollywood genres with which the film engages. With their witty banter and hypermasculinity, the 'American' trio appear superior to the dense, traditional British soldiers who have already been victims of the cult that will serve as the film's primary antagonists – an identification Stevens underscores by filming MacChesney and Ballantine entirely with low angle shots and Higginbotham in high angle during the introduction sequence.

In this opposition between the traditional British officers and the three rebellious friends, *Gunga Din* echoes Ray's conceptions of Hollywood cinema's outlaw hero – who 'valued self-determination and freedom from entanglements' – and the official hero – the teacher, politician, or family man with a belief in 'collective action and the objective legal process that superseded private notions of right and wrong' – who often work together to defeat an antagonist, especially in westerns and disguised westerns.[28] Yet, *Gunga Din* presents a much more nuanced and conflicted official/outlaw hero dynamic rare in such an early Classical Hollywood film – largely as a result of its associations with Kipling's colonial India. Although Cutter, MacChesney and Ballantine act as the narrative's outlaw characters, the scope of the British Empire is so all-encompassing that they are as tethered to military duty as Higginbotham. At the same time, Weed and Mitchell constantly rely on the three to neutralise outside threats throughout the film, burnishing their reputations as the only capable soldiers in the entire regiment: they investigate the remnants of Tantrapur together and fend off a Thugee attack using dynamite and they discover the temple base of the cult and capture the Guru. As Weed says to the trio after their introductory brawl: 'I ought to take away your stripes' . . . 'But unfortunately, I need all three of you', a line that echoes the mutualistic relationship of colonial and settler identity. Even when the cavalry appears during the film's climactic battle, Stevens presents the unit as more victim than savior by centring the scene's suspense on the need to warn it about the ambush. Given their conformity to the traits of outlaw heroes, Cutter, MacChesney and Ballantine's ability to defeat the Thugees without support seems as plausible as their penchant for escaping from the film's four other action scenes unscathed.

Though the film endorses the trio's heroics and endows them with the same traits as Hollywood's western heroes, it also demonstrates an anxiety stemming from the obvious limits of their individualism. [29] Despite the dangers of the Thugees and other hazards of military life, the narrative's central conflict stems from Ballantine's upcoming discharge and impending marriage to Emmy (Joan Fontaine), the daughter of a wealthy tea trader. Upon returning from Tantrapur and revealing the Thugee plot, Ballantine is dismissed by Weed because the operation will extend far past his discharge date, causing MacChesney to call Ballantine 'indispensable' and Cutter to bargain with Weed: 'Well, Ballantine would be a great help, sir. If I may remind you, sir, the three of us have always brought off things very well together.' When Weed expresses his powerlessness in the situation, Cutter and MacChesney spy on Ballantine and Emmy in the hall, remarking on their friend's marriage as the film crosscuts between them and the couple:

MacChesney: Oh, that's horrible. She's charmed him like a snake.
Cutter: Siren!
Cutter: I wouldn't believe it if I didn't see it with me own eyes. You know it?
MacChesney: Me neither.

While Cutter and MacChesney's reaction to the union seemingly mirrors a standard example of homosocial behaviour, one must keep in mind Eve Kosofsky Sedgwick's own claim that,

> . . . 'patriarchy' is not a monolithic mechanism for subordinating 'the female' to 'the male'; it is a web of valences and significations that, while deeply tendentious, can historically through its articulations and divisions offer both material and ideological affordances to women as well as to men.[30]

Considering Sedgwick's discussion of the complex web of significations, one must look beyond the concept of homosociality and toward the entity ultimately responsible for providing affordances to men such as the soldiers and women like Emmy: the construction and maintenance of Empire. For Cutter and MacChesney, the union does not deserve scorn because of Ballantine's love for Emmy, but because it represents his dismissal from his friends' subversive army escapades and entrance into a traditional role in the British tea trade, a fact that MacChesney makes perfectly clear when Ballantine offers to help him rescue Cutter from the Guru: 'It says here that Thomas Anthony Ballantine is restored to the rank of citizen of Great Britain and his duty to her Majesty's service is over and done with . . . I'm saying goodbye, Pal. And I wish you luck in the tea business and your matrimony both.' Though the soldiers realise the immense scope of Empire and their inability to extricate themselves, membership in the army provides them with a role that allows for enough independence for the trio's hijinks in contrast to direct participation in the economy of Empire such as that of the tea trade. Similar to the American ideals and settler colonial identities they are intended to embody, the three soldiers express an open hostility toward Empire despite requiring aspects of its infrastructure to maintain some semblance of independence.

Reflecting the complexities of America's own relationship with British culture, Cutter and MacChesney do not resist the infringement on their autonomy that Emmy's family tea business directly represents through appeals to Ballantine's obligation to Her Majesty or overt statements concerning their fraternity. Instead, they appropriate the conventions of the Hollywood screwball comedy to both mock the rigidity of British culture and remind Ballantine of the potential for subversion inherent in military service that would be unavailable to him in the tea trade. As a genre intended, according to Schatz, to 'reaffirm faith in the traditional American ideal of a classless utopian society', screwball comedies unite protagonists from different socioeconomic standings through the discovery of their love for each other.[31] Equipped with Grant – already famous for entries in the genre such as *Topper* (1936), *The Awful Truth* (1937), and *Bringing up Baby* (1938) – Stevens employs screwball comedy's central convention of mocking upper-class mores to shed light on their hypocrisy, which the film translates into its military context by juxtaposing the trio's rebellious natures against the refined manners of the other officers.[32] However, given *Gunga Din*'s imperial adventure dynamic, the film acts as an inversion of the screwball comedy with Grant and company's antics opposing marital unity – a strategy to maintain the prestige of its British associations while preserving a popular Hollywood genre.

When they find out that Weed has groomed Higginbotham as Ballantine's replacement, Cutter and MacChesney hatch a plan to remove him from service. Borrowing a heavy sedative that MacChesney uses to care for Annie, his work elephant, Cutter and MacChesney spike the punch at Ballantine's engagement party so that their new colleague will have to take sick leave. Stevens executes the gag as a prolonged farce lasting nearly seven minutes: MacChesney prevents Weed and Mitchell from drinking the punch by pretending to fish a fly out of the bowl with his bare hands, Cutter initiates a long-winded toast to initiate Higginbotham into the group as he and MacChesney feign drinking, and MacChesney drops a large plant in the punch bowl that immediately droops when it meets the liquid. While this subplot is explicitly borrowed from *Gunga Din* screenwriters Ben Hecht and Charles MacArthur's 1921 Broadway smash *The Front Page* (which original *Gunga Din* director Howard Hawks remade as the Grant screwball comedy *His Girl Friday* in 1940), the humour in Stevens' film is not meant to unmask an upper-class rival, but to allow Cutter and MacChesney to expose the ineptitude of the most stereotypically 'British' character in the film while setting the plot in motion to dissolve Ballantine's engagement.[33] Within the colonial context of *Gunga Din*, the importance lies not in unifying two opposite positions, but in advocating the ingenuity and independence of the outlaw hero over stolid British traditionalism.

Stevens furthers his employment of screwball comedy convention in the film as Ballantine makes his final decision to stay in the army. Though Higginbotham's sickness allows Ballantine to attend the expedition, his tenure as a soldier still reaches its expiration date. As a result, when Ballantine offers to help MacChesney rescue the captured Cutter, he only agrees to take Ballantine along if he signs reenlistment papers: 'When we get Cutter, we'll tear up the papers. It'll be neat and according to regulation.' Despite Ballantine's objections that MacChesney is 'getting clever again', he consents to the plan, but only if he can keep the papers. MacChesney agrees, and after a fight with his wife in which Ballantine tells her that he 'hates the blasted army, but friendship, that's something else,' the reenlistment is not remarked on. However, when Ballantine and MacChesney are captured, MacChesney tricks the Guru by telling him that the papers in Ballantine's pocket contain the regiment's location. While he is distracted with the papers, MacChesney overpowers the Guru and takes them, stating 'Sergeant Ballantine hereby reenlists.' Ballantine feigns anger and playfully calls MacChesney a 'turncoat', but he has made the decision to forego his marriage and stay with his friends, contrary to both his statements of love for his wife and his alleged hatred of the army.

Through the execution of this screwball scheme, the film reveals its most developed depiction of the ambivalence innate in the relationship between Britain and America. Pitting the marriage contract against the reenlistment papers, MacChesney subverts the power of British law to preserve the trio's own moral and interpersonal codes, an ideology so important to maintain that even through his own torturous beatings and Cutter's untenable safety, MacChesney perceives it as the utmost priority. In addition, Ballantine can only become the mark of one of the trio's pranks at the point in the film when he is most British, riding with Emmy on his way to their civilian life. Such screwball conventions are meant to unite a couple and, according to Ray, resolve difficult choices such as those between marriage and military service by 'refusing to acknowledge that a choice is necessary' or 'by blurring the difference between the two sides'.[34] However, MacChesney's prank not only destroys Ballantine's marriage plans but also, in stark contrast to Hollywood convention, presents Ballantine's choice as substantial and not without consequence. With the shadow of the British Empire unshakeable, Ballantine is forced to make the right choice, maintaining his allegiance to the 'blasted army' for the sake of friendship while rejecting the marriage plans that would place him directly in the economic centre of Britain's imperial project.

'VERY REGIMENTAL, DIN': INSIDE/OUTSIDE THE 'OTHER'

While *Gunga Din* serves as a pivotal film that documents the dissolving of British cultural supremacy, its dismissal as merely, in the words of Richards, 'one of the greatest fun movies of all time' may have resulted from the problematic representations of its Indian characters.[35] In addition to being banned in India and other international markets, it became the victim of censorship by Washington's Office of War Information during its proposed re-release in 1942 for fear that it might lend credence to arguments that Britain was fighting merely to retain its colonies.[36] Much of the controversy stemmed from the film's disclaimer regarding the Thugee religious cult during the opening credits:

'Those portions of this picture dealing with the worship of the goddess Kali are based on historic fact.' At the time of its debut, historians discovered that India's roving band of Thugee stranglers was largely mythologised and acted, in the words of Mark Brown, as 'a lightning rod for British anxieties about their capacity to govern in India'.[37] Likewise, the film's implication that the worship of Kali was a fringe activity steeped in extremism became diluted not only because Kali is one of the most common goddesses in the Hindu religion but also because the goddess is worshipped in multiple places in multiple ways for specific regional purposes, rarely ever in a pure and abstract way, a factor that also had the effect of displacing Kali's feminine power as a form of deviancy.[38] Coupling the obvious inaccuracies of the film's 'historical presentation' with actors such as Sam Jaffe (Gunga Din) and Eduardo Ciannelli (the Guru) performing in blackface, the film's depictions of Indians, at worst, embody the most obvious kind of Orientalism, which Stevens ultimately apologised for along with what he saw as the film's complacency toward British colonialism.[39]

Gunga Din's appropriation of Kipling's India falls victim to the same Orientalist tendencies of Empire literature, but it also recalls Veracini's party of settlers run amok dressed as natives as it relates to Hollywood's Cinema of Empire. Though outlaw heroes, the film's central trio must retain their associations with Empire despite their predilection for subversion. However, as evidenced by the film's use of American actors in blackface, its Indian characters embody settlers dressed as natives exhibiting a similar sense of ethical nuance and rebellious spirit as the soldiers three. Like the trio at the film's centre, America cannot entirely erase its settler colony ties to the British Empire despite its attempts to negotiate methods of resistance against it. In addition, because of its settler colony inception and own imperialistic pursuits, the nation cannot quite identify with the legacy of colonialism underlying British control of India. As a result, *Gunga Din* problematises these depictions by endowing its Indian characters with the same sense of moral superiority and individualism thought self-evident in America's founding ideology. Though such a choice may foster a sense of solidarity between the trio and their Indian counterparts that facilitates a settler colonial identity attempting to differentiate itself from British culture, it also runs the risk of replicating the colonial discourse of the British Empire while exposing the mutualistic support inherent to the relationship between colonial and settler nations that Veracini discusses.

Although Stevens depicts the Guru as the primary antagonist of the film, the character resembles neither the British Empire's brutish Thugee stereotypes nor the 'noble savage' mentality customary of America's depiction of its own natives.[40] Instead, the Guru displays a talent for military strategy and justifications of war that conform more to the traits of Ray's 'official heroes' than an indigenous antagonist in a B-western. From the beginning of the film, the

Guru's soldiers use the British military's latent racism as their primary weapon, performing the roles of slyly civil Indians who engage in what Bhabha calls, 'the native refusal to unify the authoritarian, colonialist address' rather than the stereotypically unscrupulous others they appear to be at face value.[41] These undercover Thugees beg for sanctuary to fall in with units, overhear orders and eventually exterminate the soldiers – a similar, although more extreme, version of the deception that Cutter and company deploy throughout the film. In addition, the Guru uses the military's own tactics against it demonstrating his use of English and service protocol as primary ways to oppose his enemies. While Ballantine ultimately fools him with his American screwball shtick, the Guru can read Ballantine's papers himself, realising MacChesney's trick moments too late. Even when captured by the trio, the Guru is able both to save his own life and to buy time for the army to walk into the ambush, calmly letting his captors know that 'as long as I am alive, you live' and laughing off their threats to kill him: 'You would throw away your shield, brave soldier?' Throughout these sequences, Stevens consistently shoots the Guru from low angles, conveying his power and prestige, in sharp contrast to the high angles he uses in his compositions featuring Higginbotham and the other British officers.

While Stevens' focus on the Guru's talents for strategy elevates the character above typical 'savage' antagonists of western and imperial epics, the film complicates the Guru even further by depicting him as a mouthpiece for the arrogance and hypocrisy of the British imperial project. After defining his brutal lashing of Cutter as 'a lesson in the error of false pride,' the Guru reveals his place in the history of India's warriors: 'You seem to think warfare an English invention. Have you never heard of Chandragupta Maurya? He slaughtered all the armies left in India by Alexander the Great. India was a mighty nation then while Englishmen still dwelt in caves and painted themselves blue.' As he completes his monologue, he shows the trio his artillery units and the layout of his ambush for the British from the roof of the temple – a plan that uses the Guru's intricate knowledge of the landscape to defeat his enemies. Speaking in refined English not out of place on a theatrical stage, the Guru not only exposes Britons' primitive history but also reveals his nation's own heritage to agents of a colonial project, which functions on the false premise that colonised lands were unchartered territories free from history. While the conflict then shifts from the heroic British defeating the Thugee army to the need to save a regiment ignorant of its territory from a plan far superior to any conceived by the British Army, Stevens enriches his comparison of civilisations through the Guru's speech pattern. Mocking the British for their ineffective battle strategies and primitive origins, the Guru espouses a clear anticolonial politics. Yet, in delivering his dialogue through a distinct English accent, Stevens depicts him as an amalgamation of British influence, Orientalist thought and American independence.

Not content with shattering the illusions of superiority of his captors, the

Guru challenges their own dedication to their nation as he sacrifices himself to a pit of vipers so the battle can commence more quickly: 'You have sworn as soldiers if need be to die for your faith, which is your country. For England. Well, India is my faith and my country, and I can die for my faith and my country as readily as you for yours.' Considering that the three soldiers spend the entire narrative mocking British authorities, seeking treasure and lambasting the 'blasted army', as was customary of Anglo-Indians who often viewed their service as, in the words of B. J. Moore-Gilbert, a prison of 'banishment' and 'bondage', the Guru's parting words unravel the illusion of nationalism at the foundation of Empire.[42] However, the Guru's love of country and intense patriotism parallel the spirit of self-sacrifice that defined both America's own struggle for independence and Indian anticolonial politics. As the only character in the film dedicated to the preservation and restoration of his nation, the Guru occupies a contradictory position, deserving of vilification for his violent assaults on seeming innocents, but respected for his steadfast belief in an autonomous nation free from Britain's control.

Departing from his revisionist depiction of the Guru, Stevens uses Gunga Din as a cipher to highlight the racism and strict hierarchies of the British military. Speaking in broken English and dressed in a turban, Din embodies the Indian stereotypes customary of Victorian adventure tales and Empire cinema. Though the film's soldiers – including MacChesney and Ballantine – scoff at Din's desire to join the army, Din maintains a friendly camaraderie with Cutter throughout the narrative. In one of the film's most famous sequences, Cutter discovers Din mimicking military marching patterns fully knowing that the highest Din could rise in the army would be leader of an Indian unit. Slightly amused, Cutter assumes the role of commanding officer, instructing Din how to march and salute, an action which forms a bond between the two (Figure 1.2). When MacChesney throws Cutter in jail to stop him from seeking out the treasure, Din hatches his own screwball plan to spring Cutter by borrowing Annie the elephant to destroy the cell and ride to a treasure site

Figure 1.2 Cutter (Cary Grant) and Gunga Din (Sam Jaffe) mimic the unit's marches.

that turns out to be the Thugee temple. While the scene appears to adhere to criticisms of Kipling such as Tim Christensen's contention that Kipling's distinction between whiteness and other ethnicities, 'allows what has often been labeled racial "anxiety" to become a form of enjoyment that strengthens, rather than threatens, the racial hierarchy of imperial India', the film's settler perspective complicates this ethnic dynamic.[43] Through creating an alliance between Din and the British character played by the film's biggest star, Stevens invokes an association between the most Americanised soldier in the film and its most stereotype-riddled character.[44] Noticing that he and Din share the same talent for rebellious scheming and dedication to their friends, Cutter develops a relationship with him unencumbered by the military duty and matrimony that have trapped his cohorts, allowing Stevens to depict them as two individualised subjects bound to subservient roles within the British Empire.[45]

Despite his bond with Cutter, the Din of the film – as is true for the Din of the poem – is most important to the narrative after death. However, unlike the Din of the poem who dies while dragging the wounded speaker to safety when 'a bullet came an' drilled the beggar clean', Din succumbs to multiple wounds after an act of supreme bravery in the film.[46] With Cutter wounded and Ballantine and MacChesney overcome in battle, Din climbs one of the temple's pillars and plays his bugle to warn the approaching soldiers of the ambush. The regiment hears the bugling and changes formation in time to overtake the Thugee army, but not before Din dies a violent death and his corpse dangles from the scaffolding. After the battle, Stevens cuts to a shot of Din dressed for burial in full uniform as Weed and Kipling hover over the body. Taking a paper from Kipling, Weed recites the last lines of the poem:

So I'll meet 'im later on
At the place where 'e is gone –
Where it's always double drill and no canteen.
'E'll be squattin' on the coals
Givin' drink to poor damned souls,
An' I'll get a swig in hell from Gunga Din!
  Yes, Din! Din! Din!
You Lazarushian-leather Gunga Din!
  Though I've belted you and flayed you,
  By the livin' Gawd that made you,
You're a better man than I am, Gunga Din![47]

Considering Din's relationship with Cutter, Stevens' choice to make Weed the speaker of the poem seems to violate the narrative trajectory of the film. Yet, the choice permits Stevens to both maintain the plausibility of the source text and absolve the trio from their complicity in the colonial project. Kipling's speaker honours Gunga Din's bravery, but he appears to believe that colonial hierarchy will remain intact in the afterlife, leaving Din in the same role he held in the military even as he is damned for eternity for his lack of Christian faith. Likewise, the speaker also assumes he will 'get a swig in hell' from Din, though his reasons for damnation are unclear – either an expression of guilt over his role within Empire that justified his abuse of Din or a manifestation of the metaphorical 'hell' that Kipling used to describe military service.[48] Within the context of the film, attributing such lines to Cutter, or even MacChesney or Ballantine, is antithetical to their admiration for Din and their Americanised resistance to Empire. With Weed delivering the eulogy, the ambivalence of Empire and its seemlier characteristics rest solely on the British character with the highest military rank. Avoiding compromising the prestige that Kipling's attachment provides, Stevens interrogates the differences between colonial and settler culture, subtly conveying his Hollywood depictions of the soldiers three as ideologically opposed to the Empire and removed from culpability despite their inability to escape its structures.

Resulting from its simultaneous legitimisation of and resistance to the literature of the British Empire, *Gunga Din* serves as a seminal film for understanding the political foundations of Hollywood adaptations of Victorian literature. Although attempting to trumpet its own cultural forms, Hollywood cemented itself as a hegemonic force in cultural production that would have a similar scope and influence over the world as the literature of the British Empire did at the height of its power. However, by positioning Hollywood cinema's origins as a form of settler resistance to colonial identity, one can see not only the lingering importance of the British Empire's cultural impact but also the complexities of contemporary Empire's mechanisms of reappropriating and repackaging methods of resistance with which contemporary postcolonial filmmakers working within and against the Hollywood system must contend.

CHAPTER 2

'He Is Not Here by Accident': Transit, Sin and the Model Settler in Patrick Lussier's *Dracula 2000*

In the sixty years between *Gunga Din*'s 'Golden Year' release and the dawn of the 21st century, Victorian literature adaptations endured as staples of Hollywood despite a litany of industry disruptions: the onset and aftermath of World War II, the massive declines in ticket sales due to the widespread adoption of television, the rise of the summer blockbuster with the releases of Steven Spielberg's *Jaws* (1975) and George Lucas' *Star Wars* (1977), and the advent of VHS and DVD home-video technology. As the industry evolved, so did film adaptation of colonial texts, a shift on full display in the work of David Lean as he moved from the nostalgic postwar nationalism of *Great Expectations* and *Oliver Twist* (1948) to the 70mm Hollywood spectacle of *Lawrence of Arabia* (1962) and the Merchant Ivory prestige of *A Passage to India* (1984). Though Lean provides a potent example of the Cinema of Empire's longevity, perhaps the most prominent figure in Hollywood film's ongoing devotion to the Victorian era is Count Dracula, who is not only likely the most filmed character of all time (with the possible exceptions of fellow Victorians Tarzan and Sherlock Holmes) but also has amassed a body of academic criticism that has made Bram Stoker's 1897 novel one of the most studied texts of the 19th century.[1] Such insights are especially true when considering that, while the vampire has a range of origins from early accounts of demon possession to the legacy of Vlad the Impaler, Stoker's Count has dominated the image of the vampire in popular culture and academic criticism with even autonomous nosferatus from different narrative universes owing a debt to Dracula.[2] That Stoker's novel appears just two years after the first public film screening to offer commentary on the state of the body in the age of the cinematographic image further establishes its legacy as forever intertwined with the cinema.[3]

Dracula made his film debut in Murnau's German Expressionist classic *Nosferatu*, though Stoker's estate successfully sued for infringement as

Murnau had never secured the rights to the novel.[4] The first official adaptation would arrive nine years later in 1931 when Tod Browning's *Dracula* became an instant phenomenon for Depression audiences and sold out theatres nationwide. *Dracula*'s success was so resounding that Universal Studios mogul Carl Laemmle, Jr immediately followed up the film with a quickly produced secession of horror adaptations based on 19th century British novels. The success of James Whale's *Frankenstein* eclipsed even *Dracula*'s popularity in the last months of 1931, thus establishing the legendary Universal Monsters that transformed the studio into a major Hollywood player.[5] The character experienced an endless cycle of iterations throughout the 20th century: British company Hammer Films' *Dracula* (1958) starring Christopher Lee and Peter Cushing and its seven sequels (including *Dracula A.D. 1972*); Paul Morrissey's Andy Warhol-produced *Blood for Dracula* (1974) with Udo Kier as a Dracula starving from a dearth of virgin blood in the midst of the counterculture; John Badham's misfire *Dracula* (1979) starring Frank Langella as a heartthrob Count more akin to John Travolta in Badham's breakout film *Saturday Night Fever* (1977) than Stoker's vampire; Werner Herzog's remake of Murnau's film, *Nosferatu the Vampyre* (1979), starring Klaus Kinski; Francis Ford Coppola's *Bram Stoker's Dracula* (1992), which used 19th century film technology to position Gary Oldman's Dracula as an aristocratic enemy of the Catholic Church who is equal parts Stoker and Vlad.[6] Such a list does not even begin to broach the ubiquitous presence of the Count beyond the horror film in outright parodies such as Stan Dragoti's George Hamilton vehicle *Love at First Bite* (1979) and Mel Brooks' *Dracula: Dead and Loving It* (1995) or Fred Dekker's cult classic *The Monster Squad* (1987), a family-friendly Universal Monsters reboot featuring Dracula (Duncan Regehr) facing off against a group of kids who befriend Frankenstein's monster.

As Hollywood entered the 21st century, filmmakers continued to mine Stoker's narrative with three variations of *Dracula* that are both a testament to the enduring popularity of Stoker and indicative of Hollywood film industry economics leading up to the Great Recession [the financial crisis of 2008]. As Miramax's *Scream* trilogy came to its conclusion with the release of *Scream 3*, Bob Weinstein, the company's co-founder and head of its genre label Dimension Films, hoped to continue a working relationship with horror legend Wes Craven and establish another successful franchise. After hearing about an offhand idea to modernise Dracula from Craven's long-time editor Patrick Lussier in late 1999, Weinstein greenlit the project as *Dracula 2000*, offering Lussier the chance to direct if he could conceive the concept and complete a final cut in time for a holiday release within the next year.[7] Shooting in Lussier's native Canada as well as New Orleans in the summer of 2000, Dimension released the film six months later to largely negative reviews and an international box-office take of $47 million on a budget of under $40 million.[8]

Initially set in contemporary London, *Dracula 2000* traces the Count's accidental resurrection by a group of American thieves who plan a heist of an antiquities dealership owned by Van Helsing (Christopher Plummer) and staffed by his protégé Simon Sheppard (Jonny Lee Miller). When Dracula (Gerard Butler) is released amid a transatlantic flight, he crashes in the bayou outside New Orleans and begins a search for Mary Heller (Justine Waddell), Van Helsing's estranged daughter, who also shares Dracula's lineage as a result of her father's reliance on leeches filled with the Count's blood to achieve immortality and stave off Dracula's inevitable return. As Van Helsing and Simon follow Dracula to New Orleans in the middle of Mardi Gras, the Count rebuilds his vampire army and sires three new brides in hopes of turning Mary to the darkness and extinguishing the human race. The film was popular enough in its home-video release to spawn two direct-to-DVD sequels, *Dracula II: Ascension* (2003) and *Dracula III: Legacy* (2005), unrelated to the narrative of the first film but also directed by Lussier. Although *Dracula 2000* did not transcend the horror genre to achieve the crossover appeal and blockbuster box-office of Craven's iconic trilogy, it serves as an example of midbudget, R-rated studio horror that added a sense of gloss unavailable to its pre-*Scream* slasher movie forbearers and contemporary $5-million-and-under descendants from companies such as Blumhouse (*The Purge* franchise [2013, 2014, 2016, 2018], *Sinister* [2012, 2015], *Get Out* [2017]).

Briefly discussed in this book's introduction as an example of indie Victorian adaptations, fellow Canadian Guy Maddin's *Dracula: Pages from a Virgin's Diary* was released 18 months after *Dracula 2000* to much better reviews, but the negligible box-office domestically and abroad customary of a Canadian cinema where such fiercely local projects are, in the words of Jerry White, 'foreign films in their own country'.[9] Perhaps the most critically successful adaptation of Stoker's text since Herzog's remake of *Nosferatu*, the film, as Sarah J. Heidt writes, is 'an admirably specific critical reading of the novel and also a musing on the history of film itself', with its melodramatic satire of xenophobia and subtle commentary on migrancy in Canada.[10] Maddin's settler colony roots and intertextual play make it relevant for this project's purposes, but as a film situated outside the scope of Hollywood yet ultimately absorbed under the banner of indie.

As Maddin's film played American festivals and art houses, Universal Studios began an early marketing blitz for Stephen Sommers' *Van Helsing* (2004), a tangential adaptation of *Dracula* more akin to its writer/director's *The Mummy* (1999) and *The Mummy Returns* (2001) than a late-Victorian period piece. Depicting the Dutch doctor of Stoker's novel as a monster-slaying assassin in the employ of the Vatican, the film's Van Helsing (Hugh Jackman) faces off against Count Dracula (Richard Roxburgh). Incorporating other Universal horror properties in a similar manner to *The Monster Squad*, the plot revolves around the Frankenstein monster and the various wolf men whom Dracula and his brides use as energy sources to hatch a vampire army. Despite the seeming ludicrousness of its B-movie plot, the project was not merely a halfhearted attempt for Universal to recycle its 1930s monster icons for a summer tentpole cashgrab. With its $148 million budget, it was the studio at its synergistic pinnacle, a product intended not only to spawn sequels, video games and a television series but also to turn the film's Prague set into the Disneyland of horror cinema by resurrecting the Universal Monsters: Dracula, Frankenstein, the Wolf Man and, in what amounts to a cameo, Dr Jekyll and Mr Hyde.[11]

Van Helsing's disappointing $120 million domestic gross and general critical drubbing curtailed the studio's reboot hopes for a decade until it tried to revive the Universal Monsters again as the 'Dark Universe' franchise with Gary Shore's moderately successful *Dracula Untold* (2014) and Alex Kurtzman's disastrous 2017 reboot of *The Mummy* starring Tom Cruise.[12] However, the film remains pivotal to discussions of the sheer dominance of Hollywood's cinematic style and business practices at the height of global Hollywood.[13] Rather than rely on the cultural clout of a canonical work, Sommers' film exists in a context in which classic Hollywood's iterations of Stoker's, Mary Shelley's and Robert Louis Stevenson's characters have completely dislocated traces of the source texts, an example of Hollywood's usurpation of the British Empire's former cultural prowess that began with films such as *Gunga Din*. In addition, the film's production and ultimate economic success hinged upon a global presence both through its on-location shooting in the Czech Republic and its international cast and crew, including the Australians Jackman and Roxburgh, American Sommers, and British Kate Beckinsale, who plays Anna Valerious, a Transylvanian aristocratic monster hunter and Van Helsing's sometime love interest. Perhaps most importantly, the film relied on international grosses, which would eventually total $300 million, to become profitable.[14] With its CGI action sequences and successful international dissemination, a film such as *Van Helsing* expresses the mass media industry's own preservation of its form of administration via the spectacle of Hollywood magic and lays claim to British cultural forms to extend the concerns of US-based multinational corporations. Sommers' film all but erases its character's true origins. Within the world of *Van Helsing*, there is no place for resistant reading of Empire literature, nor is there a need for familiarity with the underlying social critique of 'otherness' present in the original Universal Monsters films. There is only commodity – produced, packaged and distributed with no regard for history or national community.

Though it is the epitome of synergised Hollywood, one should not dismiss *Van Helsing* as merely empty spectacle. In its finer moments, the film quite effectively captures contemporary anxieties over the ethics of hierarchal institutions such as the Catholic Church and the nation state. Yet, its demonstration of Hollywood's international dominance is of central concern to the current wave of postcolonial, diasporic and settler colonial filmmakers to which Maddin and Lussier belong. With its abundance of critical praise and clearly Canadian concerns, Maddin's film has become the go-to settler colonial reimagining of Stoker. However, when considering Lussier's status as a Canadian filmmaker working in Hollywood and – due to tax incentives – his home country on a studio project, his reimagined *Dracula* appears as an integral text to both the interfidelity approach and the role of Victorian adaptations in the 21st century.

This chapter examines *Dracula 2000* as both a resistant text of settler colonial identity and as an example of Hollywood's influence on the Canadian film industry. Focusing on a Dracula who is revealed to be an undead Judas Iscariot and a Van Helsing sustained through the 20th century by injections of Dracula's blood, the film engages with a poststructuralist cycle of the settler/subject/colonial dynamic. Likewise, the film's relocation from the imperial centre of London to New Orleans not only positions America as a contemporary imperial power but also harkens back to the port city's legacy as a former hub for slavery and global trade during Stoker's time. Within this context, Lussier articulates a model for the ideal global settler colonial through the character of Mary Heller, Van Helsing's daughter who is marked with Dracula's blood and torn between her family's legacy in past and present imperial centres. Shot primarily on Canadian sound stages that doubled for London and New Orleans, *Dracula 2000* also embodies contemporary production politics in which Hollywood's relationship to settler nations such as Canada provides economic support for national cinemas while still dominating domestic box-office.

VAMPIRES, SETTLER COLONIALS AND GLOBAL CONSUMPTION

In his pivotal article, 'The Occidental Tourist', Stephen Arata deems Stoker's novel a fantasy of reverse colonisation in which subjects of the British Empire see the violence of imperial practice mirrored in Dracula's arrival to Britain.[15] For Arata, Dracula is the most Western character in the novel, a reverse coloniser who has fully mastered the art of mimicry to such an extent that it takes an ensemble of model sons and daughters of Britain to unite and ultimately defeat him.[16] In light of such postcolonial readings of *Dracula* over the past two decades, Lussier's most radical break from his source text is the total absence of British characters with the exception of Simon, who assumes the function of Jonathan Harker, though now as a supporting player in the battle against Dracula to both Van Helsing and Mary Heller. Likewise, Mary becomes the narrative's Mina Harker, though she has no romantic ties to anyone beyond a subtle flirtation with her priest and childhood friend, Father David (Nathan Fillion). Her origins are also transnational as she has lived in New Orleans for most of her life after her mother fled London upon discovering Van Helsing's secret. With Lucy (pop star Vitamin C) now a New Orleans Gen-Exer, Lussier eliminates her fiancé Arthur Holmwood from the narrative. Dr. Seward, Lucy's second suitor and the other British member of Van Helsing's 'Crew of Light', who kills the undead Lucy and defeats Dracula in the novel, becomes merely an allusion in the film, the name of the coroner (Robert Verlaque) who Dracula slaughters when his first victims become the subject of a murder investigation.[17] Subsequently, Renfield, Seward's patient and Dracula's human minion, is also entirely absent in contrast to his recurrent appearances in other Hollywood adaptations.

Despite the film's numerous deviations from the novel, its Van Helsing largely resembles the source text's depiction. Writing to Holmwood about Lucy's fading health in Stoker's novel, Seward convinces his rival of Van Helsing's unparalleled expertise:

> He is a seemingly arbitrary man, but this is because he knows what he is talking about better than any one else. He is a philosopher and a metaphysician, and one of the most advanced scientists of his day; and he has, I believe, an absolutely open mind. This, with an iron nerve, a temper of the ice-brook, an indomitable resolution, self-command, and toleration exalted from virtues to blessings, and the kindliest and truest heart that beats – these form his equipment for the noble work that he is doing for mankind – work both in theory and practice, for his views are as wide as his all-embracing sympathy.[18]

Similar to all of Europe's contribution to the making of Kurtz in *Heart of Darkness*, Van Helsing is the paragon of European civilisation, which Stoker underscores by referring to him in correspondence as 'Abraham Van Helsing, M. D., D. Ph., D. Lit., etc., etc.'.[19] Yet, like Kurtz, Van Helsing's polymorphous identity prevents him from becoming the model British subject, and he is the perfect foil for Dracula's otherness. As Robin Wood writes, 'The good and noble British (and the American) cannot cope with Dracula – to cope with him requires access to knowledge that would threaten their innocence . . . Van Helsing has possession of that knowledge; the novel also gives him connections as close to Dracula as Budapest.'[20] Similar to the Count, Van Helsing remains at the margins of the Empire, a traveller whose knowledge fuels the imperial centre – as evidenced by his mentorship of Seward – but who is also severed from the

British culture whose pure imperial imagination he must guard. He serves as the embodiment of how, for Paul Gilroy, 'The imperial and colonial past continues to shape political life in the overdeveloped-but-no-longer-imperial countries.'[21]

Lussier's film retains Van Helsing's intellectual prowess and uncompromised allegiance to Europe. However, achieving immortality by leeching Dracula's blood also positions Van Helsing as the lone witness to the anxieties Arata discusses coming to fruition. Although he has kept London safe from Dracula, the Empire the vampire threatened to disrupt a century ago has crumbled. As a result, Van Helsing undertakes the roles of guardian against Dracula, heir to Empire and mentor for Simon, the film's lone and rootless progeny of the imperial project. His expansive antiquities trade and 'personal collection acquired by means not always befitting of the law' serve as a repository of the weapons of imperial force as well as the commodities of global culture, reflecting, in the words of Benedict Anderson, the 'alternative legitimacies' that substitute for conquest embodied in the imperial project's desire to 'museumize' its subjects.[22] Legendary Canadian actor Plummer further emphasises Van Helsing's assumed role as imperial protector, working with Lussier on a hybrid accent that bears a faint trace of Dutch, and which becomes increasingly English as his immortality wears on.[23]

For Van Helsing and the British heroes of Stoker's novel, the ultimate goal is to eradicate the Count and ensure the safety of the Empire and Mina's Victorian femininity. In her closing journal entry written after she is delivered from vampirism, Mina recalls the Crew of Light's final interaction with Dracula in which 'almost in the drawing of a breath, the whole body crumbled into dust and passed from our sight' after Jonathan shears through the Count's throat and Lucy's American suitor, Quincey Morris, plunges a bowie knife into the vampire's heart before succumbing to the wounds he incurred in the battle.[24] Not undercutting this series of events, Lussier's film incorporates Stoker's ending as an alternate history. Early in the film, Simon meets with Van Helsing to discuss his latest acquisition: a Slavic crossbow that shoots silver and is not bad 'for Eastern Europe'. Complaining about the weapon's utility, Simon remarks how it pales 'to what they were using in England at the time' and that it seems like something his boss' grandfather would have used to hunt vampires in Bram Stoker's book. Laughing off the ludicrousness that his country doctor grandfather could have inspired Stoker's novel, the immortal Van Helsing buffers Simon's offer to resell the weapon, responding that he will keep what he likes because 'We turn a profit, do we not?' (Figure 2.1).

Yet, in the aftermath of Dracula's first attack in America, Van Helsing admits to Simon that the ultimate destruction Mina relates in the novel is a ruse to relegate Dracula to the realm of myth. In flashback, Lussier reveals Dracula's real fate: lured into a cage by Van Helsing's trickery with mirrors, he is commodified and consigned to the bowels of Carfax Antiques, his nemesis feeding

Figure 2.1 Van Helsing (Christopher Plummer) and Simon (Jonny Lee Miller) make light of Stoker's novel.

off his vampiric blood for the better part of a century to maintain his own immortality. Consequently, rather than arrive from Eastern Europe to engage in a project of reverse colonisation in the imperial centre, Lussier's Dracula begins the narrative as a possession of Empire. In this revisionist treatment of Van Helsing and Dracula, Lussier echoes Veracini's classification of vampire stories as inherently settler colonial narratives 'about the specific difference between discrete groups and processes of assimilation that can only proceed in one direction'.[25] As, in Veracini's words, 'pale and exotic beings that empty the land and are obsessed about owning it', both Van Helsing and Dracula serve as settler vampire figures on eternal quests for ownership of antiquities, bodies and the land of past and present imperialisms.

Resulting from the film's settler colonial associations, its treatment of Dracula acts as an obvious exception to what Milly Williamson deems the 20th- and 21st-century trend of the 'sympathetic vampire' that, though popularised by Anne Rice's Lestat, the Cullens from *Twilight*, and Angel and Spike from Joss Whedon's *Buffy the Vampire Slayer* universe (1997–2004), has its roots in Byron.[26] Unlike the aforementioned vampires in contemporary popular culture or even the Asian-Canadian Dracula of *Pages from a Virgin's Diary*, Lussier's Count is an unapologetic and unbridled force with which not even Van Helsing can contend. Much of Dracula's rage (and his hatred of silver and crosses) stems from his origins as Judas Iscariot, who upon attempting suicide following his betrayal of Jesus, was left wandering the earth undead and cast out of God's kingdom. Lussier's intertextual bridging of the New Testament and Stoker admittedly appears erratic, especially in light of the mockery in the film's more scathing reviews, including *The New York Times* critic Stephen Holden's outright assault on the plot as implausible 'sewage.'[27] Yet, this left-field narrative turn also allows Dracula to go beyond Stoker's original colonial context to foster comparisons between the novel's postcoloniality and readings of the Gospels as biblical or postbiblical discourses of ancient colonial relationships.[28] Such readings position Christ as a postcolonial figure whose resurrection after death on the colonial cross marks the first step for a revolution in which, as Stephen D. Moore writes, 'it is not just the invaders who must be swept away, but the comprador class who have made the continuing control of the land and its people possible'.[29] Postcolonial readings of the Jesus narrative as a cosmic showdown between Rome and Christ have inherent caveats due to the host of anti-imperial messiah figures in Judaism as well as Christianity's integral role in European colonialism.[30] At the same time, they allow for a multi-dimensional view of Judas, not merely as Jesus' betrayer, but as a Jew entrenched by a host of imperial forces, from the Roman Empire to local politicians such as Pontius Pilate, to a self-proclaimed messiah who defied the expectations of prophecy. In these readings, Judas appears less a villain and more akin to Thomas Macaulay's 'interpreter class' of natives, caught in-between imperial rule and national autonomy with blurred allegiances.[31]

Consequently, Lussier's Dracula becomes Empire's eternal precipitate, his guilt over the betrayal and anger of a Christ who has damned him fuelling his rage and unrepentant evil. The film's pitting of Dracula against characters whose names are allusions to the mother/female companion of Christ and two of the disciples, (Simon and 'Matthew' Van Helsing) underscores such connections. Lussier further complicates this depiction of Dracula by also associating him with the figure of the Wandering Jew who, in medieval Christian legend, Jesus cursed to roam the Earth until the second coming for mocking him on the way to the Crucifixion. Though the Wandering Jew has no fixed identity (various iterations have assumed him to be a range of minor biblical characters from Pilate's doorkeeper Cartaphilus to King Ahasuerus), he assumes the role as, according to Hyam Maccoby, the embodiment of the Jews' necessary function in Christianity as 'An Executioner, who, like the hangman once in England, was shunned by ordinary people and banned from their homes, just because he performed for them an act which they regarded as necessary, but had not the courage to perform themselves.'[32] Similar to the Wandering Jew, the film's Dracula is an executioner unbound by time, with obscure origins, his true identity only alluded to in the Aramaic he scrawls both on the deck of *The Demeter* in the film's opening credits and after he successfully massacres Van Helsing in Mary's bedroom.

While Lussier's location of Dracula as an amalgamation of these two Jewish figures roots him in the Empires of antiquity, it also recalls the link between Marx's characterisation of capital as vampiric and the anti-Semitic associations between Jews and the banking system in the Victorian Era.[33] Additionally, this Jewish context evokes readings of *Dracula* as allegorical and indicative of Stoker's own Irish-Victorian heritage in which, as Joseph Valente writes,

> The Irish and the Jews split the distinction between of being white-skinned specimens of the other in fin de siècle Britain, and Dracula's 'extraordinary pallor' underlines this shared estate (27), which factored heavily in the sort of domestic cosmopolitanism current among Stoker's devolutionist compatriots.[34]

The Count of *Dracula 2000* then becomes a cyclical settler, simultaneously a product of and participant in a linked trajectory of imperial force.

Given Dracula's multifaceted settler identity, the film's shift from London to New Orleans for the majority of the narrative places him in a region that is perhaps most representative of the US's own imperial history. Characterising Louisiana as a 'borderland of American culture', Thadious M. Davis writes that the state 'represented the permeable cultural boundaries and melding of the racial, linguistic, culinary, artistic aspects of several cultures' as well as a region in which port cities like New Orleans were sights of commercial exchange and body flows.[35] Such port cities are vital connections both for the colonies of Europe in the Caribbean and the fraught settler relationships not only between dominant US culture and the often overlooked Creoles of Louisiana but also the English settlers in the North and the largely Scots-Irish migrants to the South of particular importance to a vampire film based on an Irish author's work starring a Scottish actor as Dracula.[36] As a city that links two geographies of British imperialism and came to prominence in the 19th century, New Orleans is also indicative of the US's increased power during the Victorian era that was a central concern of Stoker's novel. In his discussion of Quincey Morris, Andrew Smith views Lucy's American suitor as representative of 'An American desire for the subjugation of Europe' that suggests an even larger threat for Victorian England than the Eastern Count.[37] With his 'kind of belief in a Winchester when there is any trouble of that sort around', Morris acts as a hybrid of intimidating American masculinity with a head that Van Helsing remarks 'is level at all times, but most so when there is to hunt.'[38] Suggestively, he is also the only member of the Crew of Light to die vanquishing Dracula, a final battle that functions to annihilate both threatening foreign interlopers and restore order to the imperial centre. Yet, Morris' presence continues after death when Jonathan and Mina name their firstborn Quincey Harker, a child who shares his birthday with the anniversary of Morris' (and Dracula's) death, and whose name also conveys the inevitable ascension of the US in the twilight of the Victorian era.

Although Morris is absent from Lussier's film, Americans abroad are represented by the techno-savvy thieves led by Marcus (Omar Epps) and Van Helsing's turncoat assistant Solina (Jennifer Esposito) who unwittingly release Dracula. No longer lending their strength to defend the Empire, Marcus' operation assumes the Count's role of reverse coloniser, pilfering Van Helsing's vault and stealing the silver coffin that holds the vampire. Unlike Morris with his rugged whiteness, the thieves are a diverse lot: African-Americans Marcus and Trick (Sean Patrick Thomas), Hispanic Solina, Asian-American Dax (Tig Fong) and the Irish Nightshade (Danny Masterson). Resuscitated by the corpses of Dax and his hacker friend Eddie (Lochlyn Munro) when Van Helsing's booby traps splatter their blood over the Count's coffin, Dracula butchers the remaining crew aboard their getaway plane, returning to his primary form and creating the core of the vampire army he will unleash on Simon and Van Helsing in New Orleans. In substituting the plane for *The Demeter*, the film combines the novel's Gothic imagery with the force of global transit to convey Dracula not as a reverse coloniser but as the ultimate settler who unmasks the Americans' colonial desires and redeploys them in the South's quintessential port city. Consequently, Dracula both liberates and exploits his army of colour, echoing Jodi A. Byrd's concept of 'the transit of Empire' in which indigenous populations are deferred and displaced into a nonexistent past and impossible future. As Byrd writes:

> The deferred 'Indian' that transits U.S. empire over continents and oceans is recycled and reproduced so that empire might cohere and consolidate subject and object, self and other, within those transits. In the process, racialization replaces colonization as the site of critique, and the structuring logics of dispossession are displaced onto settlers and arrivants who substitute for and as indigenous in order to consolidate control and borders at that site of differentiation.[39]

In his invasion of New Orleans, Dracula uses a host of racially diverse vampire bodies to consolidate his control and ascend to power, perpetuating a cycle of imperial violence from Jesus' crucifixion to indigenous genocide to the slave trade and anti-immigrant sentiment. In their transition to vampires, the thieves become unified, their difference partially erased as they are subsumed into the arrivant Dracula's designs. Such a transition also serves as a perversion of the Good Thief narrative in which the gang's members are not unified in a heavenly kingdom, but in the brute force of vampirism – the newest iterations of in-between settlers with roots, like Judas, in marginalised communities.

Unlike the vampires of the 1980s and 1990s who are, in the words of Stacey Abbott, 'born and bred within the urban milieu', this 21st century Count finds himself in an urban milieu born and bred by the cycles of oppression of which he has belonged for two millennia.[40] As Dracula arrives in New Orleans for the first time, he stops in front of a Jumbotron playing a music video (Figure 2.2) that intercuts the metal band Monster Magnet with stock footage of crosses, nuclear bomb explosions, riots, World War II combat and softcore pornography. The film's featuring of Monster Magnet also serves to connect this visual

Figure 2.2 Dracula (Gerard Butler) watches music videos at the Virgin Megastore upon arriving in New Orleans.

collage of imperialism to global capital, suggesting the importance of the film soundtrack as a way to reflect the identities of niche audiences and initiate a cycle of media industry texts that, like the Count, live on beyond the film.[41] Transfixed, a smiling Dracula deems the pastiche of fetishised imperialism 'Brilliant'; he is at home and unbridled in his surroundings. Othered by Van Helsing's crumbling London and settling in a vital trade hub of its imperial successor, Lussier's Dracula evolves into a global coloniser.

GENDER, HOLLYWOOD HORROR AND THE MODEL SETTLER

Readings of *Dracula* in a postcolonial context have become more prominent over the past two decades, but it remains a work largely approached through the lens of gender and its presentation of Victorian womanhood. For Judith Weissman, the novel is 'A man's vision of a noble band of men restoring a woman to purity and passivity, saving them from the horrors of vampirism, it is an extreme version of the stereotypically Victorian attitudes toward sexual roles.'[42] Central to such readings of the novel is Lucy Westenra, the 'Light of the West', whose lament 'Why can't they let a girl marry three men, or as many as want her?' has positioned her as the epitome of the emerging New Woman in the late 19th century.[43] As Lucy succumbs to Dracula's appeal and becomes the 'Bloofer Woman' that the Crew of Light ultimately dispatches as, notes Sally Ledger, punishment for Lucy's sexual deviancy, Mina emerges as the ideal Victorian woman, not only surviving Dracula's siring of her due to her innate purity but also transcribing the various journal entries, letters and newspaper clippings that form Stoker's novella.[44] Expressing his admiration for Mina, Van Helsing proclaims, 'She is one of God's women, fashioned by

His own hand to show us men and other women that there is a heaven where we can enter, and that its light can be here on earth. So true, so sweet, so noble, so little an egoist – and that, let me tell you, is much in this age, so skeptical and selfish.'[45] Considering Mina's narrative and social importance, the relative absence of other female characters beyond Mina, Lucy, Dracula's brides, and Lucy's mother – who dies soon after the novel begins – allows for an easy hierarchy of Victorian female purity.

Amid the litany of radical alterations and character erasures to the source text, Lussier's film retains the novel's preoccupations with its female characters while also extending them into the realm of the Hollywood horror film. Lucy (now Westerman) remains Mina's best friend and confidante. However, since her suitors are absent, her transformation into the Bloofer Woman, the Crew of Light's blood transfusions (and their gang rape connotations) and her eventual execution that have become so central to Stoker criticism are entirely absent. Instead, Lucy assumes a more minor role, transformed into one of Dracula's brides midway through the film when the Count follows her to the house she shares with Mary and states, 'I don't drink . . . coffee' before taking her upstairs.[46] Deviating sharply from the novel in which Lucy's dalliance with Dracula is implied by Mina's discovery of 'two little red points like pin-pricks, and on the band of her nightdress was a drop of blood', Lucy and Dracula passionately consummate their relationship levitating above a bed before Dracula sires her offscreen.[47]

Rather than update the dichotomy between New Woman and model Victorian, Lussier employs the film's female characters to playfully subvert the conventions of the novel and the Hollywood horror film. In addition to the vamped Lucy, Dracula's other two brides include Solina – the only survivor of Van Helsing and Simon's first two altercations with Dracula's army – and Valerie Sharpe (Jeri Ryan), a news reporter for the New Orleans market who stays a little too far past sunset to cover the plane crash in Bayou Celeste. In Stoker's text, Harker describes his first impression of the brides before the seduction, which leaves him in 'languorous ecstasy': 'Two were dark, and had high aquiline noses, like the Count, and great dark, piercing eyes that seemed to be almost red when contrasted with the pale yellow moon. The other was fair, as fair as can be, with great wavy masses of golden hair and eyes like pale sapphires.'[48] Beyond the incestuous implication that Dracula sired relatives, the brides are all amorphous constructions, leaving Lucy and Mina as the only women whose transformations earn context.[49] In contrast, all of Dracula's female victims in the film are fairly developed characters that, while ultimately sexualised and unceremoniously dispatched after their transformations, elaborate on the more positive aspects of the Victorian New Woman. Solina and Marcus act as equal partners in their underground operation, leaving Solina to brandish a gun at her surviving subordinates when they threaten to abandon

Dracula's coffin after Van Helsing's traps activate. Valerie jokes with her cameraman JT (Shane West) about her low-cut top while filming a promo for the plane crash story, mockingly saying 'Turn me on at 11' and calling attention to the inherent sexual performativity and objectification characteristic of her role as female reporter. Even Lucy articulates a fierce independence as Mary's roommate and co-worker, suitor free and enjoying a blissful, albeit conservative, single life in the Big Easy before Dracula's seduction.

Since Craven produced *Dracula 2000* in the wake of *Scream*, the film's frequent self-reflexive relationship with Stoker and the horror genre is expected. Valerie's character is an obvious nod to tabloid reporter Gale Weathers (Courtney Cox) in Craven's franchise. This becomes even more apparent when Lussier stages her and JT's death scene as a shot-for-shot homage to the moment in *Scream* when Gale watches from a television in her news van as the Ghostface killer sneaks up behind her cameraman, Kenny (W. Earl Brown) – with the obvious exception that Dracula cannot be picked up on camera, leaving JT to be dashed against the ground by an invisible force. However, as a Canadian filmmaker working in Hollywood, Lussier hails from a national cinema tradition with a history of politicised genre play. As Jim Leach writes, 'it was precisely because of the close association between popular genres and American culture that Canadian filmmakers could use these genres to explore the impact on Canada of the powerful cultural influences from south of the border.'[50] Such is especially true for the horror film largely because of Canada's 100% Capital Cost allowance of the late 1970s, which allowed investors a complete write-off for film investment, and led to an influx of cheap horror productions to the nation.[51] While the allowance launched the career of David Cronenberg and led to heralded horror films such as George Mihalka's *My Bloody Valentine* (1981) – which Lussier remade as a 3D film to a $100 million international gross in 2009 – it also spawned a host of badly received and made efforts that eventually curdled the industry. This focus on genre becomes even more potent as a result of Hollywood North – the pejorative for the host of runaway Hollywood productions shooting in Canada for tax breaks, which, for critics such as Mike Gasher, implicate local filmmakers like Lussier in the Hollywood system while stunting interest in and opportunity for a healthy national cinema.[52]

However, in its intersections of gender and genre, Lussier's film challenges such binaries between Canadian and Hollywood cinema, harnessing the revision of his source text to create an evocative intertextual Dracula that forges a transnational Canadian identity. Beyond the film's metafilmic references to Stoker and Craven, Lussier's depiction of Mary Heller serves as a distinct alternative to the gender constructions of source text and American horror. While the absence of British characters beyond Simon in *Dracula 2000* is a conspicuous alteration, that an adaptation of a Victorian novel set in the US would feature no American heroes directly contradicts the ideological implications of Hollywood films such as *Gunga Din,* becoming a central point of integration for the film's Canadian perspective. Further, with the exception of Van Helsing, every one of Dracula's victims is American, either seduced by his settler colonial charisma as is true of his female victims like Lucy and Valerie or unable to contend with his unbridled masculinity forged from millennia of imperial knowledge and experience, a fate that befalls Marcus and Nightshade. In dispatching Van Helsing, Dracula extinguishes the last relic of Europe's colonial might; in killing the Americans, he threatens the rugged individualism of a US as ambivalent about its supremacy as the Britain so threatened by Quincey Morris.

In contrast, Mary Heller is not quite American or European, which the South African Waddell underscores in her performance by not hiding her accent. She is the progeny of a mother with unnamed origins, but a fervent Catholic faith that carries over to her daughter. She is also equally Van Helsing and Dracula's offspring who sets the film's plot in motion by settling in New Orleans, the initial arrivant in the US after fleeing from both her biological and spiritual fathers' eternal imperial power struggle. Significantly, she is also the film's only character who cannot become fully vampire or human, constantly communicating telepathically with Dracula against her will but also fully able to fend off his invasion of her body when he attempts to turn her at the end of the film. If, as Eric Kwan-Wai Yu argues, Stoker's novel was fueled by a Protestant work ethic called to sacrifice the sexual female to cultivate male bonding and exterminate the ultimate other, then Lussier's film centres on a hybrid, catholic female who facilitates a model settler alternative to Dracula's cyclical imperial force.[53] That she and Lucy work at the New Orleans branch of the Virgin Megastore music chain owned at the time by British entrepreneur Richard Branson only punctuates her transnational and transhistorical identity.

In assuming this role as the model settler, Mary also upsets the traditional role of the female in the Hollywood horror film. In her famous conception of the 'final girl,' Carol Clover aligns the vampire and slasher films due to their symbolic displacement of genital sex in their acts of violence.[54] As Clover writes, the slasher in particular operates by 'eliminating the woman (earlier victims) or reconstituting her as masculine (Final Girl). The moment at which the Final Girl is effectively phallicized is the moment the plot halts and horror ceases. Day breaks, and the community returns to its normal order.'[55] Given the film's focus on gore and the flouting of Craven's attachment as a marketing tool, *Dracula 2000* merges the vampire and slasher film, thus highlighting Clover's parallels. Yet, while Mary does, in effect, become the film's Final Girl, her actions openly subvert the genre's typical gender representations. Though Mary externally transforms after Dracula bites her, she also gains full access to the Count's memories, learning his true identity. Fending off her transformation, Mary pretends to behead a bound Simon as a ruse to free him. Decapitating Lucy instead, Mary lunges at Dracula and stabs him with Van Helsing's knife, stating, 'For my father,' as she plunges it in. When Dracula lunges at her, proclaiming that he cannot die because Christ will not let him while gesturing toward an enormous neon crucifix on an adjacent church roof, Mary flashes back to Judas' rope breaking after his suicide attempt. As Mary inquires whether he has asked forgiveness, Dracula throws her next to the crucifix. Grabbing some exposed electrical cables, she ties them around Dracula's neck, pulling them both off the roof. Dracula writhes in pain as he once again hangs – this time from the downed crucifix – while Mary recovers from the fall on the street below. As the sun rises, she watches Dracula's body burst into flame, which Lussier shoots from a low angle with the cross looming over the vampire.

Despite certain tendencies of the Final Girl, it is ultimately Mary's femininity that triumphs over Dracula, permitting her to succeed where her immortal father failed. In stabbing Dracula with Van Helsing's knife, she realises that phallicisation is an ineffective tool, opting instead to deploy the Count's accrued imperial knowledge against him. Forcing him to confront his violence against Christ's liberation from Rome, Mary initiates Dracula's return to dust at the Ash Wednesday sunrise. She takes on the role of exterminating Lucy from the Crew of Light while also saving a Simon from the brides who is much less capable than his counterpart in the novel. Likewise, rather than ceasing the horror and returning the community to normal after Dracula's death, Mary assumes her father's role at Carfax Antiques with Simon as second, guarding Dracula's ashes and ending the film by saying, 'I am Mary Van Helsing. I am my father's daughter, and nothing can ever take that away' as a lightning strike makes her eyes momentarily appear vampiric. As opposed to a Final Girl, Mary mirrors the tensions and anxieties of Canadian horror. As Ayla Ahmad writes:

> . . . we could say that, in Canadian horror, the settler is confronted in a variety of ways with the presence of the Indigene, the relationship calling into question his or her complacent sense of ownership over the land and his or her privileged position as the 'normality' by which the monster is defined. Horror therefore, produces an *unsettled* Canadian identity, one in which the boundary between monstrous wilderness and brutish 'civilization' becomes blurred with violence, death, and atrocity . . .[56]

In her defeat of Dracula, Mary confronts the count not as a global settler force but as the indigenous member of the 'interpreter class' who betrayed his anticolonial leader. She recognises his otherness and the full extent of her complicity in the imperial cycle. Yet, in her unsettled identity, she comes to terms with her hybridity. No longer colonising Dracula's body as her father did, she fully acknowledges both Van Helsing's duties and Dracula's existence while remaining vigilant about his return and her own vampiric traits. She has also rejected the legacies of violence taken up by both men. Though she claims to be her father's daughter, Lussier's visual cues undercut the obviousness of her statement. She ends the film the ultimate daughter of the father Dracula betrayed, aware of her anticolonial potential and global reach.

Although overlooked amid the litany of contemporary vampire narratives, *Dracula 2000* is perhaps as indictive of contemporary anxieties over settler legacies and global capital as Stoker's novel was for the Late Empire at the close of the last century. As a Canadian filmmaker adapting a British narrative to a US setting largely recreated on Canadian soundstages, Lussier is fully ingrained in the cycles of imperialism clearly on display in transnational Hollywood. At the same time, his radical adaptation of the source text preserves its colonial critique while extending its concerns to Hollywood's conventions and industrial practices, harnessing horror film's potential to negotiate settler and national cinematic identities in an industry endlessly preparing for Dracula's inevitable return.

CHAPTER 3

Those Other Victorians: Cosmopolitanism and Empire in Jane Campion's *The Portrait of a Lady*

As Hollywood's shift from *Gunga Din* to *Dracula 2000* indicates, the US film industry's early experiments with Victorian narratives had proven effective to such an extent that, by the end of the century, even an adaptation of a novel as important to British colonial discourse as Stoker's text appeared seamlessly American despite being largely shot in Canada. Such an overwhelming influence has severe implications for English-language postcolonial national cinemas that, in contrast to industries like Bollywood and Nollywood, invite direct comparison to Hollywood's output.

For Tom O'Regan, 'Producing in the English language also encourages a sense amongst audiences, distributors and exhibitors that the local cinema is interchangeable with US and to a lesser extent British films.'[1] Such is especially true in settler nations such as Australia in which only 5–7% of annual box-office revenue comes from locally made films, which are trying to compete with Hollywood's latest releases.[2] In addition, this problem of interchangeability is compounded in Australia because of its popularity as a location for Hollywood productions such as the Wachowski's *The Matrix* (1999) and George Lucas' *Star Wars* prequels. In addition, Australian filmmakers who left the Australian film industry for successful Hollywood careers, such as Peter Weir, George Miller, Gillian Armstrong, Baz Luhrmann and P. J. Hogan, often bring their studio projects back home – much more prodigal sons and daughters than directors of the 'runaway productions' that transformed the Canadian film industry.[3] This trend also holds true for the host of Hollywood acting talent hailing from or with ties to Australia, beginning with 'golden age' swashbuckler Errol Flynn and including Nicole Kidman, Hugh Jackman, Mel Gibson, Eric Bana, Geoffrey Rush, Naomi Watts, Margot Robbie, Cate Blanchett, Rose Byrne and Chris and Liam Hemsworth among others.[4]

Resulting from its dynamic and internationally recognised film culture as well as its often-tendentious ties to both Britain and the US, Australia serves as an integral nation to defining the postcolonial elements of settler cinemas. While Australia has the distinction of producing the first feature in film history with Charles Tait's largely lost *The Story of the Kelly Gang* in 1906, its cinema has largely worked within many of the same genres as Hollywood, though accented with localised concerns: the western, the road movie, and the 'Ocker' film – a hybrid of the rural fish-out-of-water trope and sex comedy typified by Peter Faiman's international blockbuster *Crocodile Dundee* (1986).[5] Yet, in the wake of the 1992 Mabo decision that acknowledged indigenous land rights for the first time in the nation's history, Australian national cinema underwent a marked transformation in which it instigated a process of 'backtracking' through its settler history. According to Felicity Collins and Therese Davis:

> Genre films function for their generic audience as either mythic or ideological solutions to ongoing, unreconciled social conflicts. In this sense, Australian films might appeal to particular local and international audiences for the way they backtrack over the dilemmas of a minor English-speaking nation negotiating a place for itself in global politics on the basis of its former status as a far-flung dominion of the British Empire, and, since the Second World War, as a South Pacific deputy to the current world superpower, the United States of America.[6]

This backtracking had significant repercussions for Australian genres, leading to a series of films like Rolf de Heer's revisionist outback narrative *The Tracker* (2002) with indigenous Australian screen legend David Gulpilil, as well as Baz Luhrmann's musical pastiche *Moulin Rouge!* (2001) and epic *Australia* (2008) that meditate on a 21st century Australian identity (both starring Nicole Kidman). However, the concept has largely eluded discussions of adaptation within an Australian context.[7]

The consistent wave of migration to Hollywood exploded with the directors of the late 1970s Australian New Wave such as Weir (*Picnic at Hanging Rock* [1975], *Witness* [1985], *Dead Poets Society* [1988], *The Truman Show* [1998]); Miller (*Babe* [1995, 1998], *Happy Feet* [2006, 2011], the *Mad Max* franchise [1979, 1981, 1985, 2015]); Bruce Beresford (*Breaker Morant* [1980], *Driving Miss Daisy* [1989]), and Armstrong (*My Brilliant Career* [1979], *Little Women* [1994]), with the result that Australian filmmakers – more than any other transnational group – have sustained lucrative careers as some of the most lauded Hollywood directors of the past four decades. Yet, despite their prominence, they have largely ignored undertaking adaptations of Victorian literature as projects once established in Hollywood, opting instead to focus on classic American texts from the 19th and early 20th centuries such as Armstrong's *Little Women*, Luhrmann's *The Great Gatsby* (2013), and Campion's *The*

Portrait of a Lady. Considering Australia's status as 'South Pacific deputy' to the US, the politicised adaptation strategies that are the focus of this project easily apply. If, as Julie Sanders contends, 'the full impact of film adaptation depends on the audience's awareness of an explicit relationship to the source text . . . The desire to make the relationship with the source explicit links to the manner in which the responses to adaptations depend upon a complex invocation of ideas of similarity and difference', then the domestic and transnational audiences for such films bring variations of awareness to such works by Australians in Hollywood.[8] As a result, the full impact for an Australian audience may differ from the American fan of Louisa May Alcott or F. Scott Fitzgerald because the former views such films' relationships to their sources transnationally.

This transnational context is especially important to Campion's adaptation of Henry James' 1881 novel *The Portrait of a Lady* as it serves as an example of an American work largely set in the European metropolises of London and Rome that features a host of cosmopolitans who do not quite belong on either continent. Detailing Albany-native Isabel Archer's rise to wealth after inheriting a fortune from her deceased uncle, the novel traces her various romantic entanglements with British and Euro-American suitors that ends in a loveless marriage to preening dilettante Gilbert Osmond. James made frequent trips to Europe largely because, once he embraced his lack of commercial success, he cultivated a persona as a detached Master of high culture who catered to a discerning readership.[9] Regardless, he valued what he saw as the idealism and innocence of America, which served in sharp contrast to the moral decay and decadence of Europe's imperial centres.[10] Catalysed by the end of the Civil War, James intensified his preoccupations with American heritage and idealism in spite of the European sensibilities and Victorian structures of his works during the late 19th century.[11]

Resulting from his fiction's ambivalent relationship to Europe and articulation of American ideals, one could situate James in an early postcolonial context, his Victorian fiction working toward an American conception of the novel that would rival the work of his British contemporaries. As Bill Ashcroft, Gareth Griffiths and Helen Tiffin write in their pioneering work of postcolonial studies, *The Empire Writes Back*:

> The American experience and its attempts to produce a new kind of literature can be seen to be the model for all later post-colonial writing. The first thing it showed was that some of a post-colonial country's most deeply held linguistic and cultural traits depend upon its relationship with the colonizing power, particularly the defining contrast between European metropolis and 'frontier'.[12]

Yet, in contrast to the works of frontier writers such as Mark Twain, Willa Cather, Sherwood Anderson, and Bret Harte, James elected to define these contrasts with the British Empire through a host of American expatriates and tourists in the imperial centres – less Gothic incarnations of Stoker's reverse coloniser.

Given James' postcolonial undercurrents and European focus, *The Portrait of a Lady* serves as a unique source text for a filmmaker like Campion. Hailing from New Zealand, but working in Sydney, Campion has ruminated on her own transnational settler status in films such as *The Piano* (1993) and *Holy Smoke!* (1999).[13] While she often identifies as Australian despite setting films in New Zealand, including *The Piano* and her adaptation of Kiwi writer Janet Frame's autobiographies *An Angel at My Table* (1990), her work embodies the increasing 'mixed production' in Australasia that illustrates settler colonial concerns.[14] Not able to establish her career in New Zealand's industry – which has produced less than 300 films, even after the international success of Peter Jackson and Taika Waititi (*What We Do in the Shadows* [2015], *Thor: Ragnarok* [2017]) – Campion made internationally renowned shorts through the Women's Unit of Film Australia that began her tenure as the nation's perennial representative at Cannes, which she cemented with her debut feature *Sweetie* (1988) and the Palm d'Or-winning *The Piano*.[15] As her follow-up to *The Piano*, which parlayed its success at Cannes with three Academy Awards and a $100 million international gross, expectations were high for Campion's foray into the Hollywood costume drama.[16] However, though the film received Academy Award nominations for costume design and Barbara Hershey's supporting performance, reviews for Campion's take on James were often hostile, largely due to, as Deb Verhoeven notes, the film not conforming to its prefigured critical profile, proving too middlebrow for proponents of Campion's unique style and too heretical for fans of the novel and period pieces.[17]

Over the past decade, scholars have begun to revise critical appraisals of *The Portrait of a Lady*, placing it into a universal feminist context consistent with readings of Campion's previous efforts and her later works like *Holy Smoke!* and the John Keats/Fanny Brawne biopic *Bright Star* (2009). However, little attention has been paid to the film's examinations of colonial identity despite its singular status as a narrative that meditates on the relationship between the settler and imperial centres. As the first film Campion made after Mabo, her James adaptation engages in the process of 'backtracking' through Australian history via comparative analysis of its settler colonial characters as they inherit fortunes and form family alliances throughout England and Italy. In addition, it serves as a unique example of a postcolonial adaptation of an American Victorian novel, opening a space for Campion to address the Americanisation of Australia's film industry.

AMERICAN SETTLERS AND EUROPEAN PERFORMANCE

Throughout his career, James expressed an ambivalent relationship with cosmopolitanism, deploring its tendencies toward salacious content in literary form, but heralding it for its sophistication and artistic contributions to the Western world.[18] For James, cosmopolitanism was a force that, if employed properly, could make a better American through offering sensual experiences and, as Adeline R. Tinter writes, 'use of the continent for its art, for its museum world, which can be appropriated and brought back' to the states.[19] As Tinter indicates, much of James' cosmopolitan writing was itself a radical reworking of the style and concerns of writers such as Émile Zola and Alphonse Daudet.[20] In undertaking the similar strategies of revision and appropriation applied to postcolonial works in the later 20th century, James lays claim to an American literature than can compete with the urbane continental works of his time while asserting the burgeoning culture of his native land.

Within this context, *The Portrait of a Lady*'s Isabel Archer serves as the epitome of James' American cosmopolitanism. When James introduces Isabel in the wake of her father's death, her Aunt Lydia has come to visit the family's Albany estate and discovers the girl in the office reading. Distracted as Lydia Touchett enters, Isabel thinks to herself:

> It had lately occurred to her that her mind was a good deal of a vagabond, and she had spent much ingenuity in training it to a military step and teaching it to advance, to halt, to retreat, to perform even more complicated manoeuvres, at the word of command. Just now she had given it marching orders and it had been trudging over the sandy plains of a history of German Thought.[21]

Though she has never left Albany, Isabel demonstrates an intellectual vagabondism that will manifest when Lydia invites her to cross the Atlantic and join the 'amiable colonists' of American expatriates James refers to throughout the novel.[22] While the passage illustrates Isabel's budding cosmopolitanism, it also suggests a tension between the sophistication of European philosophy and the realities of the Civil War that shaped Isabel's generation the decade before. Much of James' fiction reflects his own guilt over evading fighting in the war, a connection Kristin Sanner sees as integral to Isabel's identity in the novel as, 'a naive proponent of democratic ideals' that 'sets her up perfectly for a plot that eventually shows how those same ideals victimize her, much as he may have felt personally victimized by falsified ideals and familial politics.'[23] Neither experiencing the trauma of war directly or the idealised worlds contained in her continental volumes, Isabel exhibits an innocent Americanness that could fulfill its potential with the necessary experience provided by cosmopolitan exposure.

While Isabel remains hungry for knowledge and the experience of life abroad in Europe, her democratic sensibilities and American perspective are already so entrenched that she rationally rebuffs her two most tenacious suitors for failing to live up to her lofty ideas despite their outwardly respectable traits. Throughout the novel, James couches his descriptions of Isabel's primary suitors, Parliament radical Lord Warburton and New England industrial scion Casper Goodwood, in the terms of colonialism. Talking with her uncle and eventual benefactor, Daniel Touchett, about her dual marriage proposals, Isabel thinks about her prospects: 'however she might have resisted conquest at her English suitor's large quiet hands she was at least as far removed from the disposition to let the young man from Boston take positive possession of her.'[24] Isabel slights both suitors with vague references to her desire for independence and uncertainty over ever marrying, but James' depiction of both men subtly implies that Isabel's reticence largely results from their failure to live up to Isabel's idealised conception of American cosmopolitanism. James consistently characterises Warburton through references to his travels to England's colonial holdings. Remarking on the consumption that plagues Isabel's cousin, Ralph Touchett, Warburton proclaims that the only time he ever fell ill was 'once, in the Persian Gulf'.[25] Likewise, when he unexpectedly shows up in Rome, Warburton has just returned from Turkey and Asia Minor, regaling his company with tales of Persia. As James writes:

> He was splendidly sunburnt; even his multitudinous beard had been burnished by the fire of Asia. He was dressed in the loose-fitting, heterogeneous garments in which the English traveller in foreign lands is wont to consult his comfort and affirm his nationality; and with his pleasant steady eyes, his bronzed complexion, fresh beneath its seasoning, his manly figure, his minimising manner and his general air of being a gentleman and an explorer, he was such a representative of the British race as need not in any clime have been disavowed by those who have a kindness for it.[26]

This affirmation of his nationality is central to Warburton's identity and authority, which James underscores late in the novel as he tries to woo Pansy, Isabel's stepdaughter, by telling her 'all about India' where he helps shape colonial policy and his brother serves in the British Army.[27] While not possessing a complete grasp of imperial politics, Isabel's democratic ideals are fixed enough to see through this 'nobleman of the newest pattern, a reformer, a radical, a contemner of ancient ways' who was born into England and 'owned a considerable slice of it'.[28] As she playfully tells Warburton toward the end of the novel, he has no right to amuse himself 'with the affairs of the British Empire on your hands'.[29] Regardless of intentionality, Isabel refuses to allow Warburton's genteel colonisation to extend into the realm of the marriage union, reinforcing her unwavering American perspective even as she gains experience on the continent.

Although rooted in the US and hesitant about Europe, Casper Goodwood represents an unwitting American iteration of imperial connection that contradicts Isabel's ideals about her native land. Before Lydia invites Isabel on her grand tour of Europe, the young woman had tentatively agreed to marry Goodwood often imagining that, 'he might have ridden, on a plunging steed, the whirlwind of a great war – a war like the Civil strife that had overdarkened her conscious childhood and his ripening youth.'[30] However, as the heir to a cotton fortune and inventor of cutting-edge mill technology, Goodwood is much more in line with the US's colonial past than the patriotic preservation of democracy Isabel imagines, a dissonance that highlights what for Sigi Jöttkandt is a persistent 'fundamental disjunction between representation and reality that Isabel is, at least initially, unable or unwilling to perceive'.[31] Though Goodwood pursues Isabel across the Atlantic, she continues to reject his advances because 'She cared nothing for his cotton-mill – the Goodwood patent left her imagination absolutely cold.'[32] Not an active participant in Empire as is Lord Warburton, Goodwood heralds a vision of America that deviates sharply from Isabel's own in its view of the nation as capitalistic successor to Britain's imperial prowess. In one of his more botched proposal attempts, he lashes out at Isabel when she mentions Warburton as a rival:

> 'Well then, as you have companions in misfortune, make the best of it.'
> 'I don't call him a companion,' said Casper grimly.
> 'Why not – since I declined his offer absolutely?'
> 'That doesn't make him my companion. Besides, he's an Englishman.'
> 'And pray isn't an Englishman a human being?' Isabel asked.
> 'Oh, those people? They're not of my humanity, and I don't care what becomes of them.'
> 'You're very angry,' said the girl. 'We've discussed this matter quite enough.'
> 'Oh yes, I'm very angry. I plead guilty to that!'[33]

Firmly entrenched in New England's elite, Goodwood serves as an American Warburton, lacking the title and political power, but possessing a savvy industrialism and insularity that clashes with Isabel's intellectual ambitions and view of her native land. His lack of appeal lies in his rejection of the cosmopolitan American viewpoint, which is so pervasive that, even at novel's end, she rejects his final advance and returns to Rome and her loveless marriage with Osmond.

As the innocent American abroad who cherishes experience and democratic ideals, Isabel defines herself by rejection of obviously imperial mindsets, which leaves her vulnerable to Osmond's ruthless desire to possess that masquerades as an aloof cosmopolitanism. In revising the cosmopolitan novel from an American perspective, James positions Osmond and his co-conspirator Serena Merle as embodiments of the darkest impulses of European cosmopolitanism and a satirical comment on late-Victorian aestheticism.[34] James introduces Osmond as 'an elegant complicated medal struck off for a special occasion' with a beard 'cut in the manner of the portraits of the sixteenth century' who 'used the Italian tongue, and used it with perfect ease; but this would not convince you he was Italian.'[35] Yet, as Ralph reminds Isabel, Osmond is, in truth, 'a vague, unexplained American who has been living these thirty years, or less, in Italy.'[36] Similar to Madam Merle, who proclaims she, 'was born under the shadow of the national banner', Osmond serves as the pinnacle of cosmopolitanism for the naïve Isabel, which solidifies her attraction to him despite his lack of future or occupation.[37] As Isabel remarks, 'he is a specimen apart.'[38] However, Isabel's description of Osmond as specimen foreshadows his own seemingly benign assertions of imperial control and obsession with ownership. As he tells Isabel, 'I've a few good things . . . indeed I've nothing very bad. But I've not what I would have liked.'[39] Revering Merle's cosmopolitan identity that she claims comes from the 'old, old world' before the French Revolution, Isabel falls victim to her secret plan to unite her and Osmond in order to provide a mother figure for Osmond and Merle's illegitimate daughter, Pansy.[40] The ultimate indicator of Osmond's imperial underpinnings, Pansy is a perpetual blank slate different from American girls and the maidens of England who, as Isabel concludes is, 'so formed and finished for her tiny place in the world . . . yet so innocent and infantine.'[41] Consequently, in marrying Isabel and receiving access to her fortune under the guise of his unassuming cosmopolitan mask, Osmond achieves what his more obviously imperial rivals failed to, marrying Isabel and rearing his child 'as I wished, in the old way.'[42]

In contrast to Isabel, both Merle and Osmond hide their American origins, preferring to bask in the things of the old world while underplaying their complicity with its imperial logic. Much of Osmond's desire to evade his American heritage originates from, as his sister Amy Osmond (the Countess Gemini) reveals, the family's 'Creole' ancestors, whose accents the siblings repress in favour of a more continental dialect.[43] In this shift from Creole to cosmopolitan, Osmond manufactures an insubstantial self that severs him from the hybrid nature and democratic potential of the American experiment. This performance becomes even more apparent when taking into consideration the novel's sly implications that American writer Margaret Fuller is the mother of Gilbert and Amy, which Kathleen Ann Lawrence views as a choice that 'reveals the hidden anatomy of the novel, the intellectual underpinnings that form the basis of the moral battle between Isabel and Osmond and the cultural context that provides the matrix of its realism.'[44] In referencing another writer who was working toward a dynamic national literature (despite his often critical assessments of her), James further renders Osmond and Merle's brand of cosmopolitanism outmoded, demonising Osmond for binding Isabel and Pansy to his intellectual hollowness and leaving Merle to return in disgrace to America when her secret is revealed.

Isabel's marriage to Osmond prevents her from reaching her cosmopolitan potential. However, her relationships with her cousin Ralph and American journalist Henrietta Stackpole serve as alternatives to both Goodwood's latent nationalism and Osmond's aesthetic façade. In Henrietta's view, Ralph is an 'alienated American' unable to assume control of his father's banking empire because of his illness but carving out an even-tempered and compassionate life as an observer.[45] Yet, Ralph does not forcefully alienate himself by masking his heritage like Osmond and Merle. As a student at Harvard, he became 'redundantly native', spurring his father to place him at Oxford for further refinement. As James writes,

> Ralph became at last English enough. His outward conformity to the manners that surrounded him was none the less the mask of a mind that greatly enjoyed its independence, on which nothing long imposed itself, and which, naturally inclined to adventure and irony, indulged in a boundless liberty of appreciation.[46]

Ralph's boundless liberty of appreciation places him the closest of all the novel's characters to achieving James' ideal cosmopolitanism. Unlike Goodwood's capitalistic pursuits and Osmond's desires for control, Ralph actively convinces his father to give half of his inheritance to Isabel so that she can do 'Absolutely what she likes'.[47]

As Isabel's closest friend, Henrietta lacks Ralph's discretion but more than compensates with an amalgamation of international experience and honesty that endow her with unapologetic American identity. A correspondent for the American tabloid *The Interviewer*, Henrietta has, as Isabel notes 'travelled over the whole American continent and can at least find her way about this minute island.'[48] Not approving of lords, Henrietta is the American experiment's greatest proponent, consistently positioning her native country within the empires of the past. As James writes, 'Henrietta Stackpole was struck with the fact that ancient Rome had been paved a good deal like New York, and even found an analogy between the deep chariot-ruts traceable in the antique street and the overjangled iron grooves which express the intensity of American life.'[49] Similarly for

Henrietta, 'Michael Angelo's dome suffered by comparison with that of the Capitol at Washington.'[50] Even though she ends the novel by relocating to London and accepting a marriage proposal from the English Mr Bantling, she retains her American outlook, only succumbing to the Englishman's advances after taking him to the US, which had 'opened his eyes and shown him that England wasn't everything.'[51] Though her marriage and abandonment of her country saddens Isabel, Henrietta exhibits perhaps the greatest change in the novel, shifting from a nationalistic American to a more refined cosmopolitan outlook, echoing Ralph's remark to her early in the novel that, 'one doesn't give up one's country any more than one gives up one's grandmother. They're both antecedent to choice – elements of one's composition that are not to be eliminated', advice that Isabel clearly does not heed in her marriage to Osmond.[52]

Establishing Ralph and Henrietta's American cosmopolitanism, James situates them as Isabel's guardians as she makes her first trip to London, the pivotal step in her continental transformation. However, before the trip, the duo argue about the others' influence over their charge as Henrietta asks for Ralph's help in setting Isabel up with Goodwood:

> 'I shall enjoy that immensely!' Ralph exclaimed. 'I'll be Caliban and you shall be Ariel.'
>
> 'You're not at all like Caliban, because you're sophisticated, and Caliban was not. But I'm not talking about imaginary characters; I'm talking about Isabel. Isabel's intensely real. What I wish to tell you is that I find her fearfully changed.'
>
> 'Since you came, do you mean?'
>
> 'Since I came and before I came. She's not the same as she once so beautifully was.'
>
> 'As she was in America?'
>
> 'Yes, in America. I suppose you know she comes from there. She can't help it, but she does.'
>
> 'Do you want to change her back again?'
>
> 'Of course I do, and I want you to help me.'
>
> 'Ah,' said Ralph, 'I'm only Caliban; I'm not Prospero.'
>
> 'You were Prospero enough to make her what she has become. You've acted on Isabel Archer since she came here, Mr. Touchett.'[53]

In their designs for Isabel, both Americans tellingly self-identify as the marginalised characters from Shakespeare's *The Tempest*. However, Ralph bristles at Henrietta's comparison of him to Prospero, the Italian who settled on the play's New World island, appropriated magic from Caliban's deceased mother Sycorax, and enslaved both Caliban and Ariel. Even as the most attuned characters in James' novel, they exhibit an implicit knowledge of their inferior position in Europe and an anxiety over becoming continental Prosperos. In agreeing to accompany Isabel on her trip to London after her rejection of Warburton – a journey that Casey M. Walker deems central to Isabel's liberation as she walks 'An itinerary that makes the city not "geographical" London but her own signification of it' – Ralph and Henrietta act as realistic cosmopolitans, guides through the imperial centre that understand their place in Victorian England and fully believe, despite their differing methods, in Isabel's individual American experience.[54]

FRAGMENTED FIDELITY AND AN AMERICAN-AUSTRALIAN ISABEL

In his pioneering work of adaptation studies *Novels into Film*, George Bluestone cites James' admiration for the fifty-hour-novel and its 'solidity of specification' that allows readers to live with it longer. Bluestone writes of the 'contrast between the loose, more variegated conventions of the novel and the tight, compact conventions of the film', that typically govern the adaptation process as fifty hours turns into two.[55] Yet, when Campion released *The Portrait of a Lady*, much of the ire directed at her adaptation hinged on three loose and abrupt digressions from the text that she and her screenwriter Laura Jones added to James' already sprawling narrative: 1. A documentary prologue of Australian and New Zealand women discussing being kissed, 2. A dream sequence in which Warburton (Richard E. Grant) and Goodwood (Viggo Mortensen) caress Isabel on a bed while Ralph (Martin Donovan) watches on (Figure 3.1), and 3. A black-and-white pastiche of Isabel's world travels (Figure 3.2) that Mark Eaton sums up as, 'a bizarre montage sequence which mixes cinematic styles such as early twentieth century newsreels and travelogues, the silent-era Orientalist films starring Rudolph Valentino, the

Figure 3.1 Campion's quadrangular traffic in women.

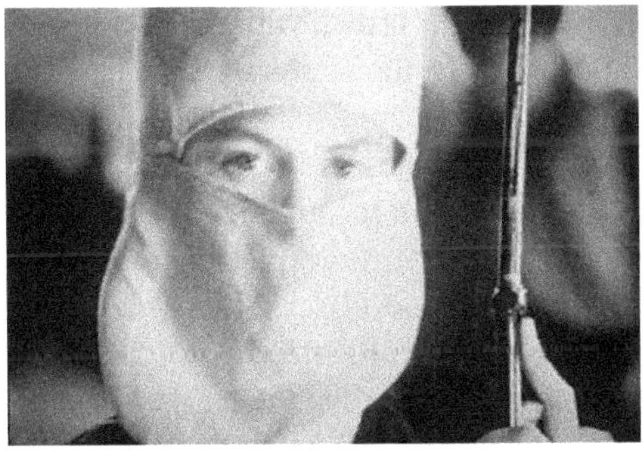

Figure 3.2 Isabel (Nicole Kidman) on her world tour.

surrealist films of Luis Buñuel, and the psycho-sexual suspense films of Hitchcock.'[56]

Citing Jones' screenplay as a 'marvel of compression', Michael Anesko observes that the majority of the film's scenes are derived almost verbatim from James' definitive New York Edition text of the novel.[57] Nevertheless, contemporary reviews from critics such as Cynthia Ozick and Janet Maslin eviscerated the adaptation on the grounds of its lack of fidelity and took the director to task for making the film her own.[58]

Such responses to Campion's film indicate that a concept as seemingly forthright as fidelity becomes muddled in the adaptation process. Campion and Jones do not explode James' narrative in a manner similar to Stevens and Lussier. Moreover, they do not undertake a revisionary strategy that directly writes back to imperial centres as do the films this project discusses later, largely because James' novel provides multiple points of centrality. Instead, they undertake a process of resettlement, shifting James' narrative further into its cosmopolitan milieu while using cinematic style and industrial practice to extend it into the 20th century, an adaptation strategy that makes it a pivotal illustration of the interfidelity approach. In a similar manner to James' forging of an American cosmopolitanism, Campion pushes the text's innate postcolonial resistance, refracting it back toward the US and the Americanisation of the global film industry.

Campion's stylised departures may have captured the attention of most of the film's detractors, but her most radical break from James's novel is the total erasure of the American cosmopolitism that was the subject of the previous section. As a result, the screenplay excises the first 20% of the novel that covers Isabel's time in Albany and the majority of Ralph's banter about American identity, instead beginning with Warburton's marriage proposal. In opening the film with the voiceovers about the intimacy of kisses that transition to black-and-white and colour shots of multiethnic Australian and New Zealand women, Campion creates a direct link between the women of these

South Pacific settler nations and Isabel, who the film reveals in close-up as the documentary sequence ends. In the words of Priscilla Walton, Campion's cut from the title sequence to Isabel, 'positions the ensuing Jamesian narrative on and through a post-colonial screen.'[59] While Walton's reading demonstrates Campion's postcolonial intervention, it elides that the sequence is a replacement for James' meditations on American cosmopolitanism, serving a similar purpose for a different population of settler colonials. In addition, the scene also provides a unique rendering of the 'othering' of Australia in the nation's films that O'Regan views as invitations for locals to laugh at stereotypes and play domestic anthropologist while adding an 'extra richess' and appeal to international audiences.[60] Campion's opening clearly others and decentres James' text for viewers expecting a 19th century period film. At the same time, it collapses the difference between settler cultures, mirroring what Jeffrey T. Nealon views as an 'alterity politics' that goes beyond identity barriers to forge a situation in which, 'the specific other and the socio-historical realm of others cannot be separated in the revelation of the face-to-face.'[61] In her near graphic match between the women and Isabel, Campion orchestrates this face-to-face moment of productive alterity among the diverse women the film features. That Kidman herself is an Australian actress gazing back at Warburton while portraying an American in a cosmopolitan narrative set in the British Empire only deepens the choice's complexity.

While the narrative follows James' novel closely through Isabel's repeated rebuffing of Goodwood and eventual acquiescence to Osmond (John Malkovich), Campion injects an askew settler perspective into the proceedings through her blocking and camera angles, fostering a dialogue between narrative fidelity and stylistic intervention. In the wake of Mabo, Australian cinema refocused its conception of the landscape cinema that mined Australian anxieties about the wild bush and proved successful as cinematic tourism for international audiences. According to Collins and Davis, 'The resurgence of the image of the desert landscape in Australian films at the end of the same millennium is a case of the image of a pre-historic, empty landscape suddenly becoming recognizable, post-Mabo as a land with a history.'[62] Campion would directly tackle such anxieties in her follow-up to *The Portrait of a Lady,* the cult-deprogramming outback drama *Holy Smoke!* However, she also imbues the various landscape scenes Isabel traverses with a post-Mabo perspective, calling attention not to indigenous presence but to the frailty of Empire. Known for her use of angled camerawork since her early shorts, Campion sparingly employs them throughout the film, relegating them to the establishing shots of the various imperial cities Isabel visits to disrupt their historical imperial authority.[63] Likewise, she frames Daniel Touchett (John Gielgud) from the same angle during his death scene, coding him as complicit with the Empire – a characterisation underscored through casting a British actor as Isabel's American benefactor. In addition, she shifts the scene in which Osmond professes his love for Isabel from the lobby of her Rome hotel to the Roman catacombs, a choice that, notes Alistair Fox, serves as the counter to the Australian bush, a place of 'sterility, lifelessness, disillusionment, and death.'[64] Deepening the scene's melodrama, Campion structures it around Isabel's attempts to retrieve her parasol, which Osmond flaunts throughout as he delivers the dialogue perfectly faithful to the novel, highlighting his obsessions with consumption and accumulation through an object used to shelter from the elements. What results is a multifaceted interrogation of geography that backtracks through an imperial history in a way befitting of the post-Mabo film.

In her study of Campion and adaptation, Estella Tincknell considers *The Portrait of a Lady* along with *The Piano* and *Bright Star* as a trilogy of 'anti-heritage texts, refusing to conform to the conventions of the genre, and insistent on their disengagement from its structures', with Campion's take on James as the most radical.[65] Although Tincknell characterises structure as related to such genres as the period melodrama in Hollywood film, her assessment is especially applicable to the manner in which the film addresses James' American Victorian past and Hollywood's influence over Australia. Feminist critics have long pointed out how Campion's film visualises Isabel's repressed sexual desire – most notably in the voyeuristic dream sequence involving her unsuccessful suitors – but also in her kiss with the dying Ralph at the film's end. While the film does not shy away from repressed eroticism, it also employs these additions to further engage its settler colonial context. As Isabel fantasises about Warburton and Goodwood in her dream, Ralph is left to gaze before priming himself to pounce in a fit of jealousy as the men dissolve into the ether and Isabel comes back to reality. Yet, throughout the film, Campion blocks Ralph and Isabel's scenes to cultivate a sense of intimacy absent from the novel: she playfully brushes his hair when they are alone together, she slaps him when he objects to her union with Osmond, she constantly moves toward him in their conversations. Given Henrietta's (Mary-Louise Parker) drastically reduced narrative centrality and the reduction of the novel's first chapters, Ralph becomes Isabel's only deep connection to the American facet of her increasing cosmopolitanism. Yet, he also views her as the object of a gaze, as the dream sequence indicates, locating him as a figure of flawed American benevolence toward Campion's American-Australian Isabel.

Despite its intense stylisation, Campion's most nuanced interrogation of settler identity is the travelogue scene. While James consistently associates Warburton with travel to colonial territory, he also includes a brief depiction of Isabel's own formative voyage:

> Isabel, on her side, had not been a fortnight in Rome before she proposed to Madame Merle that they should make a little pilgrimage to the East. Madame Merle remarked that her friend was restless, but she added that she herself had always been consumed with the desire to visit Athens and Constantinople. The two ladies accordingly embarked on this expedition, and spent three months in Greece, in Turkey, in Egypt. Isabel found much to interest her in these countries, though Madame Merle continued to remark that even among the most classic sites, the scenes most calculated to suggest repose and reflexion, a certain incoherence prevailed in her. Isabel travelled rapidly and recklessly; she was like a thirsty person draining cup after cup.[66]

Discussing the 'impulses' she received staring at the Pyramids and Acropolis, James contrasts Isabel's international experience to Warburton's. While Warburton is motivated by the preservation of Empire, Isabel travels to the sites of former empires, draining cup after cup of knowledge to increase the depth of her cosmopolitan worldviews, which places her in opposition to Merle's incoherence and inability to transcend the inauthenticity of her continental identity. In contrast, Campion shifts Isabel's journey from a passing mention to the stylistic centrepiece of the film, a sequence Anna Despotopoulou views as, 'Juxtaposed to the constriction that Isabel encounters on her return; the constriction, filmed in normal colour, represents her current reality while the travels are shot in early twentieth-century newsreel fashion – they are short and fragmented which stresses their temporariness and otherness.'[67] While such a juxtaposition does occur, within the context of post-Mabo cinema, the scene's use of otherness also presents Isabel as a settler intruding on colonised lands in a purposefully Orientalised style, complete with shots of Kidman in a headscarf as she traverses the Middle East. With Madam Merle (Barbara Hershey) lingering behind her aboard the ship's deck in Gothic horror fashion, Isabel undergoes an experience that, as opposed to James' novel, fragments her settler identity, pushing her far from the realm of James' idealised cosmopolitan and toward the domineering impulses of Osmond and his Freudian fever-dream encroachments into the sequence.

Although Campion's film often conforms to its radical 'anti-heritage' status, it also ends on a much more ambiguous note than the novel, which finds Goodwood resoundingly rejected and learning from Henrietta that Isabel has returned to Rome wiser, but trapped in her marriage. After shifting Ralph's funeral to the winter and covering Gardencourt in a dense snow, Campion shoots Goodwood and Isabel's final encounter in close-up with a constantly moving camera, lingering on their passionate kiss. Isabel runs away toward the house and frantically tries to open the doors to escape but hesitates. The camera follows in a slow-motion tracking shot that assumes Goodwood's perspective. Turning around, Isabel lingers in front of the door looking out of the corner of her eye as the film fades to black. Stripping away the finality of the novel, Campion nudges Isabel further into the Australian settler tradition. Gardencourt has grown cold and alienating since Ralph's death, Rome has become the territory of Osmond's patriarchal control over Pansy (Valentina Cervi) and Goodwood remains an impossible match. As a result, Isabel realises she has become defined by failed connections with men, which Campion enhances through the added intimate scenes with Goodwood and Ralph. The camera lingers on Isabel's face with her back toward the English estate as she purposely averts both Goodwood's and the audiences' gazes. In this ambiguous ending, Campion presents what Glenn Lewis refers to as the preoccupation with national failure innate to the Australian cinema that stands in opposition to American cinema's aspirant heroes.[68] James' Isabel clearly failed by returning to Osmond, but she returned wiser and more self-actualised. Campion's Isabel inhabits a cosmopolitan world with no place for her; she has clearly attained a new level of agency but is unsure of her future, trapped between two suitors who fail to note these shifts in her character, but retain their desire for her docility and commodification.

Despite the radical nature of Campion's adaptation, its strategies to assert Australian settler identity rely on a substantial fidelity to James' source text. Yet, through imposing her post-Mabo Australian perspective on the Victorian-American novel, Campion constructs a unique context that both unites disparate settler identities and interrogates the historical limits of cosmopolitan thought. Rather than move the adaptation into the present, Campion backtracks not only through Australia's settler past but also the layers of Empire at the core of James' idealised Americans and their contemporary globalised counterparts.

CHAPTER 4

Imperial Vanities: Mira Nair, William Makepeace Thackeray and Diasporic Fidelity to *Vanity Fair*

Like her Australian contemporary Campion, Mira Nair occupies a dual space in film culture, fully integrating herself within the Hollywood film community while making films in and about her native country. Nair has built her career on films that contribute to the Indian identity in diaspora while attesting to the prominence of Indian filmmakers in international cinema. For a filmmaker so concerned with the contemporary Indian experience, Nair's adaptation of William Makepeace Thackeray's 1847–8 novel *Vanity Fair* (2004) appears to be a departure. Its seeming outlier status may explain why, of all the films under discussion in this project, it is the only one to have amassed consistent critical notice as a postcolonial adaptation of Victorian literature, although primarily through anecdotes in Hutcheon's *A Theory of Adaptation* and Leitch's *Adaptation and Its Discontents*.[1] Critics such as Helen Machalias have deftly analysed the contrapuntal strategy Nair uses in the adaptation, which ultimately led to controversies over the film's fidelity: 'While Nair asserts that she is *faithful* to the novel, she overturns the nostalgic visualization of the English past that is customary for costume dramas, and includes voices that were marginalised in Thackeray's panoramic view of Regency England.'[2] For Machalias, Nair's fidelity to the novel belongs in italics, a 'professed reverence' contradicted by the film's focus on Indian servants and the revisionary politics it applies to characters of colour such as the Caribbean Jew Rhoda Swartz.[3] Yet, Nair had a personal connection to the novel after first encountering it when she was sixteen at an Irish-Catholic school in Simla, going so far as calling its heroine, Becky Sharp, the greatest female character in literature and the adaptation a dream project, sentiments that call into question assertions of her hypercritical approach to the source material.[4]

Given Nair's affection for the novel, her adaptive strategy goes beyond merely refashioning it for the postcolonial era or flagrantly criticising the text for its colonial discourse. While Nair's films, including her debut feature *Salaam Bombay!* (1988), *Kama Sutra: A Tale of Love* (1996) and *Monsoon Wedding* (2001), probe the connections between India's traditions and history and its contemporary cultural climate, her other work such as *Mississippi Masala* (1991), *The Perez Family* (1995), *The Namesake* (her 2007 adaptation of Jhumpa Lahiri's Pulitzer Prize-winning novel), *The Reluctant Fundamentalist* (2012) and *The Queen of Katwe* (2016) discuss the ethnic and diasporic conflicts inherent in a globalised society dominated by Western influences.[5] Within the context of an oeuvre so concerned with diaspora and globalisation, questions of fidelity in Nair's film version of *Vanity Fair* become complicated; non-Indian film critics may quibble over how unfaithful the adaptation is (even pointing out discrepancies) while adaptation theorists may decry any discussion of the film within the context of fidelity as irrelevant.

Yet, Nair's self-proclaimed adherence to fidelity is central to the politics of her adaptation in a manner unique from the other adaptations under discussion in this study. Positioning Nair's work as an example of 'accented cinema,' Hamid Naficy writes:

> The current globalization and deterritorialization have made Nair's films part of the cultural identity of Indians everywhere. As such, her films are part of not only accented cinema but also Indian cinema because all accented films contribute to constructing both what is exilic and diasporic and what is national.[6]

Hailing from Orissa, India, Nair moved to the US at 18 to study film at Harvard, making student work about Indian subcultures on location in her native country. As Nair told Stephen Lowenstein, 'I made my difference my strength. You know: "I am an Indian woman who has access to worlds that you will never have access to."'[7] Often working within the realm of domestic drama, Nair's films subtly convey the conflicts and consequences of immigration and assimilation through the accents her Indian-American perspective bring to her work, which is especially true of *Vanity Fair*. Understanding her Thackeray adaptation means understanding the importance of what I call diasporic fidelity, an ambivalent affinity for a colonial text that takes into account Stanley Fish's concept of interpretive communities, 'made up of those who share interpretive strategies not for reading (in the conventional sense), but for writing texts, for constituting their properties and assigning their intentions.'[8] In viewing adaptation studies through a postcolonial context, the concept of interpretive communities is vital because it directly applies to the writing (or rewriting) of texts through the adaptation process by a filmmaker such as Nair who provides an accented perspective that conceptions of fidelity largely ignore.

This chapter argues that Nair's film maintains an overarching diasporic fidelity to the source text's plot as a strategy to imbue the narrative with an Indian perspective. Nair subtly rewrites the narrative by eliminating the novel's omniscient narrator and his complicity with the imperial project in favour of her own diasporic narrative position through her use of cinematic style and the camera's point-of-view capabilities. In asserting India's physical presence in her adaptation, Nair also incorporates elements of Bollywood cinema into the production, including the film's much-discussed item number dance sequence that brings Hollywood and Bollywood convention in dialogue with each other. As a result, Nair wedges images into the narrative that directly challenge both the power of the British Empire and its agents as well as Hollywood's continuing influence over Indian cinema.

BECKY SHARP, BOLLYWOOD AND THE POLITICS OF DIASPORA

Despite her critical acclaim and diasporic perspective, Nair is also a filmmaker whose early career was steeped in controversy, largely because of her dual associations with the US and her homeland. As Alpana Sharma writes:

> Nair approaches filmmaking with a high level of tolerance for complexity, irony, contradiction, and ambiguity, qualities in short, which demand a subtle, sideways approach . . . Criticisms of her have generally targeted her orientation to the West, maintaining that her films are made with an eye toward Western consumption; she has been accused of a class-based replication of racist colonial gestures; her increasing use of Hollywood style budgets and formulas of glamour and romance has also come under attack, as has her presumed arrogance in assuming she can speak for those who cannot speak for themselves.[9]

In her assessment of the problematic aspects of Nair's career, Sharma highlights an issue facing filmmakers who traverse the East/West dichotomy that we have, up until now, not encountered in this study: the question of the subaltern's ability to speak, which Gayatri Chakravorty Spivak has so thoroughly discussed. Working with Macaulay's 'interpreter class,' Spivak exposes the contradictions of postcolonial intellectuals from nations such as India representing subaltern groups:

> For the (gender-unspecified) 'true' subaltern subject, whose identity is its difference, there is no unrepresentable subaltern subject that can know and speak itself: the intellectual's solution is not to abstain from

> representation. The problem is that the subject's itinerary has not been left traced so as to offer an object of seduction to the representing intellectual . . . The question becomes: How can we touch the consciousness of the people even as we investigate their politics?[10]

Spivak's discussion of intellectuals who share Nair's positionality exposes the potential problems of representations of India in Nair's cinema. However, it also evokes questions regarding political criticisms of postcolonial cinema in general. As we have seen in the previous two chapters, while representations of ethnic minorities by settler colonials like Lussier and Campion are certainly open to criticism, their depictions have not led to a general dismissal of their work.

Though it may be true that Nair's subject matter and representations of her homeland are diluted by her intellectual position and complicity with a Western, even Orientalist lens, such contradictions make her work fruitful to an interfidelity approach and indicative of the globalised postcolonial subject. Spivak's contention certainly still serves as an important caution for postcolonial theory, but it runs the risk in the globalised world of dismissing important work from ethnic and gender groups that, while privileged, are still marginalised – such as a female Indian filmmaker with a transnational presence.[11] For a filmmaker so consumed with and criticised for her representations of India, Nair's film adaptation of *Vanity Fair* serves as an ideal text to examine how Britain's colonial past informs the contemporary Indian diaspora.

Published at the height of Britain's pre-Rebellion (Indian Mutiny, 1857) imperial endeavours in India, the novel centres on Becky Sharp, the daughter of an impoverished artist, and her attempts to rise in England's rigid class system through her interactions and associations with the noble Crawley family and the wealthy merchant-class Sedley and Osborne families. Born in Calcutta to a father who amassed his wealth through military and independent economic endeavours in Indian territory, Thackeray enjoyed a life of prosperity and prominence as a result of his father's imperial successes.[12] Working as a journalist and humourist for *Fraser's Magazine*, Thackeray ridiculed the British class system and its concern for title over wealth in biting satires for the conservative publication before beginning his career as a novelist.[13] However, though Indian culture permeates his novels and journalism, Thackeray's work ignores detailed discussions of India, portraying it simply as a foreign land ripe with financial opportunity for his English characters. Through his depictions of India in his work, Thackeray's writing echoes Said's claim that the 19th century European novel contains allusions to Empire more regular and frequent than any other cultural product.[14] As Said writes in *Culture and Imperialism*:

> One of my main reasons for writing this book is to show how far the quest for, concern about, and consciousness of overseas dominion extended

> – not just in Conrad but in figures we practically never think of in that connection, like Thackeray and Austen – and how enriching and important for the critic is attention to this material, not only for the obvious political reasons, but also because, as I have been arguing, this particular kind of attention allows the reader to interpret canonical nineteenth and twentieth-century works with a newly engaged interest.[15]

Through her film adaptation, Nair far exceeds Said's call to interpret the imperialism embedded in Thackeray's novel. Dispatching with Thackeray's omniscient male narrator and infusing the *mise-en-scène* of the film with costumes, props and set decorations inspired by India as well as by shooting scenes on location in her native country, Nair endows India with a voice in the narrative that both challenges Britain's cultural dominance and critiques the imperial power for its consumption, working toward her stated goal of demonstrating that the Victorian upper-classes were built on the backs of the colonies without, as John Kenneth Muir writes, perverting 'the novel's intent or ethos'.[16]

While Nair may actively criticise imperialism in a manner that echoes Said's statement, her efforts to integrate India into Hollywood cinema seem to fall victim to a caution Said made much earlier in his career: depictions of the Orient as a fragmented and unusual experience. Resulting from the Orient's alien relationship to the West, representations of countries such as India appear as fragments to the West in which 'The Orientalist is required to *present* the Orient by a series of representative fragments, fragments republished, explicated, annotated, and surrounded with still more fragments.'[17] As a result, while Nair's focus on India cultivates a space for the nation that the source text denies, her Indian representations are fragments surrounded by the context of the narrative's colonial discourse, a version of India that, though present and self-aware, remains tied to Orientalist structures. Yet, Nair's seeming conformity to Orientalist tropes permits a more complex representation of India when taking her diasporic perspective into consideration. Writing about the web of relationships between Caribbean writers and filmmakers, Black British filmmakers, and the avant-garde directors of America and Europe, Stuart Hall discusses the 'tense and tortured' nature of diasporic dialogue: 'It is nowhere to be found in its pure, pristine state. It is always-already fused, syncretized with other cultural elements. It is always-already creolized . . .'[18]

Within this context, Nair's surface Orientalism and its fragmented inclusion becomes another strategy to convey an ambivalent reading of the novel from a diasporic Indian perspective. At the same time, it is rooted in what Homi Bhabha refers to as a 'sly civility' in which Nair's adaptation seemingly adopts the Orientalist bent of Victorian and Hollywood representation, but contains strong subversive undercurrents, engaging with a projection of colonial and neocolonial discourse that, as Bhabha writes:

> May compel the native to address the master, but it can never produce those effects of 'love' or 'truth' that would centre the confessional demand. If, through projection, the native is partially aligned or reformed in discourse, the fixed hate which refuses to circulate or reconjugate, produces the repeated fantasy of the native as in-between legality and illegality, endangering the boundaries of truth itself.[19]

Adopting a slyly civil attitude toward Orientalist discourse, Nair approaches the text from an 'in-between', diasporic perspective, revising a colonial text for which she has an affinity and opening a dialogue about an authentic India between Thackeray's novel and Hollywood convention.

Distributed by Focus Features – the art-house film distribution arm of NBC/Universal – Nair's adaptation of *Vanity Fair* also provided her with a forum to address the globalised film industry that has further asserted its presence on Bollywood in the last decade. Originating as an attempt to define cultural identity during English occupation, the Hindi film industry has become India's primary model of national unity, using its immensely popular 'item numbers' – musical scenes reminiscent of Hollywood films from the studio era – to foster nationalism and highlight similarities among its ethnically diverse population.[20] Since the Indian state declared the film industry approved activity under 'industrial concerns' in 2000, Bollywood has increased its financial strength and film output, producing more than 300 films a year and seeking coproductions and other financing structures with Hollywood and European studios.[21] With Bollywood films such as Rajkumar Hirani's *3 Idiots* (2009) and *PK* (2014), Anurag Basu's *Kites* (2009), Karan Johar's *My Name is Khan* (2010), and S. S. Rajamouli's two-part *Bahubali* (2015 and 2017) becoming international box-office successes, Western public relations firms, distributors and critics began devoting increased attention to Bollywood. Consequently, recent releases within the industry have demonstrated a greater Western influence, adopting an MTV-inspired sexuality and cinematic style.[22] Likewise, Bollywood productions have eschewed the lip-synced item numbers to appeal to the West because, in the wake of Ashutosh Gowariker's *Lagaan* (2001) not winning the Academy Award for Best Foreign-Language Film after becoming the first Bollywood film nominated, many in the industry felt that, according to Tejaswini Ganti, 'Indian cinema was simply too alien and its songs a form of cultural baggage that kept Indian filmmakers from competing globally.'[23] While such alterations to Bollywood films may increase their marketability internationally, the conformity to outside influence has alienated many members of the working-class audiences within India that constitute a substantial portion of Bollywood's domestic demographic.[24]

Using her clout after the international success of *Monsoon Wedding* to achieve more creative control over her adaptation of *Vanity Fair*, Nair comments on the increased corporate influence on Indian cinema by making the adaptation an amalgam of Hollywood and Bollywood style, allowing Bollywood to influence the dominant Hollywood narrative conventions within her film. Embedding India's presence onto the narrative even further, Nair added several scenes to the film she shot in her native country with the goal of avoiding, according to screenwriter Julian Fellowes, 'That same old palm tree and man-in-a-tent with cicadas going in the background always telling you so clearly that the whole thing was shot in Surrey.'[25] Through including the stylistic conventions and locations of Bollywood films, Nair reasserts the cinematic identity of her country, suggesting that nations outside the dominant power centres can attain influence in the process of cultural hybridity despite the problems of subaltern agency and conformity to Orientalism on display in her adaptation.

DIASPORIC FIDELITY IN THE THRIVING EMPIRE

Subtitled 'A Novel Without a Hero', Thackeray's *Vanity Fair* constantly changes the focus of its narrative, creating an epic ensemble story rather than defining a central protagonist. Yet in his narrative construction, Thackeray creates an omniscient third-person narrator that acts as an imperial voice by threading the stories together. Appearing in many of Thackeray's later works such as *The Newcomers* (1855), the narrator evolves as a character that, while separate from Thackeray, also holds a role as an Empire writer who affirms his allegiance to the power of the imperial project.[26] In *Vanity Fair*, discussing the Battle of Waterloo in which the British defeated Napoleon's forces and cemented their status as an imperial power in Europe, Thackeray writes: 'All of us have read of what occurred during that interval. The tale is in every Englishman's mouth; you and I, who were children when the great battle was won and lost, are never tired of hearing and recounting the history of that famous action.'[27] Through his narrator's comments, Thackeray reveals that while the plot fails to establish a central character, his audience already possesses the characteristics necessary to identify with the novel: a shared reverence for the military and cultural prowess of Britain as Empire. *Vanity Fair* acts as a novel without a hero, because the British Empire and its subjects already act as heroes by default as a result of their mutual allegiance to their native country. Thackeray's narrator continues to cement his omnipotence throughout the text, reaffirming his ethos through statements such as 'The novelist, who knows everything, knows this also' in reference to Becky writing all of her husband Rawdon Crawley's correspondence, and, 'The novelist, it has been said before, knows everything' when discussing how Becky and Crawley lived extravagantly without an income.[28] Taking into consideration Said's advocation of reading colonial discourse contrapuntally, one can perceive Thackeray's narrator as an unseen imperial force who controls the novel's narrative in a manner similar to the way Britain's colonial endeavours enhance the wealth of the characters in the novel.

Throughout her adaptation, Nair uses the camera's objectivity to strip the novel's narrator of his agency, eliminating the presence of a third-person narrator from the film. However, Nair's use of point-of-view conforms much more to Seymour Chatman's definition of slant – a term that captures 'the psychological, sociological, and ideological ramifications of the narrator's attitudes, which may range from neutral to highly charged' – than the vague connotations of the term point-of-view.[29] As Chatman writes:

> Attitudes, of course, are rooted in ideology, and the narrator is as much a locus of ideology as anyone else, inside or outside the fiction. The ideology may or may not match that of any of the characters. And it may or may not match that of the implied author or real author. It might be argued that in a sufficiently broad definition, attitudes are *all* that 'narrator's point of view' feasibly refers to.[30]

Using Chatman's terminology, one could argue that Nair simply excises the novel's omniscient narrator in favour of a politicised implied author. Also discussing Nair through Chatman's work, Micael M. Clarke discusses both the film's postcolonial bent and point-of-view alternations, but does not link the two beyond the film's creation of 'gaps in the narrative (i.e. between what the narrator shows and what the reader or viewer interprets) that the filmmakers have charged with meaning.'[31] In his essay, Clarke does acknowledge that, as a gifted ironist, Thackeray does not construct the narrator's voice to 'represent the meaning of the novel, but rather, a series of perspectives that the reader must interpret.'[32] While the narrator may not represent meaning, his imperial complicity would not be lost on an Indian reader such as Nair, who was drawn to Becky's story, but whose experiences were outside the perspective of the British Empire. Therefore, nothing is 'implied' in Nair's elimination of the third-person narrator in favour of a voiceless presence that advances a diasporic Indian perspective through cinematic style. Instead, the narrator acts as a politicised presence actively seeking to both represent the perspectives absent from Thackeray's novel and critique their absence in the source text. As a result, Nair's silent stylistic 'narrator' integrates images into the narrative that directly interrogate the power of the British Empire and its agents while remaining faithful to her experience with the source text.

Nair opens the film's title sequence with an extreme close up of a peacock strutting on the screen against a black backdrop, an image she returns to as the titles roll. Rather than provide a direct establishment of narrative authority, Nair's focus on the peacock acts a metaphorical visual cue that presents an image of an animal associated with vanity to the audience and forces viewers to make a correlation between the animal and the film's English characters that appear in the sequences that directly follow. In addition, the peacock's origins as not only indigenous to India but also its national bird allow Nair to relate her cultural perspective directly to the audience. In Nair's words, the sequence conveys the 'vanity, beauty, mystery, and Orientalism' referenced in Thackeray's novel.[33] Through her control over the film's narrative, Nair presents a hybrid image of an Indian bird associated by the Empire with vanity, calling attention to the vanity of the Empire that originally gave the peacock its Orientalist connotations.

After establishing her control over the film's narrative, Nair uses her slant to integrate visual depictions of India into the film that are absent from Thackeray's novel. Throughout *Vanity Fair*, Thackeray portrays India as a mysterious, unknown land, omitting descriptions of the country even in the scenes that occur there. However, Thackeray includes detailed descriptions of England in the novel, claiming that its beauty far overshadows the tropical lands of India. When Joseph Sedley and Major Dobbin return home from India, Thackeray writes:

> How happy and green the country looked as the chaise whirled rapidly from mile-stone to mile-stone, through neat country towns where landlords came out to welcome him with smiles and bows; by pretty road-side inns, where the signs hung on the shadow of the trees; by old halls and parks; rustic hamlets clustered round ancient gray churches – and through the charming friendly English landscape. Is there any in the world like it? To a traveller returning home it looks so kind – it seems to shake hands with you as you pass through it.[34]

With its detailed description of the English countryside, Thackeray's portrayal of England sharply contrasts with even his most detailed depiction of India that occurs when he describes Dobbin's original deployment: 'The astonished reader must be called upon to transport himself ten thousand miles to the military station of Bundlegunge, in the Madras division of our Indian Empire.'[35] Though Thackeray designates every facet of the English landscape, touting its merits as superior to other lands, he never depicts India as an autonomous land, even denoting the foreign territory as 'our' Indian Empire. As a result, Thackeray reinforces the superiority of Britain over the colonial territory to such an extent that even a nation thousands of miles away cannot escape a definition removed from associations with its coloniser.

In her adaptation, Nair fosters a depiction of India that contrasts sharply with the scenes that take place in the dreary English countryside. As Nair writes, including India in the narrative allows her to create, 'a change of place and light for us to truly understand the impact of the colonies, how far away and utterly different it was from England.'[36] When Dobbin (Rhys Ifans) makes the decision to return to England from his post in India, Nair shoots him writing a letter in an extreme long shot, noting not only the beauty of the Indian desert but also the small stature of the agent of Empire. In addition, as Dobbin enters an Indian palace to tell his comrades of his departure, Nair frames him in a long shot, focusing her attention on the lush red decor of the building. Drastically changing the setting of the film's ending from Germany to India, Nair also includes a lengthy scene in which Becky (Reese Witherspoon) and Joseph Sedley (Tony Maudsley) ride on an elephant through the packed streets of Bombay, taking in the bright costumes of the crowd, bustle of the city and exotic animals that fill the frame. However, in both instances, India remains defined entirely by the fragments Said discusses. Rather than present a sustained depiction of India through involved sequences that capture life in the nation, Nair operates in a fragmented shorthand of vast landscape, bright colours, elephants and other Indian exotica not out of place in an advertisement for a travel company or a retail store specialising in global merchandise. Through adding depictions of India absent from the novel, Nair endows her native country with a presence ignored in Thackeray's narrative, portraying the nation as a lively culture that exists as a world independent of Britain rather than in competition with its beauty as Thackeray depicts.

Nair continues to maintain her diasporic fidelity to the novel through her treatment of the Battle of Waterloo that serves as a central narrative turn in Thackeray. As Napoleon Bonaparte returns from exile and attempts to reclaim his imperial power over Europe, Major Dobbin, Captain George Osborne and Captain Rawdon Crawley prepare for battle. Thackeray presents the battle not as a precarious conflict that threatens Britain's authority, but as a chance for British forces to demonstrate their power:

> The news of Napoleon's escape and landing was received by the gallant –th with fiery delight and enthusiasm, which everybody can understand who knows the famous corps. From the colonel to the smallest drummer in the regiment, all were filled with the hope and ambition and patriotic fury; and thanked the French Emperor as for a personal kindness in coming to disturb the peace of Europe. Now was the time the –th had so long panted for, to show their comrades in arms that they could fight as well as the Peninsular veterans, and that the pluck and valour of the –th had not been killed by the West Indies and yellow fever.[37]

Revelling in the bravery and honour that comes from belonging to the British Army, the soldiers view the impending war as a chance to cement their superiority rather than as a violent conflict that could end in death. Thackeray reinforces the patriotic fervour and faith in the British Empire through his description of Osborne's views on the war: 'Bonaparty was to be crushed without a struggle . . . People were going not so much to see a war as to a fashionable tour.'[38] Through his flippant treatment of a conflict that would eventually kill thousands of British soldiers, Thackeray reveals a strong faith in the power of the British Empire, a power so strong that, barring the death of George Osborne in battle, he never mentions the destruction and detriment the war caused for the Empire. Using the war as a simple narrative device to move his plot forward, Thackeray presents the British Empire as strong enough to withstand even one of the most difficult battles in his nation's history.

Differing from Thackeray's text, Nair's adaptation depicts the Battle of Waterloo in explicit detail, a narrative choice that allows her to expose the large death toll and horror of war for the British Empire that Thackeray's novel ignores. As the Battle of Waterloo rages, Becky walks down a street in Ostend, Belgium, flanked on both sides by hundreds of wounded British soldiers returning to the city. Though Becky remains in the centre of the frame, Nair shoots the scene in an extreme long shot that accentuates the uniformity of the soldiers while cutting to closer shots of their bloody wounds. After the British finally overcome Napoleon's forces, Nair includes a scene absent from the novel in which she reveals the death of Osborne (Jonathan Rhys Meyers) by craning the camera over a battlefield littered with the corpses of dead British soldiers until she rests the camera on his body. As a resounding defeat of the French and cementation of British authority, Waterloo became a symbol for the British of what Jeremy Black refers to as 'The fortitude of defense', an event that celebrated the power of 'the thin red line' and served as inspiration in future campaigns ranging from the Crimean War to the 1879 conflicts with Zulus in South Africa.[39] Through focusing attention on depictions of the wounded and dead British soldiers, Nair lingers on the battle's bloody and costly reality, directly undercutting the important role it would play in propagating the iconography of the British Empire throughout the rest of the century. Though thousands died for the Empire to survive the threat of Napoleon, Thackeray refuses to acknowledge the deaths in order to preserve the illusion of Britain's strength, a facet of the source text that Nair brings to the forefront of her adaptation.

Nair exerts her slant most explicitly in her deviation from the novel's treatment of native people, highlighting racism and subjugation of nonwhites by the British in the film. Throughout Thackeray's novel, the author depicts Indians and natives of other colonies as either nonentities or sources of scorn for his British characters. When Becky arrives at the Sedley house, she delights the black servant Sambo by calling him 'Sir' and 'Mr Sambo'.[40] As Becky works to cajole a marriage proposal from Joseph Sedley in the novel, the elder Mr Sedley remarks to his wife, 'Better she, my dear, than a black Mrs. Sedley and a dozen mahogany grandchildren.'[41] Similarly, as Mr Osborne tries to arrange a marriage for George to Rhoda Scwartz, a Jamaican native whose family became wealthy from trade, he laments her race, referring to her as 'a Mahogany Charmer' and 'the dark object' and to George as 'the Conqueror'.[42] Rather than neglect and mute the existence of the non-English characters in her film adaptation, Nair accents their differences, allowing them to maintain their cultural heritage while holding positions in the serving class within the Empire. Nair completely removes all references to Joseph Sedley marrying when George Osborne immediately curtails Joseph's infatuation with Becky early in the film by evoking their class difference. As a result, Joseph disappears to India for the majority of the narrative, acting as an agent of Empire free from the constraints of Britain's class structure and able to pursue what Said deems 'Oriental sex', sexual intercourse as commodity free from the societal obligations of Empire, including marriage.[43]

Nair also excises the novel's depictions of Sambo's neglect and ill treatment, instead including the Indian migrant Biju (Paul Bazely) (Figure 4.1), who, Machalias writes, 'serves no obvious ideological purpose: to emphasise the invisibility of servants in most costume dramas, as well as to draw attention to the colonial link made between language and "civilized" status: the character has no speaking lines in the film.'[44] Having no interaction with the Sedleys apart from his required duty, Biju, as Machalias implies, also serves as one of the more prominent inclusions of the film's slyly civil approach. Yet, Nair's greatest departure from Thackeray's novel occurs during the scene in which the elder Osborne (Jim Broadbent) tries to arrange George's marriage to Rhoda (Kathryn Drysdale). As she waits in the Osbornes' parlour, George

Figure 4.1 Biju (Paul Basely) looks on as Becky eats the chili.

confronts his father in his study, refusing to assent to a marriage arranged for him when he has given his word to marry Amelia Sedley (Romola Garai). During the heated argument between the two men in which the elder Osborne asks his son, 'What's a shade or two of tawny when there's a title on the table?' and tells George he must marry Rhoda to get control of her finances, Nair cuts back to a long shot of Rhoda sitting alone in the parlour with a look of anguish on her face. Despite her fortune, Rhoda remains a character denied a voice in the narrative, spoken of as an anomaly in high society by the white bourgeois. Yet, Nair's choice to cut to Rhoda sitting alone in the well-furnished English parlour as the older men argue over her in financial terms endows the young heiress with a presence that allows Nair both to demonstrate the men's rampant disregard for her and to comment on the persistence of 'otherness' fundamental to the construction of Empire that transcends even financial security.

In sharp contrast to the moral ambiguity of Thackeray's characters, Nair uses her diasporic slant to portray the bureaucratic structure of Empire as built on corruption through her treatment of Marquess Steyne (Gabriel Byrne). In the novel, Thackeray presents the wealthy Marquess as a man enthralled by Becky's wit and intelligence and angered by her inability to attain substantial status in the British class system. As a result, he attempts to better her situation by offering George a colonial appointment as a governor to Eastern Coventry Island. However, after being released from debtors' prison, Rawdon returns home to find Becky and Steyne alone, misinterpreting their meeting as a love affair. Despite his suspicions, Rawdon accepts Steyne's offer, reading about himself in the paper: 'We need not only men of acknowledged bravery, but men of administrative talents to superintend the affairs of our colonies; and we have no doubt that the gentleman selected by the colonial office to fill the lamented vacancy at Coventry Island is admirably calculated for the post which he is about to occupy.'[45] Unable to reject the prestige of his newfound occupation within the Empire, Rawdon assumes the position, abandoning reconciliation with Becky and eventually dying of a mysterious tropical fever on the island.

In contrast, Nair's use of diasporic fidelity heightens the sexual tension between Steyne and Becky, portraying Rawdon's position as governor, not as an appointment earned through Becky's social climbing, but as a manoeuvre by the corrupt upper classes to sate those whom they have wronged. From the beginning of the film, Nair depicts Steyne as a morally reprehensible figure in a scene absent from Thackeray's novel as he buys a painting of Becky's mother from Mr Sharpe (Roger-Lloyd Pack) against the wishes of the young Becky (Angelica Mandy). As Steyne reenters the narrative, Nair positions him as a figure on the periphery, gazing at Becky from afar until he makes contact with her by paying off her husband's debts in the middle of a creditor's repossession. When Rawdon (James Purfoy) catches Becky and Steyne alone together in the film, Nair alters Thackeray's narrative, shooting Rawdon in a tracking shot while he discovers Steyne attempting to seduce Becky on the parlour couch. Until Rawdon uncovers Steyne and Becky's act of infidelity, Nair makes no mention of the colonial appointment. However, once Steyne realises the extent of Rawdon's anger, he offers him the appointment, which Nair depicts as a payoff by removing all information of the appointment from the narrative until the story later runs in the newspaper.

Through her portrayal of Steyne's dubious character, Nair also situates Becky as, according to Ana Moya, 'Related to the classic Victorian hero (a Dickensian or Brontëian character), an orphan in a dark, hostile world where survival is difficult. Characters such as Heathcliff, Jane Eyre, Oliver Twist and Pip become precursors of this Becky Sharp at the beginning of the twenty-first century.'[46] The film exhibits a clear sympathy for Becky, which is the most common complaint lodged against it by fidelity-minded critics.[47] Yet, given Nair's perspective, Becky takes on the role of a diasporic figure, neither belonging in poverty nor in the world of Steyne, who Moya likens to Dickens' Fagin and Ms Havisham in the adaptation.[48] In aligning the film's slant with Becky, Nair presents Steyne as the embodiment of brute imperial force, a man who subjugates all those around him for the accumulation of commodities, whether paintings with sentimental value, or Becky's social position.

AN EMPIRE OF COMMODITY

As Steyne's obsession with possessing commodities indicates, *Vanity Fair*, similar to other novels of the Victorian era, exhibits a fascination with the growing wealth of Britain as a direct consequence of its colonial endeavours. According to Christoph Linder, 'Commodities almost jump off the page in Thackeray's writing to be fondled, touched, tasted, circulated, or lavishly gazed upon with any combination of admiration, envy, greed, or desire.'[49] Throughout the narrative, Thackeray includes a multitude of references to riches gleaned from the Indian colonies, using Indian cultural commodities as symbols of wealth and power for his characters. For Thackeray, admission to the wealthy classes carries associations with Eastern tropes such as turbans, elephants and moguls, leaving Becky and other characters to fantasise about wealth by borrowing from the imagery of Eastern texts such as *Arabian Nights*.[50] Such behaviour is indicative of what Hall refers to as 'The progress of the great white explorer', figures such as Joseph Sedley whose experiences in Africa, India and other colonies served as a catalyst for advertisements that 'translated *things* into a fantasy visual display of *signs and symbols*' and, in turn, led to the search for markets and raw materials to fuel imperial expansion.[51]

Engaging with Hall's link between commodity and Empire, Nair's film adaptation addresses the role of commodity in Thackeray's work, using visual cues to accent the Indian influence over British culture and to establish an acknowledged dialectic between the two cultures that transcends the roles of coloniser-colonised.

Thackeray most directly embodies ties between Empire and commodity through his construction of Joseph Sedley, the wealthy nabob of the Boggley Wollah Indian district and Becky's initial prospect for a husband. Characterising Joseph as an epicurean of India's finest cultural products who continually consumes hookah and Indian cuisine, Thackeray presents Indian commodities as symbols of wealth and power aspirational for individuals such as Becky. As Mrs Sedley prepares an Indian dinner to celebrate her son's return to England, Thackeray writes:

> Now we have heard how Mrs Sedley had prepared a fine curry for her son just as he liked it: and in the course of dinner a portion of the dish was offered to Rebecca.
>
> 'What is it?' said she turning in an appealing look to Mr Joseph.
>
> 'Capital,' said he – his mouth was full of it: his face quite red with the delightful exercise of gobbling. 'Mother, it's as good as my own curries in India.'
>
> 'Oh I must try some if it is an Indian dish,' said Rebecca. 'I am sure every thing must be good that comes from *there*.'[52]

Through the passage, Thackeray depicts the Indian commodity as a luxury item only available to privileged classes. Because of his imperial endeavours, Joseph acts as chief critic of his mother's imitation of the native dish, her failed demonstration of cultural awareness that exceeds her experiences. Aspiring to rise from her status as a poor girl, Becky realises that consuming the curry acts as a passage from her current class status into Joseph's. By engaging in the consumption of the curry native to *there*, the source of Empire's power, Becky participates in a method of exchange that reinforces the Victorian notion that colonisation breeds power, entering into the enjoyment of India's resources on her own domestic scale.

In her adaptation, Nair treats Becky's consumption of the curry in a humorous manner, highlighting the inability of the British to fully integrate Indian culture into the framework of the Empire. As Biju brings the curry to the table, Becky tries the dish after stating that she is 'enraptured by every scent and flavour of the East.' As in the novel, the curry proves too spicy for Becky. However, Nair breaks from the adaptation by cutting to a shot of Biju's silent (and slyly civil) laughter, a choice that mirrors Arjun Appadurai's concept of 'commoditization by diversion' in which 'value . . . is accelerated or enhanced by placing objects and things in unlikely contexts'. Within the Sedley household, the curry is a commodity diverted to middle class space for the sole purpose of engaging with 'the aesthetics of decontextualization (itself driven by the quest for novelty) that is at the heart of the display, in highbrow Western homes, of the tools and artifacts of the "other"'.[53] With their family ties to the 'great white explorer' Joseph, the Sedleys hold a direct association to the broader imperial context of which their consumption is a part. Yet, Becky, with her humble class position, lacks the ability to decontextualise and consume such commodities. After finally completing her task despite her obvious pain, Becky swallows triumphantly, deeming the dish 'delicious' to Joseph. Through these alterations to the novel, Nair accents the repressed anxiety stemming from Britain's 'commodification by diversion' of India. Though Becky attempts to mask her discomfort over consuming the spicy curry, Nair's execution of the scene for humour and shots of Biju expose her British protagonist's labours to maintain conformity to an imperialism fueled by commodity and, by extension, the illusion of Britain's seamless consumption of India and its cultural artefacts.

Nair continues to demonstrate India's resistance to the consumption of its culture through her alterations to Joseph and Becky's relationship at the end of the novel. After ending her marriage with Rawdon, Becky moves to Pumpernickel, Germany, where Joseph finds her in a casino. Still harbouring an infatuation for Becky, he immediately rekindles his relationship with her, asking her to be his companion as he travels through Europe. Thackeray writes: 'Mr Joseph Sedley went, she travelled likewise; and that infatuated man seemed entirely to be her slave.'[54] However, though the two travel together, Joseph soon dies in France under mysterious circumstances that Thackeray insinuates may involve Becky.[55] By concluding the novel with the reconciliation of Joseph and Becky, Thackeray provides a potential happy ending to his narrative, allowing Becky to achieve the wealth and privilege she has desired from her associations with a man who gained his wealth through imperial endeavours. As the relationship between the couple transitions from novel to film, Nair makes significant alterations to foreground the importance of India in Becky's rise from the lower classes. Throughout Becky's travels in the film, Nair uses her protagonist's monogrammed trunk as a motif, cutting to close-ups of it as Becky moves to new locations that mark her increase in social status, a choice that allows Becky to place her mark on the places she visits. As Joseph and Becky reunite at the end of the film, Joseph says, 'It's time to enjoy my fortune now, I'm on my way back to India', before inviting her to come. In contrast to Thackeray, Nair ends the film on the streets of Bombay with Joseph and Becky riding an elephant amid a parade of Indians, cutting to a close-up of the monogrammed trunk resting on the elephant's back before fading to black. Through her focus on the trunk, Nair directly addresses India's role in Becky's class mobility and presents Becky as a colonising force in the region whose English baggage marks her new territory. Similarly, in his decision to return to India, Joseph embraces the land that led to his fortune, transporting Becky to her ultimate living situation as she enjoys the financial comfort gained by imperial endeavours in a land responsible for the Empire's financial prowess.

Using the medium of cinema to accent Thackeray's depiction of Empire, Nair comments on the novel's lengthy references to Indian commodities by working with production designer Maria Djurkovic to cultivate an aesthetic for the film that acts as an amalgamation of British and Indian style. In the novel, Thackeray makes numerous references to Indian goods as units of exchange. Upon his return from India, Joseph gives his sister Amelia a cashmere shawl, which she tries to give to Becky: 'She determined in her heart to ask her mother's permission to present her white Cashmere shawl to her friend. Could she not spare it? and had not her brother Joseph just brought her two from India?'[56] Later in the novel, after the Sedleys' descent into poverty, Amelia buys her son, Georgy, new clothes by selling a similar shawl given to her by Major Dobbin: 'There was her Indian shawl that Dobbin had sent her. She remembered in former days going with her mother to a fine India shop on Ludgate Hill, where the ladies had all sorts of dealings and bargains in these articles. Her cheeks flushed and her eyes shone with pleasure as she thought of this resource.'[57] In both instances, the shawls from India act as commodities that allow Thackeray's characters to cement their social class. Amelia desires to give a shawl to Becky so that her friend will comply with the fashions of a higher class. Similarly, Amelia barters the shawl in order to buy her son Christmas clothes so that he will not look out of place with the wealthier boys at his school. Through his use of the shawls as commodities, Thackeray references the colonial project's power to frame English citizens' social positions, depicting them as useful symbols of prosperity within the Empire.

Elaborating on Thackeray's use of Indian goods to define social class, Nair's film presents the products of the Empire not only as integral to defining class but also as inseparable from the upper echelons of British culture. When the Sedleys take Becky on a picnic to an English park early in the film, Nair presents the setting as an Orientalist simulacrum of Indian culture, positioning her characters amid a replica of an Indian palace, shooting them riding on Indian boats, surrounding them with Indian natives playing Indian music on sitars, and even including a scene in which Joseph gives Becky a parrot as a gift. In addition, as Becky moves to a fashionable London district after her marriage to Rawdon, Nair includes a scene in which Becky accidentally drops an Oriental rug. As the rug opens in the street, Becky falls to the ground, laughing joyfully on its floral pattern. Through her subtle inclusion of Oriental commodities, Nair demonstrates the vital role Indian products play in English social mobility. Only after Becky possesses the agency to become immersed in products of Indian culture is she able to enter into the class position she has so long desired.

Nair continues to refine her commentary on the role of Indian commodity within the British Empire through her costume design in the film. Wanting to create a stark contrast from the Merchant Ivory aesthetics customary of period films, Nair hired Beatrix Pasztor, a costume designer renowned for her inventive contemporary work in Gus Van Sant's films *My Own Private Idaho* (1991) and *Even Cowgirls Get the Blues* (1994), Terry Gilliam's *The Fisher King* (1991) and Charles Shyer's *Alfie* (2004). Choosing Pasztor largely because of her lack of experience with period films, Nair desired to encourage her designer's contemporary flavour to create costumes that fused English and Indian fashions into a unified aesthetic.[58] As a result, the costumes in the film borrow elements from fashions of Indian origins popular during the time of Thackeray's novel, both subverting and conforming to Orientalist depictions. When Becky attends Marquess Steyne's ball in the film, Nair costumes the women in traditional Victorian dresses made with brightly coloured fabrics from the East, accessorising with feathers from peacocks and other exotic birds. Through costumes that turn fashions from both countries into a cohesive whole, Nair comments on the hybridity inherent in the relationship between coloniser and colonised, implying that the wealth of the British is unattainable without the contribution of commodities from the colonised nation.

HOLLYWOOD FUNDING AND BOLLYWOOD AESTHETICS

With a $23 million budget and the increased box-office prowess of Reese Witherspoon after the success of *Legally Blonde* (2001), *Sweet Home Alabama* (2002) and *Legally Blonde 2: Red, White, and Blonde* (2003), Focus Features released *Vanity Fair* in September 2004 as an early awards contender, using a similar marketing strategy that made Sofia Coppola's *Lost in Translation* (2003) a critical and commercial success for the studio the previous year. However, the film failed at the domestic box-office, earning $16 million and becoming overshadowed by Zach Braff's quirky-indie *Garden State* (2004) and Focus' Michel Gondry-helmed *Eternal Sunshine of the Spotless Mind* (2004). Critics castigated Nair for her interpretation of Thackeray's novel, criticising her for the simplicity of the adaptation and accusing her of caricaturing the British as gaudy imperialists.[59] In addition, academic reception of the film often hinged upon allegations that Nair ignored Thackeray's criticisms of his novel's heroine, allowing a blatant revisionist feminism to overshadow the novel's nuance.[60] While many critics observed Nair's attempts to address the British Empire through her retextualisation of the novel, her diasporic perspective went either largely unnoticed by critics or analysed on a superficial

Figure 4.2 Becky (Reese Witherspoon) performs Bollywood.

level by those such as Michael Agger who writes in his *Film Comment* review concerning the film's Bollywood item number sequence (Figure 4.2): 'In the wrong hands, the scene would have come off like a bad Madonna video, but it somehow works.'[61]

Despite the critical response to Nair's aesthetic choices, the director's use of conventions from her native country's cinema addresses corporate imperialism and its increasing influence on Bollywood. During a reception for King George IV at Steyne's home, the Marquess presents the sovereign with a performance in his honour that Nair refers to in the film's credits as the slave dance. Directly borrowing from the conventions of the Bollywood item number, which Anjali Gera Roy deems, 'a sequence of raunchy movements and risqué lyrics with little relation to the plotline', Nair presents the scene as a deviation, relishing in its Indian style as Becky, in Indian dress and covered with henna tattoos, dances amid an array of Indian extras.[62] However, as opposed to traditional Bollywood item numbers used to generate publicity for the films, Nair's use of the convention takes on an overtly political dimension.[63] The audience of English aristocrats looks on in a state of shock as they see Becky and a handful of other English women assimilated among the native Indians to such an extent that their ethnicities are unintelligible. Using long takes, a Bollywood-influenced score and a constantly moving camera, Nair revels in the visual spectacle of the scene, turning her period costume drama into a musical for two-and-a-half minutes. While the scene serves the narrative purpose of allowing Becky to earn the respect of King George, Nair's stylistic choices permit her to integrate the Bollywood aesthetic into a mainstream film funded by a major media conglomerate. Through Witherspoon's status as an internationally popular and marketable film star, Nair immerses the actress in Bollywood culture, turning her into a communicative tool that conveys the essence of Bollywood cinema to mainstream audiences. Yet, unlike other recent item numbers in Hollywood films such as Luhrmann's *Moulin Rouge!* or Boyle's end credits sequence from *Slumdog Millionaire*, Nair uses the number to further her diasporic perspective over Thackeray's narrative and Hollywood filmmaking. As a result, the scene becomes not merely a spectacle produced for a king, but a corporate-funded representation of a nation's culture in a commodity marketed internationally.

In adapting *Vanity Fair* to film, Nair incorporates her Indian heritage, strengthening the presence of India in a work that views Indian culture in abstract, economic terms. While the adaptation serves as a departure from the rest of Nair's oeuvre, the film preserves her thematic preoccupations with outsiders ostracised by a dominant culture and endeavouring to reconcile the Eastern and Western worlds. Nair's film allows her to infuse her own nation's culture into the confines of a text that largely denies its autonomy, writing back both to the British Empire that treated India as a source of commodity and to the contemporary Empire that threatens to homogenise Indian culture into a diluted international flair palatable enough for globalised distribution.

CHAPTER 5

Epic Multitudes: Postcolonial Genre Politics in Shekhar Kapur's *The Four Feathers*

When Miramax Films and Paramount released Shekhar Kapur's *The Four Feathers* in September 2002, the studios initiated the year's awards season race with a film that appeared ready to capture international critical and commercial acclaim. Adapted from A. E. W. Mason's late-Victorian adventure novel, the production boasted a pedigree tailor-made for awards contention. In addition to its status as Kapur's follow up to his 1998 Academy Award nominee *Elizabeth*, the $80 million epic featured up-and-coming actor Heath Ledger as well as a host of previous Oscar nominees, including cinematographer Robert Richardson (*Platoon* (1986) and *JFK* (1991)), actors Kate Hudson and Djimon Hounsou, and infamous awards campaign veteran Harvey Weinstein. However, upon release, the film grossed $29 million internationally, becoming not only one of the biggest box-office failures in Hollywood history but also receiving nearly universal critical dismissal. While many reviews lambasted the film for its lack of historical context, several critics from prominent publications attacked it both for its failure to address the repercussions of British imperialism and a narrative ill-suited to post-9/11 politics that remained raw even though the film's release was delayed for nearly a year.[1] In his review of the film for *Entertainment Weekly*, Owen Gleiberman deems it, 'A stiff-upper-lip rouser that poses the question, can a movie set during the waning days of the British Empire have its colonial cake and eat it, too? And then spit it out for good measure?'[2] Decrying the film's evasion of contemporary policies between the West and the Middle East, John Petrakis echoes Gleiberman's assessment positing, 'If *The Four Feathers* had pursued issues like these instead of falling back on a lot of charging and firing of guns, it might be a more relevant morality play for the 21st century. As it is, the film seems like a dusty period piece that has been dragged out one too many times.'[3] Even Linda Hutcheon dismissed the film four years after its release as 'an attempt to side step imperialist politics.'[4]

Though numerous box-office failures receive pointed critical drubbings, the reaction to *The Four Feathers* appears peculiar largely because, apart from its alleged elision of anti-imperialist politics critics imposed upon it, its harshest reviews largely ignore discussions of fatal failures or missteps in the film, even going so far as to praise its cinematography, direction, and performances.[5] The film's critical reception becomes even more curious considering Kapur's career-long preoccupations and stated intent of the project. Establishing his career as an actor in Bollywood before turning to directing with films such as *Mr India* (1987) and *Bandit Queen* (1994), Kapur made the transition to Hollywood after *Elizabeth*, his 1998 revisionist history of Queen Elizabeth I's early reign, became an international success. Working within Hollywood for the first time, Kapur aspired for *The Four Feathers* to both rewrite the colonial politics of Mason's novel and address the problematic depictions of the Egyptians and Sudanese in the text's six other adaptations, including *King Kong* director Merian C. Cooper's 1929 silent version and British director Zoltan Korda's much-heralded 1939 classic – the iteration Kapur most clearly addresses. As Kapur stated of his source text and previous versions of the story before his film's release, 'I was angered by them because of where I come from . . . they just did not question colonization . . . If you look at the state of the world today, you can trace it back to one cause: colonization.'[6]

With a creative team that includes Iranian screenwriter Hossein Amini, Beninian Hounsou, Australian Ledger, and Americans Hudson and Wes Bentley working for two of the most esteemed studios in Hollywood, Kapur's film is a global project that interrogates the foundations of imperialisms past and present through an internationally disseminated medium. Rather than merely addressing the lingering effects of imperialism in India and Pakistan, the film acts as a site for artists from all over the world working together to recreate and dismantle imperial ideologies at their most basic levels. In choosing a seventh adaptation of *The Four Feathers* as a project to address the legacy of colonialism, Kapur situated his political concerns within the tradition of late-Victorian adventure fiction that critics such as Elleke Boehmer describe as an example of the British national imagination growing 'extravagantly imperial in its idiom and scope'.[7] Detailing disgraced British officer Harry Feversham's efforts to salvage his reputation after resigning from the army, Mason's novel follows its protagonist to the front lines of the Sudan as he disguises himself as a Greek to demonstrate his bravery to his fellow deployed officers and fiancée after they gave him four white feathers as a symbol of cowardice. Yet, while Mason treats anxieties over going to war as a character defect that Harry must address, he opts to set the novel during the 1882–8 time period of the early Mahdi Rebellion – one of the greatest failures of the British military. Though the Sudan was largely controlled by Egypt during the period, the British Empire asserted an unofficial dominion in the area as a result of its occupation of Egypt in the wake of the Urabi Revolt in 1882.[8] Given the Suez Canal's importance to efficient travel between Britain and India, the British maintained a presence in order to preserve stability and fend off French and Russian attempts to control the canal. Yet, they largely ignored local issues such as the Egyptian support of the Sudanese slave trade.[9] Investigating these early years of British control in his cinematic depiction of Empire, Kapur creates a portrait of domestic England virtually unencumbered by imperial anxieties – until Britain's neglect of the Sudanese inadvertently serves as the context for the film's meditation on cowardice.

The catalyst of the British Empire's Egyptian blunders began when boat-maker's apprentice Muhammad Ahmad declared himself the 'Mahdi', who would abolish slavery and expunge Egyptian and European influence from the Sudan. In response, Prime Minister William Gladstone sent General Charles 'Chinese' Gordon – a former governor of the region – to quell the resulting rebellion.[10] Though ardently opposed to slavery, Gordon's Christian zeal further enraged the Mahdi, who besieged the city of Khartoum in 1884 and killed the General and his troops before a relief deployment could reach him.[11] In the wake of his death, Gordon, as Janice Boddy writes, 'became a mythic figure, the archetype of a superior race sent to battle 'heathrens' on the fringe of the settled world, a martyr for Empire and Christendom both.'[12] Set during the period after Gordon's martyrdom reached its peak, but before General Herbert Kitchener's forces defeated the Mahdi in 1896, the novel serves as allegorised historical fiction, presenting Harry as a British hero willing to atone for his previous blunders while ultimately exhibiting a Kitcheneresque bravery and dedication to regain his position of power within his military circle.

Mason's novel is ripe for the type of postcolonial revision with which Kapur engages. However, the narrative's previous adaptations provide the filmmaker with the opportunity to also grapple with the pervasiveness of imperial ideologies in the wake of World War I. While all six adaptations are firmly rooted within the discourse of the British Empire, Korda's production serves as not only the most famous and influential adaptation but also as the quintessential example of the first cycle of Empire cinema, films that, according to Jeffrey Richards, 'give glamorous celluloid life to the great folk myths of Empire' during the beginning of the end of British colonialism.[13] Though the final entry in Korda's 'Imperial Trilogy', the 1939 adaptation presents a contradictory image of the British Empire both exhibiting the director's leftist view of colonialism while maintaining fidelity to Empire's ideals.[14] A Hungarian immigrant personally affected by the fall of the Austro-Hungarian Empire, Korda and his producer brother Alexander knew firsthand of imperialism's innate violence and subjugation, but felt that depictions of the British Empire's strength were vital to combating the rise of fascism engulfing Europe during the film's production.[15] Shifting the setting to Kitchener's successful campaign, Korda presents a compromised depiction of Empire, conveying military officers as arrogant and out of place as they avenge Gordon's death in their scarlet uniforms but refusing to, in the words of J. E. Smythe, 'present the Sudanese populations with their own subjective perspective'.[16]

Considering the ample opportunity for anticolonial critique that Mason and Korda's texts provide, the disparity between Kapur's intent and his film's critical reception raises questions concerning his treatment of the legacy of British imperialism. Unlike Nair's *Vanity Fair*, Kapur's film is not based on a source text directly about his homeland, positioning his critique of the British Empire as a broad indictment of its overall structure, a factor that one could attribute in part to the influence of Kapur's favourite film as a child: a Hindi adaptation of H. Rider Haggard's Africa-set *She*.[17] In addition, Mason's novel is relatively obscure and absent from critical work on Victorian and Edwardian literature compared to texts such as *Dracula* and *Vanity Fair*, and is arguably more well-known through Korda's adaptation.[18] Given that Kapur's film acknowledges at least two iterations of the narrative from distinct historical contexts, his attempt to write back to the imperial centre may appear, as the film's detractors concur, unfocused or even relatively absent.

However, through the theoretical approach advocated by one of the film's primary critics, Kapur's primary strategy of resistance becomes apparent. In *A Theory of Adaptation*, Hutcheon argues for adaptation as a form of intertextuality in which, 'we experience adaptations (*as adaptations*) as palimpsests through our memory of other works that resonate through repetition with variation.'[19] According to Hutcheon, each adaptation has a plurality of audiences whose individual encounters with previous source texts affect the reception. Though one could dismiss Hutcheon's claim as updated reader-response criticism, it allows her to make a second claim applicable to Kapur's adaptation: each subsequent adaptation builds upon the tropes of its predecessors. In the case of Kapur's film, audience exposure to the source text and previous adaptations have a significant impact on the film's reception. A critic only familiar with the novel may excoriate Kapur for the historical inaccuracy of British soldiers wearing red uniforms in the Sudan, but fail to see how this choice allows Kapur to address the famous long shots of the British 'thin red line' in Korda's adaptation.[20] Similarly, critics well acquainted with Korda's film who attack Kapur for switching the time period to the 1884–5 botched rescue of Gordon conveniently overlook the novel's span from 1882 to 1888.

While such discussions of textual difference may appear as little more than insubstantial quibbling, they are fundamental to the revisionary approach of Kapur's film and the holistic analysis inherent in the interfidelity approach. If, as Hutcheon contends, exposure to previous source texts affects audience perception, then audiences native to former British colonial holdings experience adaptations of Empire literature through a palimpsest founded on both the source texts and the tropes of Orientalism inherent in colonial discourse. As Said writes:

> The idea of a representation is a theatrical one: the Orient is the stage on which the whole east is confined. On this stage will appear figures whose role it is to represent the larger whole from which they emanate. The Orient then seems to be, not an unlimited extension beyond the familiar European world, but rather a closed field, a theatrical stage affixed to Europe.[21]

For Said, Orientalism makes no distinction between nations, religions or ethnicities, creating a stage on which the entirety of the East is presented as a monolithic entity. As a result, postcolonial writers and filmmakers attempting to address the legacy of British imperialism face the problem of resisting a universal organisational system through experience with a colonialism that was very much influenced and governed by localised issues of their native lands. Though Kapur's *The Four Feathers* is both about a nation indirectly controlled by British policy and made by a filmmaker from a nation formerly under direct colonial rule, the Empire employed the same overarching ideology to govern both holdings. Within this context, Kapur's seeming historical inaccuracies and disregard for realistic depictions of the Sudan act not as a shallow attack on the British, but as a critique of the Orientalism that places the British Empire into a similar binary that allowed for such subjugation. By implementing such a strategy, Kapur positions the film as a subversion of Orientalism and as a way to address the confluence of capitalism and the nation state embodied by Hollywood film production and the 'War on Terror' politics that his harshest critics accuse him of skirting

In this chapter, I argue that through this collaboration with artists hailing from an array of postcolonial nations, Kapur extends the imperial politics of Mason's novel beyond its setting in the Sudan and into other postcolonial national contexts. As a result, the film presents a unified front that uses the collaborative attributes of film production to compare the totality of British rule and the global reach of Hollywood from a variety of national perspectives. Through revising his source texts' treatments of landscape, presentation of the other and veneration of the British Empire, Kapur participates in the process of intertextuality to revise the ideologies of his predecessors to expose how the structure of Empire that fueled the British imperial project remains intact in the policies and practices of a world largely governed by the hegemony of the American economy.

COLLAPSED LANDSCAPES, PURLOINED LETTERS AND DOMESTIC IMPERIAL SPACES

For a late-Victorian adventure novel, *The Four Feathers* appears out of step, largely because its primary action takes place within the confines of Britain. Rather than steep its narrative in descriptions and action sequences occurring in colonised lands as is customary of Mason's contemporaries such as Conrad, Haggard and Kipling, the novel reveals much of Harry's Sudanese experience indirectly through conversations and correspondence between his fiancée, Ethne Eustace, and his accusers in the English countryside, in effect, rendering its central figure nearly absent from the narrative. After Harry's best friend and fellow soldier Jack Durrance relates his encounter with Harry in the Sudanese city Halfa, Ethne interrogates him:

> 'So, you never knew what brought Mr Feversham to Halfa?' she asked. 'Did you not ask him? Why didn't you? Why?'
> She was disappointed, and the bitterness of her disappointment gave passion to her cry. Here was the last news of Harry Feversham, and it was brought to her incomplete, like the half-sheet of a letter. The omission might never be repaired.[22]

While such a denial of direct descriptions of Harry's interactions with the Sudanese landscape may seem like efforts to erase or eschew concrete depictions of the colonised territory similar to Thackeray's treatment of India in *Vanity Fair*, Mason's choice to reveal Harry's experiences in the Sudan through conversations and letters is indicative of what Bhabha refers to as the re-cognition of colonial authority: 'It is not that the voice of authority is at a loss for words. It is, rather, that the colonial discourse has reached that point when, faced with the hybridity of its objects, the *presence* of power is revealed as something other than what its rules of recognition assert.'[23] In the wake of the Mahdi's defeat of Gordon that frames the events of the novel, the waning Empire cannot simply disregard the agency of the 'other'. However, it can mediate its anxieties over the imperial project by presenting Harry's Sudanese adventure entirely through the discourse of Britain's military class, a strategy that removes Harry's actions from the realities of the landscape and into a near mythical metanarrative of Empire. Faced with the reality of the 'other's' agency in the Sudan, Mason's movement of Harry's imperial experiences solely to the controlled discourse of letters and conversation demonstrates both a burgeoning sense of anxiety and an acknowledgement that the colonial discourse on which the Empire previously relied is insufficient for the aftermath of the rebellion.

Though Mason mediates Harry's journey in the Sudan through such dialogue sequences between Ethne and Harry's fellow soldiers, the Sudanese landscape still remains a source of anxiety for the British in the novel largely through its harsh climate, which leads to Durrance's blindness in the middle of the campaign. After he accidentally grabs a hot pipe bowl while trying to sign a paper, Jack relates the story of his disability:

> 'There was a high wind,' Durrance explained. 'It took my helmet off. It was eight o'clock in the morning. I did not mean to move my camp that day, and I was standing outside my tent in my shirt-sleeves. So you see that I had not even the collar of a coat to protect the nape of my neck. I was fool enough to run after my helmet; and – you must have seen the same thing happen a hundred times – each time that I stooped to pick it up it skipped away; each time that I ran after it, it stopped and waited for me to catch it up. And before one was aware what one was doing, one had run a quarter of a mile. I went down, I was told, like a log just when I had the helmet in my hand. How long ago it happened I don't quite know, for I was ill for a time, and afterwards it was difficult to keep count, since one couldn't tell the difference between day and night.'[24]

An officer in the British Army with a consummate reputation, Durrance is unable to cope with the Sudan's desert atmosphere and is transformed into an inept, self-proclaimed fool chasing his hat in the wind, a victim of a colonial endeavour for which he was ill prepared. While one could read the scene as conforming to the imperial stereotype of harsh and savage colonised landscapes, the fact remains that, unlike civilians such as Marlow and Kurtz in *Heart of Darkness*, Durrance is an impeccable soldier trained to handle interactions within the various landscapes that Britain claimed, but failing miserably. The blindness serves as such an affront to Durrance's honour that he expresses the 'natural wish to hide his calamity as long as he could'.[25] Durrance's instinct to hide his injury stems largely from the embarrassment of his blindness, an affliction that, according to Sharon Sullivan, serves as a Freudian symbol of castration, in which the larger genitalia of a father figure manifests 'a threat to the child's libidinal self-investment'.[26] Considering that Durrance's failed mastery of the Sudanese landscape caused his blindness, the injury serves to invert the paternalistic dynamic of the coloniser and colonised, situating Durrance as a childlike figure prone to shame over his limited power. With his lifelong dedication to the military, Jack's blindness leaves him 'deprived of every occupation' and unable to take on a new role in British society, a striking moment of anxiety in a novel that trumpets the dominion of the British imperial project and its ability to weather even the greatest of failures.[27]

However, though blind, Durrance remains a member of the esteemed

British military class, allowing him to travel 'East' at the end of the novel to seek his fortune after Harry's return curtails his plan to marry Ethne:

> Attended by a servant, he had come back to the East again. Early the next morning the steamer moved through the canal, and towards the time of sunset passed out into the chills of the Gulf of Suez. Kassassin, Tel-el-Kebir, Tamai, Tamanieb, the attack upon McNeil's zareeba – Durrance lived again through the good years of his activity, the years of plenty. Within that country on the west the long preparations were going steadily forward which would one day roll up the Dervish Empire and crush it into dust. Upon the glacis of the ruined fort of Sinkat, Durrance had promised himself to take a hand in that great work, but the desert which he loved had smitten and cast him out.[28]

Echoing Bhabha's discussion of re-cognition, Mason's description of Durrance's return to the Sudan bridges the resounding failure to quell the Mahdi Rebellion with a fragmented statement concerning the Empire's bright future (which Mason underscores through extremely violent language such as 'crush into dust'). Drifting back to the East with no official role, Durrance is still able to reap some abstract benefit from Britain's presence in the Sudan, though bearing the physical scars of the time before the desert cast him out – reentering the colonial space blind to the ramifications and ultimate outcomes of the British imperial project. Rather than acknowledging that his blindness was a warning against intervention into the colonised territory, Durrance is drawn closer to the land, an amalgamation of wounded pride, opportunity and redemption indicative of late-Victorian British imperialism.

In the transition from the novel to Korda's adaptation, Durrance's blindness remains a pivotal scene of British ambivalence toward the Sudan campaign. However, Korda positions the sequence as his central examination of an imperfect Empire necessary to safeguard Europe from the encroachment of fascism. As Durrance (Ralph Richardson) climbs an enormous rock formation in order to survey the desert for Mahdi rebels, Korda shoots him in extreme long shots in which the vast landscape seemingly consumes the khaki-clad officer. Wiping sweat from his brow with a white handkerchief, Durrance is clearly affected by the region's intense heat, but continues to search the desert for the enemy through his binoculars. When he notices a band of Mahdi rebels approaching, a startled Durrance drops his handkerchief hundreds of feet below him, a seemingly unconscious act of surrender. Frantically looking for the handkerchief, Durrance's hat rolls down the formation, accompanied by an ominous musical score – the trappings of Western civilisation coming undone when confronted with the colonised landscape. As the rebels suddenly change direction, Korda cuts to an eyeline match of Durance looking straight into the sun. As Durrance succumbs to the heat, Korda then shifts to a subjective shot from Durrance's point of view in which the landscape before him quickly dissolves into a mirage-like blur. Not acting merely as a victim of the Sudanese desert's climate, the Durrance of Korda's film loses his sight only after he is forced to acknowledge the presence of the other. Isolated and no longer able to perceive his enemy as a faceless entity, Durrance realises that he is ill-equipped and too far outnumbered to handle the situation, unable to reconcile the limitations of the colonial discourse in which he is steeped. With his privileged imperial position dwarfed by the landscape and the presence of the enemy, Durrance's blindness sets in, an acknowledgement of the realities of the imperial project that led to Kitchener's emergency campaign.

Deviating sharply from Mason's novel, the Durrance of Korda's film does not return to the Sudan in search of some role within the colonial enterprise. Instead, he returns home to come to terms with his blindness, eventually 'learning to read this Braille stuff' (Figures 5.1 and 5.2). Sharing brandy with Dr Sutton (Frederick Culley), an old friend of Harry's deceased father,

Figure 5.1 (upper) and Figure 5.2 (lower) Korda's Durrance (Ralph Richardson) reads Shakespeare's *The Tempest* in 'this braille stuff'.

Durrance demonstrates his knowledge of Braille by reading aloud one of Caliban's speeches from *The Tempest*:

> Be not afeard; the isle is full of noises,
> Sounds and sweet airs, that give delight and hurt not.
> Sometimes a thousand twangling instruments
> Will hum about mine ears, and sometime voices
> That, if I then had waked after long sleep,
> Will make me sleep again: and then, in dreaming,
> The clouds methought would open and show riches
> Ready to drop upon me that, when I waked,
> I cried to dream again.

Through the addition of this sequence absent from Mason's novel, Korda highlights the contradictions and conflicts of his reticent endorsement of the post-World War I British Empire. Irreparably affected by British imperial endeavours, Durrance identifies with a speech the slave Caliban gives in Shakespeare's play as two of the King's servants mistake him for a monster. However, rather than align himself with a subaltern figure in the work of an author native to the Sudan or another colonised territory, Durrance opts for a native character in the work of England's most canonical author, recalling Bhabha's characterisation of the English book as a document that, 'Installs the sign of appropriate representation: the word of God, truth, art creates the conditions for a beginning, a practice of history and narrative. But the institution of the Word in the wilds is also an *Enstellung*, a process of displacement, distortion, dislocation, repetition.'[29] In addition, as Roberto Fernández Retamar writes, Caliban's name derives from a combination of the American Carib Indian tribe and the word 'cannibal', rendering the character 'a savage and deformed slave who cannot be degraded enough'.[30] Within this context, Durrance's identification with Caliban in the film represents a subtle acknowledgement of the imperial project as a deviant aberration attuned to Korda's post-World War I imperial critique. Translated into Braille, the copy of *The Tempest* from which Durrance recites becomes simultaneously a sign of the seamlessness and unity of Empire and of its variations and subversions, accenting the inability of full understanding between the coloniser and the other but positing a space of alliance so vital for Korda during the film's time period.

Working within the tradition of his source texts, Kapur excises the ambiguous anxieties over the imperial project that Durrance's blindness exemplifies for Mason and Korda, presenting it as a politicised manifestation of the British Empire's rote violence. During the film's opening, a title card stating, 'By 1884 over a quarter of the earth's surface had been conquered by the British Army . . .' appears on screen scored to Arabic music. The film then cuts to a blurred panoramic shot of what appears to be a battle, its colours desaturated except for flashes of British military red. Kapur then racks focus, revealing an intense rugby match between a regiment of British soldiers, including Feversham (Heath Ledger) and Durrance (Wes Bentley). While acknowledging that Kapur's adaptation 'lessens the starkly racial logic of its predecessors', Kamran Rastegar argues that Kapur's focus on rugby in the opening, 'amplifies the idealization of homosocial military masculinity that originates in Mason's novel'.[31] However, through his emphasis on the rugby match, Kapur also alludes to the concept of 'muscular Christianity', a Victorian movement that sought to incite fervour for the imperial project by revering, in the words of Donald E. Hall, 'Physical strength, religious certainty, and the ability to shape the world', in males domestically through activities such as sports, military drills, and religious services.'[32] From the very beginning of the film, Kapur interrogates the inseparable nature of Victorian social mores and the broader imperial project, presenting it as an extension of the economic and political relationships between metropolitan cities such as London and country towns. As Raymond Williams writes:

> The 'metropolitan' states, through a system of trade, but also through a complex of economic and political controls, draw food and, more critically, raw materials from these areas of supply, this effective hinterland, that is also the greater part of the earth's surface and that contains the great majority of its peoples. Thus a model of city and country, in economic and political relationships, has gone beyond the boundaries of the nation-state, and is seen but also challenged as a model of the world.[33]

Addressing concepts similar to those that govern muscular Christianity, Williams views domestic activities seemingly far-removed from the Sudanese landscape such as the rugby match as a microcosm of larger imperial endeavours. Despite the accusations of critics such as Rastegar, the film demonstrates Williams's characterisation of Empire's politics. Whether playing rugby in the countryside or fighting Mahdis in Sudan, the structure of Empire and the undercurrent of violence necessary to maintain it remain intact.

Through immediately establishing the interwoven nature of domestic and colonial politics, Kapur frames Durrance's blindness not as a manifestation of imperial anxieties and confusion, but as a failure of this masculine ideal. Under the impression that his regiment has fended off a Mahdi attack, Durrance leads his troops through the Sudanese desert when a group of rebels hiding in the sand ambush the army. Caught in the fog of war, Durrance shoots his rifle, but it backfires and blinds him, a stark contrast to the muscular Christian ideals of, according to C. J. W.-L. Wee, 'primitive vigor' that he displayed on the rugby field.[34] Exposed to the desert's climate, Durrance collapses – left for dead until a disguised Harry pulls him to safety and nurses him back to health. For Kapur, Durrance is not merely a victim of the Sudanese climate that eventually cements his blindness, but of the failures of British technology that, in this case, quite obviously demonstrate the deficiencies of Empire's masculine force.

In sharp contrast to the semi-enlightened veteran depictions of Durrance in his source texts, Kapur uses his return to England to expose the hollow nature of the Empire's social structure. The Durrance of Kapur's film does not return to the East to profit; nor does he come to terms with his blindness and learn to articulate British colonial discourse in a new form. He returns home a broken man, spending the remainder of the film relearning the quotidian aspects of British life. When Ethne (Kate Hudson) realises Durrance has returned to England, she stares in shock as he awkwardly rides a horse in her barn while staring blankly into the abyss. For the remainder of the film, Durrance's scenes revolve around his reintroduction to a social structure which has no place for him: he fumbles his way through his study, he takes rides with Ethne leading his horse, and, during his reunion with Harry, he proudly displays his ability to pour himself a cup of tea, an action that feminises Durrance and relegates his interactions with Empire merely to the consumption of its commodities. As Mason writes, the Durrance of Kapur's film is truly 'deprived of every occupation' – including those of a colonial nature – a figure in the margins of an imperial structure that has all but forgotten him, allowing Kapur to indict the very foundations of Empire by demonstrating how its domination extends to even those within its most esteemed ranks.

While Durrance negotiates the relationship between British and colonised space in all three adaptations, Mason's novel largely hinges on how domestic space and property ownership accumulated through marriage are vital to his characters' social statuses. Given Williams' view on the inseparable nature of imperialist policies and the internal politics of the British nation-state, the roles of marriage, financial stability and property are endowed with greater import. For much of Victorian literature, marriage functions as a competition between two male suitors over the right to claim a central female character as a bride, demonstrating, in the words of Sedgwick, 'the triangular traffic in women'.[35] According to Sedgwick:

> For each woman, the sexual narrative occurs with the overtaking of an active search for power of which she is the *subject*, by an already-constituted symbolic power of exchange between men of which her very misconstruction, her sense of purposefulness, proves her to have been the designated *object*.[36]

Sedgwick's contention opens a discourse on masculine power dynamics within Victorian literature, but the already-constituted symbolic power of which she speaks needs further clarification. Rather than serve as figures already established within the symbolic power structure of the British Empire, the male characters of many Victorian novels are – similar to Harry after his act of cowardice – partially marginalised figures themselves, suffering from inferior class positions or public economic and political humiliations that have greatly damaged their reputations.

In order to improve or restore their agency, these male characters initiate Sedgwick's triangular traffic in women, using the marriage union to fuel increased accumulation of property and status, a factor that complicates the status of the Victorian woman as object. As Jeff Nunokawa writes:

> Trauma ensues there when wives are called commodities, not because they are thus cast as property, but rather because such property is thus cast among the uncertainties of the marketplace. Trouble arises when women are cast as such property in the Victorian novel less because the proprietor's grasp goes too far when it reaches her than because that grasp is always loosened when the shadow of the commodity falls upon the object that it holds. Undoing the boundary between the woman a man loves and the property he owns, the mercenary marriage dissolves the distinction between a species of property that is normally, or at least normatively, secure and one that is bound to be lost.[37]

As a result, the females of Victorian novels occupy a precarious position in which marginalised males must simultaneously use them as objects to reenter the framework of Empire while defending them against the marketplace that fuels the imperial project at home and abroad. What arises is the creation of what I call the domestic imperial space, a situation in which the male figure such as Harry attains just enough agency to occupy a secure class position, permitting him to create an isolated holding to protect his wife and property from Empire's overarching forces, a space both inside and outside of the British Empire.

Stemming from a line of generals immortalised in portraits that 'looked down upon this last Feversham, summoning him to the like service', Harry occupies a stable position in British society with a substantial inheritance and a prestigious military commission.[38] However, Harry's greatest claim is his engagement to the Irish Ethne Eustace, a pending marital union that allows him to perceive her hometown of Ramelton 'with a great curiosity and almost pride of ownership, since it was here that Ethne lived, and all these things were part and parcel of her life.'[39] Already ingrained within the framework of the British Empire, Harry has access to its colonising force, which Mason underscores by having him lay claim to the Irish Ethne, whose status as an heiress engages with what Elsie B. Michie refers to as 'an unceasing negotiation between the material appeals readers knew individuals felt and the immaterial values novels insist they desired.'[40] As both heiress and a colonial subject, Ethne serves as a compromise in the negotiation Michie discusses, able to provide Harry with material comforts while maintaining the illusion of immaterial appeals like love because of her Irishness. Yet, regardless of Ethne's dual role as heiress and inferior, Harry eventually becomes marginalised when he resigns his military commission. Disowned by his father and sent the feathers that symbolise his cowardice by his friends and fellow officers Captain Trench and Lieutenants Willoughby and Castleton, Harry loses his claim to Ethne when she breaks off their engagement by giving him a fourth feather. Divested of his family ties and the Irish estate that his marriage would yield, Harry loses his privileged position, ousted from Empire's power structure. Viewing a renewed engagement with Ethne as central to reclaiming his place in Empire, Harry secretly follows his former fellow officers to the Sudan, hoping to prove his bravery and initiate his plan that 'if the three take back their feathers . . . why, then she perhaps might take hers back too.'[41]

In channeling his hope for redemption through the restoration of his engagement with Ethne, Harry echoes Nunokawa's concept of 'living property':

> What can't be held *to* the heart for long can be held *in* it forever: property that can't be kept up in the external world is sustained in the figure of a woman whose dimensions are defined less by the material shapes of house or body than by a lover's fond thoughts or sorrowful memory. Correlatively, the limits that the demands of circulation impose on the power of ownership are circumvented when its field of operation is not a physical object, but rather the incessant fantasies of 'living property'.[42]

Losing his claim to property because of public humiliation, Harry positions Ethne as 'living property', endowing an extremely physical mission with a symbolic dimension. Though Ethne broke off the engagement, Harry's view of her as living property circumvents the logistics of the market forces that govern Empire, giving his mission a loftier purpose. As Willoughby tells Ethne on his return home after encountering Harry in the Sudan and taking back his feather: 'Feversham's disgrace was, on the face of it, impossible to retrieve . . . No, Miss Eustace, it needed a woman's faith to conceive the plan – a woman's encouragement to keep the man who undertook it to his work.'[43]

In a similar manner to British nationalism's role in the material endeavours of Empire, the fond thoughts and memory of Ethne fuel Harry's mission, allowing him to eventually restore his engagement with Ethne and, as a result, his claim to her family estate in Ireland. He overcomes the consequences of his actions through the act of marriage, renovating Ethne's family property and using his experience in the Sudan to write a history of the war, capitalising on, as the Feversham family friend Lieutenant Sutch tells Harry's father, the fact that 'he was present while the war went on. Moreover, he was in the bazaars, he saw the other side of it.'[44] Though Harry ends the novel with his ties to the British military still severed, the agency he has gleaned from his union with Ethne leads him to a literary career in which he creates metaphorical imperial spaces for a living in the comfort of the domestic imperial space that his marriage fostered.

Considering Mason's depiction of Ethne as a largely colonised subject of Empire, both Korda and Kapur dilute her narrative importance to place more focus on the Egyptian Sudan's colonised population, changing her ethnicity and presenting her as less central to the motivations for Harry's journey. The daughter of General Burroughs (C. Aubrey Smith) and brother of Harry's feather-sending comrade Peter (Donald Gray) in Korda's film, Ethne, (June Deprez) is a fairly marginalised character, important only because Harry's marriage to her unites the film's two most powerful military families. In the wake of Harry (John Clements) resigning his commission, General Burroughs shuns his future son-in-law in the presence of Ethne, leaving her to break off the engagement: 'When you did this, did you believe that I should be proud of you? We were born into a tradition, a code that we much obey even if we don't believe, and we must obey it, Harry, because of the pride and happiness of everyone surrounding us.' Remarking that he 'quite understands', Harry tells Ethne, 'There should be four feathers here', before plucking a feather from a duster on a table. Harry raises it to Ethne's face, ordering her, 'Give it to me.' She refuses and Harry takes the feather, leaving Ethne alone in the foyer of her family estate.

Though working within the framework of Korda's depiction of Ethne, Kapur treats her in an equally marginal manner, foregoing not only a scene of her giving Harry a feather in the film but also any background into her family's history despite her consistent presence at military functions and her friendship with Jack.[45] While he retains such a depiction of Ethne, Kapur also subtly acknowledges her status from the beginning of the film. After the rugby match and a scene of homoerotic locker-room talk, the film cuts to a lavish ball. Following this parade of imperial manners and social mores, Kapur visually foreshadows the love triangle among Harry, Jack and Ethne, through the execution of a scene of the three dancing on the ledge of an estate's terrace. When Jack and Harry pass her between them – triangular traffic in action again – Ethne stumbles as Kapur cuts to a low-angle shot that reveals just how fatal the fall would have been had it occurred. Out of the arms of her two potential suitors, Ethne reaches the precipice of death, unable to extricate herself from the situation until Harry takes her in his arms.

In their depictions of Ethne, Korda and Kapur exhibit what Oyèrónkẹ́ Oyěwùmí refers to as the 'bio-logic' of Western culture in which, 'the very process by which females were categorised and reduced to "women" made them ineligible for leadership roles.'[46] Working from Oyêwùmí's colonial hierarchy of men (European), women (European), native (African men), and Other (African female), Ethne occupies a complicated role in both films, entrenched within the colonial system, but stripped of agency to the point that she can neither officially present Harry with his feather of cowardice as her brother did or escape the love triangle in which she finds herself.[47] While both Ethnes remain important to the affections and motivations of Harry and Jack, the actions of their romantic doubles take place within the masculine discourse of colonialism. As a result, the outrage both Ethnes express, but fail to fully act upon, appears much clearer. In opting to resign his military commission, Harry removes himself from the opportunities of military life and effectively destroys the only role in the colonial project for his fiancée, leaving her adrift in the world of tradition the Ethne of Korda's film so passionately defines.

While my discussion of Durrance and Ethne's relationship to the British and Sudanese landscapes may seem indirect, these two characters provide Kapur with his most intricate and pointed critique of the British imperial project. For an adaptation occurring equally in England and the Sudanese desert, Kapur's film neglects to focus any attention on the process of travel between the two locations, save the scene in which Harry surreptitiously watches his regiment's ship depart. However, transportation between England and the Sudan acts as a fundamental trope integral to the film, largely through Kapur's use of the letters Durrance and Ethne write to each other throughout the narrative. For the British Empire, the lands of the upper Nile, including the Sudan, were, according to Boddy, 'A liminal zone, capable of erupting into savagery at any time.'[48] While military mastery was certainly vital to Britain's command of such regions, the transplantation of domestic bureaucracies into the territory serves as an indicator of a much more stable control than even the most successful military campaigns. For Keith Jeffrey, 'The establishment of an organised, efficient postal service, complete with stamps, on the model of the British penny post introduced in 1840, is an important indicator (and facilitator) of modernization.'[49] In establishing such a lengthy correspondence between Durrance and Ethne, Kapur acknowledges that, despite the embarrassing losses the British suffer in the film, Empire's presence is strong enough to have already integrated its domestic institutions seamlessly into the region.

Through his focus on the British postal system, Kapur sharply strays from his source texts. While Harry's first display of bravery in the novel occurs when he retrieves and delivers a packet of letters between General Gordon and the Mahdi rebels concerning the general's surrender and conversion to Islam, the letters reside outside of the scope of the postal service, serving instead as an example of the British erasure of past failures when an officer remarks that 'they were hardly worth risking a life for'.[50] Likewise, the only letters in Korda's adaptation are those containing the feathers, which are hand-delivered to Harry and returned to their original owners. However, in Kapur's film, Ethne and Durrance begin to correspond as soon as his regiment is deployed and Harry's engagement ends. With his affection for Ethne finally manifested, Durrance begins to collect the letters in a pile that he keeps on his person at all times, a source of much amusement to his comrades who rib him when he takes them out. In the wake of the firearm malfunction and Harry's subsequent rescue of him, the blinded Durrance's first instinct upon reaching safety is frantically searching for the letters he has dropped. When Harry retrieves them for him, the action marks the first direct contact between the two friends in the Sudan.

Though this focus on the letters does attest to the vast strength and scope of the Empire within the Sudan, Kapur's depiction of the British postal service takes on a less hegemonic effect when viewed in light of Lacan's 'Seminar on "The Purloined Letter"'. For Lacan, the trajectory of a letter acts as a signifying chain that positions its writers and recipients as individuals 'more docile than sheep' who 'model their very being on the moment of the signifying chain that runs through them.'[51] Elaborating on Lacan's contention, Slavoj Žižek applies the purloined letter and its relationship to the signifying chain within the context of a message in a bottle:

> This case displays at its purest and clearest how a letter reaches its true destination the moment it is delivered, thrown into the water – its true addressee is namely not the empirical other which may receive it or not, but the big Other, the symbolic order itself, which receives it *the moment the letter is put into circulation*, i.e. the moment the sender 'externalizes' his message, delivers it to the Other, the moment the Other takes cognizance of the letter and thus disburdens the sender of responsibility for it.[52]

In applying Lacan and Žižek's discussions of the purloined letter to Kapur's film, the director's subversion of the British postal service becomes a potent and extensive critique of the colonialism he intended to demonise. For Durrance and Ethne, the importance of their correspondence is not the blossoming courtship it documents, but the fact that sending their letters irrevocably ties them to the 'big Other' of the British imperial project's chains of significations. Regardless of their privileged positions, they remain caught within the Real of a structure that subjugates them, albeit in a much less direct manner, than those colonised people of the Empire. Their sentiments, identities, and autonomy are irrelevant to the unbroken chain of significations necessary to Empire's construction, a factor Kapur accentuates when, at the film's end, Durrance only recognises the newly returned and restored Harry after he again retrieves the parcel of letters that Durrance haphazardly dropped. Far from neglecting a critique of British colonialism in the film, Kapur interrogates it at the unbroken significations that maintain its foundation, a choice that allows him to decentre the concept of imperialism from its late-Victorian iteration and apply it to the world of globalised capital in which his film was produced.

ARABIAN PERFORMANCE AND THE REINSTITUTED SUBALTERN

Kapur's *The Four Feathers* is the first postcolonial film adaptation in this book that occurs primarily within a depiction of colonised territory. As a result, its presentation of and revision to the figures of the wandering European and native are primary strategies of writing back to the imperial centre. For in his quest to reclaim his honour through his Sudanese journey, Harry Feversham must (and does) disguise himself as various natives from the region, acting as an example of a mobility Said attributes to 'The pleasures of imperialism'. As Said writes, 'What one cannot accomplish in one's own Western environment – where trying to live out a dream of a successful quest means coming up against one's own mediocrity and the world's degradation – one can do abroad.'[53] Given the severe break from his social class that his military resignation causes, Harry cannot restore his reputation through any domestic means, forcing him to travel to a land such as the Sudan. However, while travelling through the colonised landscape, Harry's disguise is fundamental to his various levels of success to disprove his accusers in the Sudan. Harry's disguise is, in fact, so necessary that it remains a central component of every rendition of *The Four Feathers*, which allows Kapur's presentation of Harry's performative state to work within and against the traditions of his source texts both by stressing Harry's difference and by providing a space of representation to previously marginalised Sudanese natives.

Though important to the success of Harry's quest in Mason's novel, Harry's disguise is not as pivotal as in the film adaptations because his time in the Sudan is largely recounted indirectly and only factors into a few of his plans to prove his bravery. In one of the instances in the novel when Mason directly discusses Harry, he reveals the disguise his protagonist has undertaken to procure Gordon's letters: '"It will be wise to speak to no one except me," said the Greek, jingling some significant dollars, and for a long while the two men talked secretly together. The Greek happened to be Harry Feversham, whom Durrance was proposing to visit in Donegal.'[54] Through mentioning Harry's Greek disguise in passing, Mason dilutes the importance of the transformation, making it seem as, if not less, important than the 'significant dollars' that

Harry jingles to the success of his mission. Such a description may mirror Said's claim about the potential to fulfill dreams in colonised lands, yet it also evokes the unacknowledged anxieties Harry, and by extension the British, feel toward the region. Unable to complete his quest under his real identity and unable to pass as Egyptian or Sudanese, Harry settles on an 'in-between' ethnicity that recalls Mustapha Chérif's argument that, for European colonialism, proximity to the Mediterranean is directly proportional to otherness from the imperial centre.[55]

In addition to foregrounding Harry's inability to inhabit either the role of coloniser or colonised in his interlocutor state, his disguise attains a near prophetic pronouncement of his nation's fate in the region through allusions to the fallen empires of the past. For Britain, the Empires developed during the classical period served as fertile models that founded the nation's own imperial ideology. As Boehmer writes: 'In their plans for enlightened service and development the British discerned the makings of a new Rome. The Romans had laid roads; the British now built railroads and laid telegraph cables. Their rule exhibited inspirational continuities with the past.'[56] By traversing a land unable to be governed by the remnants of the Egyptian Empire in the guise of a Greek, Harry retrieves the packet of Gordon's letters, which highlights an embarrassing breakdown of British imperial control – Mason's ambivalent presentation of the cyclical domination of the region.

Building upon Harry's difference from the Sudanese population, Korda's film spends a great deal of attention on Harry's transformation into a Sangali – a member of the tribe that the Mahdi allegedly branded and subjected to tongue frenectomies. Knowing that his mission in the Sudan will fail if he does not assume the role of a native, Harry visits an Egyptian doctor who dyes his skin and, in Harry's first act of bravery in the film, brands Harry with a hot iron. Through feigning muteness and assuming the role of Sangali, Harry is able to blend into the local culture and to experience the savagery of the British Army.[57] As the disguised Harry pulls Durrance to safety and slips the envelope containing the feather into his pocket, a group of soldiers mistakes him for a pickpocket and subjects him to a savage beating. Though the disguise is successful, it leaves Harry branded for life with his own battle scar. At the same time, it forces him to surrender his use of English and the agency of Empire built upon it. Becoming a victim of Empire's violence and unable to reveal his ethnicity without foregoing his plan to re-enter Empire's society through redemption, Harry's identity becomes contradictory, an ideal opportunity for Korda to insert his compromised views of British imperialism into the film.

Sharply contrasting with his predecessors, the Harry of Kapur's film never even comes close to passing himself off as anything but English. Despite his attempts to become the 'other' by foregoing shaving, growing out his hair and exhibiting a natural tan, it is not Harry's disguise that keeps him safe early in the film, but his employment of a French trafficker and scout who leads him toward Durrance's regiment. Yet, a Sudanese slave and her partner kill the Frenchman in a scene that emphasises the latent anxieties of the British Empire. When the slave spares Harry because of his earlier role in stopping the trafficker's beating of her, he is left to navigate the desert on his own and quickly succumbs to the heat, which Kapur shoots in extreme long shot to underscore the isolation. Even when Harry finally reaches the British outpost, he awkwardly plays dumb as the Egyptians and Sudanese slaves around him speak in languages he does not know, a scene that allows Kapur to satirise the relative ease of Harry blending into the Sudan in Korda's film. While Kapur uses Harry's failed transformation as an intertextual criticism of his predecessors, he also employs it to engage with the lingering impact of Orientalism on contemporary film audiences. Through the casting of Ledger as Harry, Kapur executes a situation in which an actor from a settler colony in the Pacific Rim acts as a bridge between the Occident and the Orient, exposing the falsity of the binary construction so important to colonial discourse. Harry cannot successfully travel the region on his own, requiring the aid of a Sudanese character who presents the opposition to continuing Orientalist discourse as a global unity of colonised peoples rather than the efforts of an individual.

Though Harry's disguise is an abject failure, he still completes his mission in the Sudan and returns home to marry Ethne. But, Harry's success has much more to do with the help he receives from the Sudanese slave Abou Fatma (Djimon Hounsou) than his military training or personal heroism (Figures 5.3 and 5.4). As *National Review* film critic John O'Sullivan points out in his pan of the film, 'Without his [Fatma's] protection, Harry would be a goner, his attempt to redeem his honor and return the four feathers ending in an unknown grave in the desert.'[58] A minor character in Mason's novel, Abou Fatma is a native of the region whom Mason introduces as 'sleeping under a boulder on the Khor Gwob'.[59] Despite his brief appearances in the text, he serves as Harry's informant and assistant, helping him retrieve Gordon's letters and providing knowledge of the landscape without which Harry would have no access. While Abou Fatma is absent from Korda's adaptation, Kapur positions him as arguably the central figure of his film, shifting his ethnicity from the mysterious Arab of Mason's novel to a slave who learned English working for the British and who has eluded traders, the Mahdi and Egyptian forces. In the wake of rescuing Harry after his collapse in the desert, Fatma continues to aid him, protecting him from other slaves and Egyptians who are not fooled by Harry's disguise, helping him track down the regiment, giving him and Colonel Trench (Michael Sheen) a sedative that allows them to escape

Figure 5.3 (upper) and Figure 5.4 (lower) Harry (Heath Ledger) and Abou Fatma (Djimon Hounsou) find Jack's letters.

from a Mahdi prison by feigning death, and even suffering an intense lashing after his warning to Durrance's troops of ambush leads to accusations from feathergiver Lieutenant Willoughby (Rupert Penry-Jones) that he is a Mahdi spy.

One could easily read Kapur's reintroduction and focus on Abou Fatma as either simply giving voice to a marginalised figure in the source texts or, as Richard A. Voeltz writes, conforming to the stereotype of 'the best black buddy sage'.[60] Yet Abou Fatma's expanded role in the film allows Kapur to suggest the unresolved conflict between Islam and the West so indicative of the narrative's setting. Kapur depicts Abou Fatma as a devout Muslim who responds to Harry's constant inquiries into his motivations for help with the refrain, 'I had to. God put you in my way.' Kapur's character mirrors Chérif's support of the acknowledgement of a 'friendship' between Islam and the Judeo-Christian world:

> There is no inevitable confrontation nor intrinsic clash of civilizations between the two worlds. On the contrary, Islam has participated in the emergence of the modern Western world; through its cultural and spiritual values, it is close to Judeo-Christian and Greco-Roman ethics, norms, and principles, regardless of the very real differences, divergences, and uniqueness of each.[61]

Through his depiction of the relationship between Harry and Abou Fatma, Kapur presents a portrait of the Islamic faith largely absent from Hollywood cinema – post-9/11 or otherwise. Harry and Abou Fatma make no efforts to convert each other despite openly discussing their religious and cultural beliefs; nor do their beliefs ever appear fundamentally at odds with each other. Instead, the two characters celebrate their differences while forging the bonds of friendship so important to Chérif. As Harry and Abou Fatma sit around a campfire with a group of British-employed Sudanese, Harry enquires about a feather Abou Fatma wears. He responds by informing Harry that he received the feather, not as a symbol of cowardice, but as reward for killing an enemy, an inversion of the Eurocentric discourse that originally led to Harry's journey. Likewise, when resting after tracking the British Army, Abou Fatma responds to Harry's laughter over God forcing a Muslim to protect an English Christian by telling him that he 'laughs like an Englishman'. When Harry inquires, 'And how does an Englishman laugh?' Fatma explodes into an exaggerated guffaw. Harry bursts into genuine laughter, soon followed by Abou Fatma as Kapur cuts to an exterior shot of their cave while their blended jollity echoes through the desert. Though the scene began as confrontational, the two allies forge a unity free from the domination of the imperial project.

Kapur's central depiction of Harry and Abou Fatma's relationship occurs through a seemingly extraneous moment of culture-clash humour. Awakened by the march of troops, Harry bursts out of the cave in search of Abou Fatma and freezes when he finds him engaged in his morning prayers. Waiting for a moment to cut in, Harry embarks on a series of false starts before realising the length of the prayer. Not wanting to disrupt his partner, Harry resigns himself to observing the prayer until Abou Fatma finishes. In this moment, Harry accepts Abou Fatma's difference and recognises Islam as something other than the fundamentalist Mahdi savagery he and his fellow soldiers remarked upon before deployment. Through this experience, Harry can return to England with a restored reputation and a changed outlook. As the film ends, he holds hands with Ethne, telling her that 'God put you in my way' before cutting to the film's final scene of Abou Fatma riding through the Sudan. Through the juxtaposition of the sequences, Kapur cultivates a model for a relationship between 'Islam and the West' that preserves differences while fostering a sense of unity capable of overcoming hegemonic forces – be they British, Egyptian, or (within the context of the film's transnational cast) multinational and corporate.

Through his engagement with Mason and Korda's previous iterations of *The Four Feathers*, Kapur uses his adaptation as an interrogation of the evolution of imperial ideologies from the dominance of the British Empire to the rise of global capital. Yet, Kapur does not seek to reject or excoriate the work of his predecessors. Instead, he crafts a site of intertextual understanding that evaluates historical precedence and bridges the legacy of colonial discourse with the ramifications European imperialism has had on contemporary politics. In a similar manner to Harry and Abou Fatma's attempts at understanding and an ultimate bond, he reaches out on a global scale to collaborators and audiences to forge a new discourse within and opposed to the founding ideologies of the imperial project.

CHAPTER 6

Gentlemanly Gazes: Charles Dickens, Alfonso Cuarón and the Transnational Gulf in *Great Expectations*

The final section of this study examines the relationship between Charles Dickens and postcolonial film adaptations made within and in the shadow of Hollywood's global scope. As the most adapted writer in all of literature, Dickens has maintained an integral influence over not only adaptation studies, but also the history of cinema. Dickens was one of the first authors adapted to film with *The Death of Nancy Sykes*, the 1897 dramatisation of the climactic scene from *Oliver Twist*.[1] Much of Dickens' appeal for filmmakers lies in both the rich history of theatrical adaptations of his work and George Cruikshank's iconic illustrations that accompanied the serial release of all of Dickens' novels.[2] Consequently, an association between the movies and Dickens' status as a cultural icon began that countered the low standing of cinema at a time when its novelty was wearing off and it faced increased scrutiny from politicians and religious institutions.[3] Dickens also holds the distinction of authoring the most adapted work of all time with *A Christmas Carol*, published in 1843, including versions as disparate as Edwin L. Marin's 1938 MGM classic, Richard Donner's contemporary Bill Murray vehicle *Scrooged* (1988), children's classics featuring Mickey Mouse (1983) and the Muppets (1993), Robert Zemeckis' 2009 motion-capture animation experiment starring Jim Carrey in all the major roles, and Indian director Bharat Nalluri's *The Man Who Invented Christmas* (2017), an Irish-Canadian pseudo-biopic that details Dickens' writing of the book and features Christopher Plummer as Scrooge.[4] Such a list does not even take into account the hundreds of film and television adaptations of his other works ranging from Lean's *Great Expectations* and *Oliver Twist* (which I discuss at length in the next chapters), Cukor's *David Copperfield*, Ralph Thomas' *A Tale of Two Cities* (1958), Carol Reed's *Oliver!* (1968), Disney's Billy Joel-penned musical *Oliver and Company* (1988), and the numerous BBC, PBS and ITV miniseries that are themselves part of a lucrative niche industry.

Yet, Dickens' influence over the cinema goes far beyond the popularity of his stories. As Grahame Smith writes, 'his work played some part, however small, in the cultural and material movements and transformations that eventually made it possible'.[5] The international pioneers of the early film industry saw Dickens not only as a fertile source of material but also as a trailblazing stylist whose narrative innovations were foundational to the advent of filmic story technique. In his seminal essay 'Dickens, Griffith, and The Film Today,' Soviet film icon Sergei Eisenstein firmly articulates Dickens' towering influence over the developing medium:

> Dickens' nearness to the characteristics of cinema in method, style, and especially in viewpoint and exposition, is indeed amazing. And it may be that in the nature of exactly these characteristics, in their community both for Dickens and for cinema, there lies a portion of the secret of that mass success which they both, apart from themes and plots, brought and still bring to the particular quality of such exposition and such writing.[6]

As Eisenstein indicates, Dickens and his narrative style wielded a transnational influence that, though proving central to the development of international cinema, was also illustrative of a form of cultural imperialism felt beyond the reaches of Victorian-era colonial discourse. Similar to Hollywood cinema, Dickens and his legacy served as a touchstone to which national cinemas defined themselves within and against, making him perhaps the most important figure to a study of postcolonial filmmakers adapting Victorian literature in Hollywood.

Chapters 7 and 8 will focus on two divergent adaptations of *Oliver Twist*: one, *Boy Called Twist*, made as an independent South African film with play at international film festivals and the other, *Slumdog Millionaire*, an Oscar-winning global phenomenon and adaptation of a postcolonial rewriting of Dickens' work directed by one of Britain's most famous contemporary filmmakers. However, before shifting from the category of postcolonial adaptations of Victorian literature made in Hollywood, this chapter turns to Mexican filmmaker Alfonso Cuarón's contemporary adaptation of Dickens' *Great Expectations* (1998), a studio film that undertakes a much less overt postcolonial adaptation strategy than Nair or Kapur despite radically altering one of the most important Victorian novels in postcolonial studies.

Cuarón's renegotiation of the imperial centre and focus on a setting once colonised by Spain makes the adaptation a cogent commentary on immigration and class mobility within a globalised US particularly conducive to the interfidelity approach. By paring down the narrative to focus on Pip and Estella's romantic and sexual liaisons, Cuarón exposes how the waning Empire embodied by Ms Havisham uses the young people's emotions and sexuality to further its agency. Employing the camera's seemingly objective gaze to dilute Pip's first-person narration, Cuarón depicts his protagonist as a powerless spectator in the world around him whose status and sexuality are defined by imperial authority. Resulting from his lack of agency, the sexual relationship between Pip (called Finn in the film) and Estella acts as a mechanism of control that defends imperial power, a narrative choice the director uses to negotiate the cultural tensions between America and Mexico.

WRITING BACK TO EMPIRES: DICKENS AND CUARÓN'S GLOBAL SCOPES

Opening weeks after the release of James Cameron's *Titanic* (1997) and its four-month reign over the North American box-office, Cuarón's Dickens update grossed a disappointing $26.4 million domestically and faced open hostility from critics who attacked its style-over-substance approach as, in the words of Owen Gleiberman, 'postmodern Cliffs Notes with an alt-rock soundtrack.'[7] Although the film did receive praise from a minority of critics, including Roger Ebert, Cuarón has publicly spoken of it as a failure, routinely citing intense studio interference from 20th Century Fox meant to capitalise on Gwyneth Paltrow's rising stardom. As he told Pamela Katz when asked about demands to make Paltrow's Estella softer and more likeable: 'No one was at all interested in this class element except me. And once we began rewriting scenes for Paltrow on the set, well, that was it.'[8]

While *Great Expectations* received near-universal dismissal – including from its director – film scholars have frequently revisited it over the past decade, especially after Cuarón's reputation grew with his critically revered *Children of Men* (2006) and his Academy Award for directing *Gravity* in 2013. Much of this critical appraisal echoes a softer version of Gleiberman's remarks, positioning the adaptation as a savvy postmodern nostalgia film that, according to Shari Hodges Holt, 'fuses different elements into a cultural pastiche' to erase historical boundaries.[9] Others, such as Latin American cinema scholar Deborah Shaw, view the project as a transitional film that fostered, 'the idea of Cuarón as unable to escape the status of director-for-hire in his Hollywood career prior to the return to Mexico, and his need to make a film that had an authorial stamp on it beyond a sophisticated use of *mise-en-scène*.'[10] More pervasive than either of these positions is discussion of how the film employs the male gaze to characterise Estella, a tactic that, notes Raffaella Antinucci, uses cinematic style to exalt its male protagonist's 'partial and distorted gaze'.[11] Such critical readings indicate that Cuarón's film is far more nuanced than its immediate reviews reflected, some even going so far as to meditate on the director's motif of green throughout the film, which he dismissed as simply a way to make his artistic mark on the project.[12] However, they also perceive it as an aberration unrelated either to the thematic preoccupations of Cuarón's other work or his reputation as a Mexican filmmaker.

In his nearly three-decade film career, Cuarón has crossed genres and national boundaries to create an oeuvre of stylistically distinct films that has cemented his (and his director of photography Emmanuel Lubezki's) status within the American and Mexican film industries.[13] However, while Cuarón has garnered a reputation as a director who alternates between independent and blockbuster productions, he remains, first and foremost, a filmmaker who has infused all of his work with questions of Mexican identity in a postcolonial context.[14] Cuarón's debut, *Sólo Con Tu Pareja* (1991), is his foray into the Spanish sex farce that, despite a topical depiction of the AIDS crisis, failed to gain international success due its provincial appeal and an abandonment of what Shaw calls 'transnational modes of narration not suitable to art cinema programmers', a factor which caused Miramax to renege on a tentative US distribution deal.[15] Following the dismal experience of *Great Expectations*, Cuarón returned to Mexico to make the teen road movie *Y Tu Mamá También* (2002). Unlike *Sólo Con Tu Pareja*, the film garnered international acclaim and an Academy Award nomination for Best Original Screenplay, serving as a comeback that relaunched Cuarón's Hollywood career.

Despite newfound artistic acclaim, Cuarón's Hollywood work has maintained the same resistant outlook. He interrogated imperialism by highlighting the connections between the British Empire, India's colonisation and the US in his adaptation of Frances Hodgson Burnett's *A Little Princess* (1995) using a focus on race and colonial education he would again evoke in *Harry Potter and the Prisoner of Azkaban* (2004) almost a decade later. In allegorising contemporary immigration and terrorism policies in *Children of Men* (2006), Cuarón piloted the undercurrents of what Nicolas Brindi calls 'A critical appraisal of the triumphal rhetoric of American Exceptionalism' in *Gravity* and its presentation of a wildly different colonised space.[16] Though not as direct as other filmmakers under discussion in this project, Cuarón's filmography typifies 'accented cinema' in its transnational appeal and concerns while extending them into the realm of the critically acclaimed blockbuster, making him a vital figure in understanding the relationship between cinema and diaspora.

Within this context, Cuarón's choice to, in the words of Susan Johnston, erode 'historical distance' to reel *Great Expectations* into the present appears less as an exception to and more a natural extension of the traits that cemented his lofty place in transnational cinema.[17] Published in 1861 as an emergency intervention to counter a sales slump for Dickens' periodical *All the Year Round*, the novel focuses on country boy Philip 'Pip' Pirrip, a future blacksmith's apprentice, and his desire to earn the love of his childhood playmate Estella by becoming a proper English gentleman through the financial support of a mysterious benefactor.[18] In wrenching the Victorian sensibilities of Dickens' novel into a contemporary context, Cuarón employs the novel's status as a work of Empire to address Mexico's tumultuous relationship with the US. Although Mexico declared independence from the colonising forces of Spain during the early 19th century, the fluid boundaries and conflicts over issues ranging from land disputes to illegal immigration have led to a form of internal colonialism in which the US's political dominance asserts a substantial amount of control over Mexican culture.[19] In addition, the dominant role of Hollywood in the international marketplace and the industry's close proximity to Mexico make it the most influential force in defining international perceptions of Mexicans and Mexican culture for global dissemination.[20]

Despite Cuarón's clear strategy of writing back to the imperial centre, the use of a Victorian text to navigate the colonial relationship between Mexico and the US appears much more indirect than the other projects under discussion in this book. As Cuarón has pointed out in past interviews, the novel is not required reading at Mexican schools in the same way it is for British and American high-school students, a cultural difference that significantly impacted his vision for the film.[21] Such comments call attention to what Klaudia Hiu Yen Lee refers to as the recent global turn in Dickens studies that too often falls into viewing translations and adaptations of Dickens' works 'as merely part of a global phenomenon or a localized cultural practice'.[22] For 'Global Dickens Studies,' *Great Expectations* is a central text both because of its prominence in Said's *Culture and Imperialism*, which contemplates Pip's benefactor Abel Magwitch making his fortune in the penal colony of Australia and because Magwitch's journey is one of the first instances of Victorian fiction to address what Jonathan H. Grossman deems the 'increasingly everyday condition of a globally networked simultaneity to which individuals must adapt.'[23] Within the context of this 'Global Dickens', Cuarón uses the adaptation to position Mexico in an imperial framework that calls attention to its Spanish colonial past and its contentious ties to the US during the Victorian era.

Mexico occupies a unique position in North America because its governing structure shares much in common with British and French territories such as India and parts of the Caribbean. According to Lora Romero, 'Spanish deployment of mestizo descendants of colonisers to govern New World territories created a class of colonial subjects for which US history offers no exact equivalent.'[24] With their lineage traced back to both Spanish settlers and indigenous Mexicans, mestizos retained a sense of otherness from American frontiersmen, which led to a series of clashes that culminated in the Mexican–American War (1846–8). Given the 'polyglot character' of a border populated by indigenous Mexicans, Hispanics, and mestizos, the conflict is better characterised, notes Walter L. Hixson as, 'a war for the extension of settler colonialism into the colonial space of California and the contested borderlands of the Southwest'.[25] In addition, the war became the catalyst that would shape contemporary US-Mexican relations and immigration policy while serving as the starting point for the US's own colonial endeavours during the Victorian era, including the escalation of Native American resettlement, the Civil War, and the annexations of Hawaii, Puerto Rico, Guam and the Philippines. Given the various imperial tensions between the US and Mexico, designations such as colonial, postcolonial and settler colonial seem imprecise. As Rosara Sánchez and Beatrice Pita write,

> . . . multiple situations as Latinos/as within the US cannot be sufficiently explained in terms of colonialism or decolonisation, much less postcolonialism. Clearly, we need to examine the frameworks with which we grasp our history and explain our multiple situations, full of nuances and contradictions as they are.[26]

As an adaptation of a Victorian novel that was released the same year the Civil War began, set in the US and helmed by a Mexican filmmaker, Cuarón's *Great Expectations* surveys a milieu of imperial contexts while navigating the contemporary relationship between the two nations.

Throughout the adaptation, Cuarón implements numerous changes to position the film's writing back to this host of imperial centres. He lays claim to Dickens' narrative by changing the names of several key characters: Pip becomes fisherman Finn Bell, a name that alludes to both Huckleberry Finn and Joyce's *Finnegans Wake* (1939) to comment on the film's geographical and stylistic play.[27] Magwitch becomes Lustig. Havisham becomes Dinsmoor, with the novel's Satis House now the decrepit plantation Paradiso Perduto ('Paradise Lost'). Likewise, Cuarón scores the film with an amalgam of American rock songs such as the Grateful Dead's 'Uncle John's Band' and David Garza's 'Slave' that are steeped in Mexican musical traditions. He also introduces Dinsmoor singing to Consuelo Velázquez's 'Besame Mucho', adding a subtle example of US commodification of Mexican culture to the film. In addition, Cuarón alters the setting of the novel from London and the country marshes of England to New York City and land on the Gulf Coast of Florida formerly colonised by Spain. Such a move to the American South directly places the adaptation's setting in a region home to a plurality of colonial situations largely because its history of Scots-Irish immigrants pushed out of the urban North endows it with its own settler colonial characteristics. This Southern settler coloniality shares much in common with nations such as Australia and creates what Fred Hobson perceives as a 'regional inferiority complex' that is also a source of pride.[28]

Consequently, the South found itself as a nexus of the US's colonial power, contending with the North's assertion of control over the region during

Figure 6.1 Young Finn (Jeremy James Kissner) and Joe (Chris Cooper) survey Paradiso Perduto.

the Civil War, continuing indigenous conflicts and territory disputes with Mexico.[29] As John-Michael Rivera writes,

> The investigation of the US 'South' in cultural and literary studies is not only a domestic inquiry into the Civil War, slavery, white women's suffrage, and African-American rights, but also a transnational study of the often overlooked but entirely related geopolitical relationship that the US has with Mexico and its inhabitants.[30]

Within this context, Cuarón's reconstruction of Paradiso Perduto (Figure 6.1) embodies the region's complicated history while also highlighting the comparisons between the plantation and the Mexican hacienda, which Jon Smith and Deborah Cohn argue is a similar colonial structure with transnational connections seen most clearly in the southern plantation novel's status as a 'model for a narrative of Mexican-American cultural memory'.[31] Through the adaptation process, Cuarón positions the planation as a site of past and present imperialisms, a decaying reminder both of the Southern past and the imperial authority Dinsmoor (Anne Bancroft) still embodies, echoing Alfred J. López's contention that, 'In the context of the postcolonial, postglobal South, however, we can read the figure of the plantation oppositionally, as a site of imagined shared struggle among subalterns otherwise unconnected by time or place.'[32]

However, Cuarón's primary method of engaging with these various imperial contexts occurs through his depiction of the relationship between Finn (Ethan Hawke) and Estella (Gwyneth Paltrow) and their respective roles as adolescents manipulated by the forces around them. Excising several supporting characters from Dickens' novel, including the angel of the house Biddy, the schemer Orlick, and the dual personality John Wemmick, Cuarón streamlines the narrative, positioning the romance between Finn and Estella as the central conflict of the text. By paring down the narrative to focus on Pip and Estella's liaisons, Cuarón exposes how the waning empire embodied by Dinsmoor uses the young people's emotions and sexuality to further its agency, depicting Finn as a working-class pawn and Estella as an ambivalent figure constructed to maintain its influence.

PIP AS THE OBJECT OF GAZES IN DICKENS' NOVEL

In this relationship between Estella and Finn, Cuarón employs the gaze of the camera to demonstrate the progression of his characters' agency. Though Cuarón integrates the novel's first-person point of view into his adaptation, he shoots the majority of the film in an objective manner, undermining Finn's narrative control by creating an opposition between Finn's voiceover and the camera's objectivity. However, Cuarón's aesthetic choice also avoids the camera's complete domination of the narrative, reflecting both Laura Mulvey's 'male gaze' that 'projects its fantasy onto the female figure which is styled accordingly' and the colonial gaze central to the work of postcolonial scholars from Said to Fanon.[33] In contrast, Cuarón's film upends both gazes, depicting Finn's narrative gaze as passive and the camera lens' gaze as active and colluding with the imperial forces that manipulate Estella's sexuality. Only after Finn attains agency through his tenuous class mobility does he acquire total subjective control of the narrative.

However, Cuarón's play with male and colonial gazes is also fundamental to his source text. Written from Pip's perspective, *Great Expectations* tells of its protagonist's rise and fall as a Victorian gentleman from a first-person point of view, endowing it with a sense of subjectivity that provides insight into the mind of a youth with working-class beginnings. Though the novel's point of view gives a unique voice to a character whose background exists outside the dominant English middle class, Pip's narration remains a product of English cultural dominance, positioning him as both the focus of the narrative and other characters' attentions. Whether acting as the object of Magwitch's gaze in the novel's opening, the audience for Wopsle and Pumblechook's lectures on manners at Christmas dinner, or the target of the lawyer Jaggers' chiding, Dickens constantly places Pip as an object the other characters evaluate and attempt to define. As Michael K. Johnson writes, 'Although the classic Hollywood film represents the male hero as the dominant gazing subject, we find Dickens' pre-Hollywood Pip more often than not positioned as the looked-at object.'[34] While such visual evaluations occur throughout the novel, no others have as great an impact on Pip's own self-image as those he encounters at Satis House. Initially arriving at Havisham's request, Pip relates her first words to him: 'Come nearer; let me look at you. Come close.'[35] Setting the stage for an inquisition of Pip's appearance, Estella later evaluates her new playmate: 'And what coarse hands he has. And what thick boots,' a criticism that serves as the first in the novel that affects Pip's own self-perception: 'I have never thought of being ashamed of my hands before; but I began to consider them a very indifferent pair. Her contempt was so strong, that it became infectious, and I caught it.'[36] Though others have defined Pip by his appearance throughout his young life, Estella's evaluation is the first to alter him, inspiring his lifelong goal of 'making himself uncommon'.[37]

As Estella's gaze continues to define Pip in the novel, Dickens shifts her power over Pip from distanced directives to physical interaction. While walking through the garden at Satis House, Pip encounters Herbert Pocket and the two boys engage in a fistfight from which Pip emerges as the victor. When Pip returns to the courtyard after blackening Herbert's eye, he finds Estella waiting for him: 'She neither asked me where I had been, nor why I had kept her waiting; and there was a bright flush upon her face, as though something had happened to delight her.'[38] Dickens clearly suggests that Estella witnessed the altercation between the two boys with Pip unknowingly the object of her gaze. When Pip meets Estella, she greets him by giving him an order: 'Come here! You may kiss me, if you like.'[39] In describing the kiss, Dickens writes: 'I kissed her cheek as she turned it to me. I think I would have gone through a great deal to kiss her cheek. But I felt that the kiss was given to the coarse common boy as a piece of money might have been, and that it was worth nothing.'[40] Through the move from passive gaze to physical interaction in the scene, Estella rewards Pip for conforming to the definition of him that she has constructed. While he is not aware that Estella witnessed his fight, Pip still feels that she uses the kiss as an emotionless unit of exchange to reward him for his continuing performance at Satis House. Regardless of Pip's physical interaction with Estella, the kiss lacks romantic meaning because of his coarse and common status, which Pip spends the rest of the novel struggling to abandon.

While Estella's evaluation of Pip may alter his self-perception and make him desire to better his social position, her negative opinions never leave him hopeless and conquered by Victorian society's rigid class structure because, despite his class, he remains a British subject. When the now gentlemanly Pip comes to the realisation that Estella plans to marry Drummle, he laments his unrequited love and deferred dreams:

> In the Eastern story, the heavy slab that was to fall on the bed of state in the flush of conquest was slowly wrought out of the quarry, the tunnel for the rope to hold it in its place was slowly carried through the leagues of rock, the slab was slowly raised and fitted in the roof, the rope was rove to it and slowly taken through the miles of hollow to the great iron ring.

> All being made ready with much labour, and the hour come, the sultan was aroused in the dead of the night, and the sharpened axe that was to sever the rope from the great iron ring was put into his hand, and he struck with it, and the rope parted and rushed away, and the ceiling fell. So, in my case; all the work, near and afar, that tended to the end, had been accomplished; and in an instant the blow was struck, and the roof of my stronghold dropped upon me.[41]

In alluding to British author James Ridley's faux Arabian tale 'The History of Mahoud', Dickens creates a convoluted metaphor for Pip's prophecy of his own downfall that serves as one of the few times in the novel that Pip fosters an introspective gaze at himself and his situation. While his unrequited love for Estella and the convict Magwitch's revelation that he is Pip's benefactor bring Pip's world crashing down like a ceiling, his dual characterisation of himself in the metaphor reveals a strange sense of agency for one whose world is about to crumble. As Stanley Friedman writes, 'Pip, therefore by stating "the roof of my stronghold dropped upon me," apparently identifies with *both* Misnar and the latter's foes, usurpers who do not belong in the bed.'[42] Though Pip fashions himself as a helpless individual, his dual status as rebel and authority figure betray his depictions as a victim. In addition, rather than make an allusion to an actual 'Eastern story', Pip chooses to mention an example of Orientalist empire literature that appropriates the *Arabian Nights*. As a result, Pip's metaphor transcends its narrator's self-pity and demonstrates a sense of agency absent from the gazes of other characters. Unlike the subalterns of the Indian and Arabian territory that the Empire dominates, Pip's status is always mobile. Despite his humble beginnings, he can shift from common to uncommon and from sultan to sycophant because, regardless of class, he is a British subject.

Pip's conversion from commoner to gentleman comes to fruition by the end of the novel as he succumbs to the various dominant Victorian gazes he encounters. Through his conformity to the gazes, Pip's transformation becomes not only a story of maturation but also the bildungsroman of an agent of the British Empire. After exposing Magwitch as Pip's benefactor, Dickens reveals that the convict accumulated the fortune that funds Pip's gentlemanly life in Botany Bay, Australia.[43] Upon hearing the origin of his fortune from Magwitch, Pip remarks, 'Once, I actually did start out of bed in the night, and begin to dress myself in my worst clothes, hurriedly intending to leave him there with everything else I possessed, and enlist for India as a private solider.'[44] Pip clearly exhibits contradictory opinions in his references to the two British colonies, abhorring his association with a fortune made in Australia that ruins his gentlemanly legitimacy while indicating ambivalence toward the colonial enterprise in India. As Said notes:

> After Pip redemptively acknowledges his debt to the old, bitterly energized, and vengeful convict, Pip himself collapses and is revived in two explicitly positive ways. A new Pip appears, less laden than the old Pip with the chains of the past – he is glimpsed in the form of a child, also called Pip; and the old Pip takes on a new career with his boyhood friend Herbert Pocket, this time not as an idle gentleman but as a hardworking trader in the East, where Britain's other colonies offer a sort of normality that Australia never could.[45]

As a subject of Empire defined by the gazes of characters with more agency than himself, Pip's renouncement of his benefactor and his eventual embrace of the acceptable means of acquiring wealth through trade in Cairo at the novel's end acts as one of the most potent examples of Pip's transformation into a gentleman. He achieves his position through a culturally acceptable channel that constructs the meaning of British gentlemen embraced by Estella, Havisham and the other characters who define him through their gazes.

Accordingly, Pip also acquires the agency to cease acting as a gazed-at object, thus gaining control of his interactions with Estella. However, Dickens' two endings for the novel depict the extent of Pip's agency in vastly different manners. In the original ending, as Pip returns to the ruins of Satis House and encounters Estella for the last time, Dickens writes 'I was very glad afterwards to have had the interview; for, in her face and in her voice, and in her touch, she gave me the assurance, that suffering had been stronger than Miss Havisham's teaching, and had given her a heart to understand what my heart used to be.'[46] Though Estella appears to have atoned for her injustices to Pip, her gaze still holds some semblance of control over him, which Dickens accentuates through Pip's passivity in the passage. Despite Pip's status as an independent gentleman, Estella maintains control over their relationship by giving him assurance, a factor that makes the original ending more open than Dickens' second and accepted ending for the novel.

In the second ending, and by contrast, Pip completely breaks from Estella's gaze, presenting himself as independent from others' definitions. Discussing Satis House's dilapidated state, Estella says, 'The ground belongs to me. It is the only possession I have not relinquished. Everything else has gone from me, little by little, but I have kept this. It was the subject of the only determined resistance I made in all the wretched years.'[47] While Estella is ostensibly referring to physical possessions, her dialogue also conveys her gaze's loss of control over Pip and his gentlemanly status as an Eastern trader. Likewise, Dickens presents Pip as a much more active character in the ending. Rather than Estella giving him assurance, Pip reverses Estella's gaze – no longer her object – becoming the dominant figure in the exchange: 'I took her hand in mine, and we went out of the ruined place; and, as the morning mists had risen long ago when I first left the forge, so the evening mists were rising now . . .'.[48] By the end of the novel, Pip has taken an active role in his own first-person narrative, achieving not only the status of colonial gentleman, but also an effective gaze on Estella.

GAZES AND RACECHANGE IN CUARÓN'S ADAPTATION

In adapting *Great Expectations*, Cuarón drastically reduces his protagonist's influence on the narrative, substituting Pip's complete control of events for Finn's role as an observer. Even though he includes Finn's voice-over narration, Cuarón uses the camera and its slant capabilities in an opposite manner to Nair in *Vanity Fair*, mimicking an omniscient presence that undercuts its protagonist's version of the story. Refusing to propagate the biases of Dickens or accusations of complicity with the male gaze, Cuarón's depiction of Estella and her deployment of sexual power dilutes Finn's narrative agency and counteracts her own objectification. Unencumbered by narrative control and acting as an agent of Paradiso Perduto's timeless imperialism, the Estella of Cuarón's film harnesses her sexuality to manipulate Finn's gaze, resulting in her subjugation of him.

Cuarón's execution of this imperial critique may seem tenuous considering that Finn, Estella, Dinsmoor and Lustig are all white Americans – though the film does position Lustig (Robert De Niro) as a member of the American mafia, thus associating him with a subculture of immigrants formed to preserve ethnic identity against the tides of assimilation and Americanisation.[49] However, the film utilises intentionally obtuse anticolonial strategies: racechange and metonymy through the adaptation process. As conceived by Susan Gubar, racechange occurs when artists traverse racial categories to create 'an extravagant aesthetic construction that functions self-reflexively to comment on representation in general.'[50] Within the confines of the Hollywood romance the studio insisted he make, Cuarón alters the lingering class elements of the novel to infuse the film with its meditations on British and US imperialism. Dinsmoor acts as a dying colonial force who manipulates an Estella that assumes a settler colonial identity torn between her allegiance to imperial privilege and her relationship with the subaltern Finn. At the same time, the film evolves beyond simple allegory grappling with what Elaine Freedgood calls the 'hapless metonym' innate to the Victorian novel, in which 'the metonym *substitutes* for those things with which it might be connected and creates a static fetish rather than a semiotic chain'.[51] For Freedgood, *Great Expectations* serves as the pinnacle of this hapless metonymy, largely through its associations with Magwitch and the 'Negro head' tobacco often taken on the long voyages that marked Britain's colonial network, a choice she argues stands in for the genocide of indigenous peoples in Magwitch's Australia.[52] Rather than opt for a direct connection between Dickens' novel and US imperialism, Cuarón's racechange allows the narrative to assume the role of metonym, a palpable shorthand for the adaptation process' web of imperial contexts.

Cuarón establishes Estella's settler colonial position when she is a child during her first appearance in the film. After young Estella (Raquel Beaudene) shows Finn (Jeremy James Kissner) to Paradiso Perduto's parlour, Dinsmoor orders her to sit for a portrait, providing Finn with an eyeliner pencil and a torn piece of wallpaper for use as drawing supplies. Sitting in a chair stiffly, Estella poses for Finn as Dinsmoor smirks at the children while swilling martinis. The scene marks the first time in the narrative that Finn exerts his drawing talent as a method of resistance, a choice that recalls Spivak's discussion of how subaltern expression, 'shares a common distancing from a self so that meaning can arise – not only meaning for others but the meaning of self to the self'.[53] Harnessing his artistic ability, Finn aims to distance himself from Estella to deflect his personal feelings onto her image on the wallpaper scrap. In addition, Finn reappropriates the eyeliner pencil and wallpaper – feminine objects – as manifestations of his phallic power through the act of drawing. Through the sequence, Cuarón alludes to the imperial practice of imbuing the colonised with childlike attributes as a way of creating a distinction between Empire and the Other. As Bill Ashcroft writes, 'The image of the child offers a filiative myth by which this repudiation directed at the Other by imperial discourse can be justified.'[54] Estella occupies a dual role within the structure of Empire, performing as its agent and subject, a contradictory identity Cuarón accents through the introductory sequence. Despite her age, Estella still deploys her sexuality to assert power over Finn. As the drawing sequence ends, Estella leads Finn to water fountain in the garden, cajoling him into taking a drink. Estella then leans into him, sliding her tongue into his mouth. Cuarón cuts to a close-up of Finn's hands letting go of the fountain in shock before cutting again to an extreme close-up of his eyes wide with surprise. Estella prolongs the physical interaction by giving Finn a series of French kisses before breaking from him and silently exiting the room. In adapting the kiss scene from Dickens' novel, Cuarón directly shifts the encounter's agency to Estella. When he drew Estella for Dinsmoor, Finn achieved a sense of agency, which Estella quickly reclaims through her active role in the performative kiss. Consequently, Cuarón presents the imperial power struggle as a contest that continues as the characters reach adolescence.

The teenage Estella's first exhibition of her sexual power occurs when Dinsmoor mandates that Finn serve as Estella's escort to a lavish party. Achieving a modest start to his artistic dreams by displaying paintings in a local bank, Finn's increasing independence allows him to brazenly suggest that he can accompany Estella. After blowing off the party immediately after

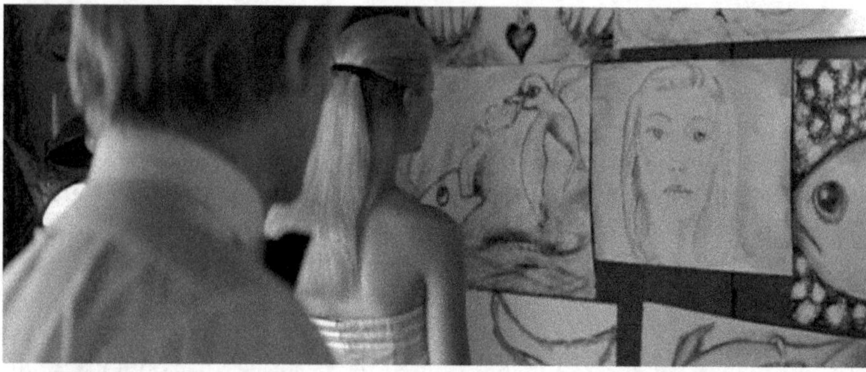

Figure 6.2 Finn (Ethan Hawke) and Estella (Gwyneth Paltrow) focus their gazes.

their arrival, Estella demands Finn take her to his house, encroaching on his personal space for the first time. As they enter Finn's bedroom, Cuarón pans to a large sketch of Estella (Figure 6.2) as she states, 'I don't wear my hair like that.' When Finn responds, 'You should,' while sitting on the bed, Estella slowly moves toward him, which Cuarón shoots from a low angle that stresses Estella's dominance of Finn. Smiling at Finn's shocked reaction, Estella guides his hand under her dress. As she climaxes, she bends over to kiss Finn, pulling away as he tries to move her onto the bed and stating, 'I have to get home. I have a million things to do.' When Finn protests, she responds in French, knowing Finn is not bilingual. Still speaking in French, Estella exits the ramshackle house, leaving a disheveled and stoic Finn looking after her as Cuarón cuts to an extreme long shot that reinforces Finn's isolation. Through the execution of the scene, Cuarón depicts Estella's sexual performance as a way to reestablish dominance over Finn and to avoid perception as a powerless sexual object. Toying with Finn at the beginning of the scene, Estella is stunned at his attempt to claim his own vision of her through the drawing. Though she has matured, Finn's drawing reminds her of his idolisation. Only after realising that Finn has rebelled against the control she had over him as a child does Estella resort to using her sexuality to reestablish her power through an act that requires no reciprocity on her part. Once she has regained complete control, Estella can again dominate him using her class and the cultural capital it provides, as evidenced by her use of French as a parting shot.

Cuarón's application of cultural capital to Finn and Estella's relationship serves as one of the most significant methods of establishing agency for both characters in the adaptation. Early in the process, Cuarón wanted to probe the intricacies of labour in the Gulf fishing industry as the region transitioned into a service economy, a way to topically juxtapose Estella's jet-set mobility and Finn's subaltern positionality.[55] Such an addition would have been especially applicable given that, in the late 1990s, a demand for cheap, nonunion labour in industries such as fishing coupled with an economic crisis in Mexico facilitated a wave of immigration in the South that, notes Raymond A. Mohl, 'produced substantial cultural and demographic change in a region where change has always been slow and received with skepticism, if not hostility.'[56] Although Fox curtailed this subplot, the film's metonymic traits still subtly convey how Estella employs her settler-colonial privilege to reinforce her sexual dominance of Finn. Still reeling from his sexual encounter with Estella, Finn returns to Paradiso Perduto in search of her, learning from Dinsmoor that Estella has left for school in Europe and a postgraduate life in New York City. Dejected, Finn abandons his artistic aspirations and assumes a position as a village fisherman, a shift Cuarón highlights by revealing Finn's career change through a scene of him painting a boat. Though Estella reclaimed the agency Finn achieved with his artistic talents through their earlier sexual encounter, she further hinders his resistance by relocating to New York City, a place where Finn cannot afford to follow. In analysing Dickens' depictions of the city, Raymond Williams discusses the potential mobility the metropolis embodies:

> In seeing the city . . . as at once the exciting and the threatening consequence of a new mobility, as not only an alien and indifferent system but as the unknown, perhaps unknowable, sum of so many lives, jostling, colliding, disrupting, adjusting, recognising, settling, moving again to new spaces, Dickens went to the centre, the dynamic centre, of this transforming social experience.[57]

In accepting his lack of mobility and embracing his class position as a fisherman, Finn also accepts Estella's complete control over his life. Consequently, he has relinquished the method of resistance his drawing talent provides and resigned himself to subalterniety. Only after Lustig's anonymous financial backing allows him the opportunity to pursue his artistic career in New York City is Finn able to undergo a transforming social experience and regain his tool of resistance in an environment that – like the Australia-funded Pip – refuses to see him as legitimate, a fact the film underscores when it reveals that Lustig also bought all of the paintings at Finn's self-proclaimed 'wild success' of a gallery opening.

With both characters entrenched in New York society, Estella again invokes her sexual performance to regain control of Finn during the film's central scene: his sketching of her. As Finn sleeps late into the afternoon, Estella bursts into his room, coyly teasing him by saying, 'Don't you want to paint me? You've slept all day, it's time to work.' Estella mechanically begins to undress, removing each article of clothing with sensual fervour as Cuarón cuts between her and Finn gazing with his mouth agape. Cuarón then executes the

Figure 6.3 Finn draws Estella.

sketching scene with a series of quick cuts between Finn drawing (Figure 6.3) and Estella posing. However, during the duration of the scene, he shoots in soft focus and frames Estella so that her nudity is always obscured, only revealing her body through Finn's interpretive drawings. As suddenly as she initiated the drawing session, Estella dresses, telling Finn: 'I have to go. I have dinner in one hour, and I look a mess.' With Estella leaving the frame, Cuarón again cuts to an extreme long shot that parallels the couple's first sexual encounter, demonstrating that Estella again has asserted control over Finn.

Though Michael K. Johnson interprets the scene as playing out 'the tension between Estella's control of her own body and Finn's visually taking possession of that body through his gaze and through his ability to turn Estella into a text, an image on his sketch pad', it assumes a new meaning when taking Cuarón's metonymic concerns with colonialism into consideration.[58] In the years since Finn and Estella's last encounter, Finn has gained independence and class mobility through his drawing talents. When Estella reenters his life, she again uses her sexuality to subjugate him, reaffirming her influence on him by making her the subject of his tool of resistance, a move that Antinucci notes, is 'a representation 'from within' an embryonic instance of a transgressive class of women as 'viewers of themselves represented'.[59] In addition, Estella not only controls Finn's craft, but also uses the sketch session to cajole her boyfriend Walter Plane (Hank Azaria) into an engagement. As Plane tells Finn when he visits his studio after the session, the nudes were 'a little push' for the proposal. Through the scene, Cuarón exemplifies the concept of approximation – the paradox of colonial subjects using the symbolic systems and language that originally hindered their freedom to resist Empire.[60] Finn has tried to rebel against his class and the hold Estella has on him through his talents. Yet, his livelihood is both a commodity sponsored by wealthy patrons who want him to create images of them and, in the case of his session with Estella, a politicised tool meant to maintain the authority of Dinsmoor's imperialism by uniting it with Plane's family.

Despite his commodification, Finn uses his flourishing art career to break away from Estella's sexual authority. As a reporter interviews Finn about his overnight success, Finn creates a persona for himself that mythologises his rise from subaltern to artistic superpower. In constructing the narrative of his life for the reporter, Finn relates a fictional account of his childhood, falsely claiming to be raised by his drug smuggling Uncle Joe (Chris Cooper). Now firmly cemented in New York City's elite, Finn actively pursues Estella, bursting in on her dinner with Walter at a posh New York restaurant and pulling her away from her fiancé as he guides her by her hand to his loft. There, Finn and Estella consummate their relationship, a scene that Cuarón shoots through alternating close-ups of the couple and of Estella's body. Though partaking in the male gaze, Cuarón uses the shift to investigate the extent of Finn's agency. With his newly acquired status, Finn takes control not only of his relationship with Estella but also of the film's narration, stripping the agency of the camera away in favour of a male gaze that is stylised by what Katz refers to as a first-person 'magical realism' that is the hallmark of postcolonial fiction, especially for Latin American authors such as Gabriel García Márquez.[61] In taking control of both his life and the film's narratives, Finn demonstrates a complete break from imperial forces, no longer presenting events as they occurred in the narrative, but as he envisions them.

Finn's control of the narrative is perhaps the most important factor when analysing the film's overtly happy ending. In stark contrast to both of the novel's endings, the film's ending completely eschews narrative ambiguity, presenting Finn and Estella's reunion at Paradiso Perduto as a happily ever after union of two lovers, which Ana Moya and Gemma López deem, Cuarón's choice of 'a "safe" Victorian closure'.[62] More than any other sequence in the film, Cuarón relishes in style to such an extent that the abandoned plantation appears more akin to an Edenic paradise than a base of imperial authority. As Finn reminisces about his childhood in voiceover while wearing a pristine white suit, the film alternates between extreme long shots of Finn dwarfed by foliage and close-ups of flowers and leaves. It then cuts to an extreme close-up of a ladybird crawling on Finn's hand, further accenting the pastoral harmony of its *mise-en-scène*. As Finn continues to ruminate about his return to Paradiso Perduto, Cuarón dissolves to an image of a blonde girl who resembles the Estella of his childhood giggling. The dissolve calls attention to the potential narrative subjectivity of the scene, but Cuarón quickly reestablishes pseudo-realism as Finn follows the girl to the plantation's dock and finds the adult Estella gazing into the sunset. Sharing a moment of recognition, Estella tells him that the girl is her daughter, saying 'I brought her here. I wanted to show her this place. What's left of it,' while looking pensively toward the plantation. As the conversation continues, Estella gazes at Finn and says, 'You're doing

Figure 6.4 The magical realist reunion of Finn and Estella.

great. I hear all about you,' and 'I think about you. A lot lately.' Awkwardly, she asks if Finn can forgive her, bearing no trace of her former self. Swaggering, Finn responds to her in voiceover: 'It didn't matter. It was passed. It was as if it had never been. It was just my memory of it.' Grabbing her hand, Finn moves closer to Estella as the couple gazes at the sunset, the music swells and the film fades to black (Figure 6.4).

Though Cuarón seemingly ends the film on a happy and unambiguous note, he complicates the scene through his earlier introduction of Finn's narrative control. Harnessing the location's dense colour palette, Finn's perfectly tailored costume and Estella's uncharacteristic dialogue delivery and actions, Cuarón constructs the ending as a magical-realist dream. As a result, the sequence retains a sense of ambiguity Dickens could not achieve on the page. Cuarón's visual cues call attention to the scene's subjectivity, framing it not as the actual ending to the narrative he began telling, but Finn's idealised ending of a narrative over which he has earned control that is so strong that the imperial site of Paradiso Perduto becomes innocuous, a place Estella and her daughter visit to view its remains. In his efforts to resist colonial authority through his artistic talents, Finn achieves an independence from Estella's dominance and, more importantly, from the metanarrative of Empire, transitioning from subaltern to politically resistant narrative authority.

While Cuarón's adaptation of *Great Expectations* suffered from a negative critical consensus and a disappointing box-office gross, the film continues the director's career-long exploration of past and current iterations of imperialism. Using Estella's sexuality and settler colonial positionality, Cuarón writes back to a canonical work of colonial discourse and subtly references the ongoing internal colonial relationships between countries such as the US and Mexico. However, though the relationship between Finn and Estella serves as a potent example of Cuarón's reframing of Dickens, it is only one of the many narrative, visual and economic choices the director has made in his career that negotiate his native culture and the Hollywood industry that has embraced him as a transnational icon of contemporary cinema.

CHAPTER 7

Indie Dickens: Oliver Twist as Global Orphan in Tim Greene's *Boy Called Twist*

These final two chapters discuss how vastly different reworkings of Dickens' *Oliver Twist* serve as examples of the problems of adaptation as a method of resistance that the interfidelity approach hopes to counter. They also diverge from the type of adaptations this project has examined thus far as they are not adaptations of Victorian literature made by postcolonial filmmakers within the Hollywood system. They are, however, examples of categories 4 and 5 of the postcolonial adaptation taxonomy discussed in the introduction that aid in further understanding of Hollywood's global reach over national film industries in postcolonial nations. We first turn to Tim Greene's 2004 adaptation of Dickens' novel *A Boy Called Twist* and the director's use of orphanhood to address both the poverty and AIDS epidemic that erupted in the wake of Britain's imperial control of the region as well as the contemporary cooption of the 'global orphan' by foreign governments and non-governmental aid organisations (NGOs) that frame transnational aid discourse.

Viewing Oliver's marginalised status within the context of postcolonial theory evokes parallels between the domestic orphans of the 'other nation' and those colonised by the British imperial project. However, for a South African filmmaker such as Greene, the orphan trope also bears strong ties to the associations between South Africa and the AIDS epidemic that has gained worldwide attention. As Helen Meintjes and Sonja Giese write,

> The notion of the orphan (read 'AIDS orphan') as the quintessential vulnerable child in contemporary South Africa (and beyond) lies at the centre both of policy and programming aimed at addressing the impact of AIDS on children and of much of the child rights discourse present in the context of AIDS.[1]

While the estimated 1.4 million children who become AIDS orphans in

South Africa each year create a host of issues ranging from orphanage funding to increased bullying and mental disorders, the group has remained largely understudied and abstractly defined.[2] At the same time, the image of the South African child orphaned by AIDS has shifted into the idea of the 'global orphan' that, while serving as a potent symbol to attract international NGO and charity resources in much the same way as the Victorian era Poor Law orphan, complicates responses to a localised issue by stripping the nuances away from such orphans living in South Africa.[3] For as the pathos-driven image of the (predominantly black and 'coloured') global orphan dominates AIDS relief discourse, vital local issues such as negotiating psychological and medical aid with the Malawian treatment of death with silence or Zulu customs of sequestering a child from the dying become neglected.[4]

With the concept of the global AIDS orphan echoing David Harvey's discussion of NGOs as 'elitist, unaccountable, and by definition distant from those they seek to protect or help, no matter how well-meaning they may be' as they propagate a form of social problem 'privatization', Greene's presentation of the South African orphan in *Boy Called Twist* appears as a viable, multifaceted alternative that eschews the transnational myths of orphanhood that control neocolonial and neoliberal representations of South Africa.[5] At the same time, it also channels the central role *Oliver Twist* played in resistance to Apartheid, especially for the students involved in the 1976 Soweto uprising. In opposition to the Afrikaans Medium Decree of 1974 that mandated schools use Afrikaans and English in the classroom, over 20,000 school children protested on 16 June 1976, taking part in what would ultimately be the largest massacre of black people by the regime in Apartheid's history.[6] As Carol Lee writes in her memoir *A Child Called Freedom*:

> The apartheid regime overlooked Dickens in its banning orders and censorship laws and, crucially, it forgot about Oliver Twist. It did not stop to think what effect this story might have on young hungry South African minds eager to be fed. Township teenagers crowded together, both in and out of school, devoured the story of this poor English boy. For them it was a revelation. Systemized oppression of children was happening in England too! They were not alone then. Workhouse conditions, random beatings, slave-labour, cruel taunts, and gruel-like rations were part of a child's life in the world outside as well. The book was not like a story from somewhere else, nor from a hundred or more years before. It seemed to describe their lives now and it gave them heart that a distinguished author should provide evidence of their plight.[7]

As Lee indicates, though Dickens' novel is representative of the legacy of colonial education the students were resisting, its seemingly benign status that did not merit censorship fostered resistance, opening up a space for a hybrid Oliver that reflected the marginalisation of Apartheid. Bridging the politics of Dickens' portrayal of Victorian orphanhood with the shadow of the global orphan, Greene's Twist acts as a distinctly local Oliver eschewing the victimisation and cypherlike purity of his predecessors.

Published in 1837 as Victoria ascended the throne, Dickens' *Oliver Twist* may appear as a novel not only tangentially related to colonialism but also critical of the imperial project. Throughout the text, Dickens only references the Empire when child thief ringleader Fagin mentions 'lagging' (exile) to Australia as a punishment for the captured Artful Dodger and when Oliver's caretaker, Mr Brownlow, journeys to the West Indies to gather information about Oliver's evil half-brother Monks, who made his fortune and owns an estate there.[8] Yet, while the novel's associations between the Empire's territories and nefarious characters seemingly function as subtle attacks on the project, it remains firmly rooted in the tradition of early Victorian literature that negotiates anxieties over both Britain's newly minted female leader and the nation's imperial endeavours. As Carolyn Dever writes, apprehension over Queen Victoria's rise to power led to an increased focus on the female body in British literature, producing an analogy between the Queen's body and Empire that led to an 'overdetermined identification of Victoria as domestic ideal.'[9] Within this context, Dickens' tale of the orphaned child struggling to find his identity in the wake of his mother dying in childbirth takes on a far greater significance for the formation of British imperialism. For while Agnes Fleming, 'imprinted her cold white lips passionately on his forehead; passed her hands over his face; gazed wildly around; shuddered; fell back – and died' in the first few pages of the novel, the force of the ensuing narrative revolves around her – much like the newly minted Queen – transcending the physical limitations of her body and becoming legitimised by the force of law in the form of Oliver's birthright.[10] Despite its seeming resignation from colonial discourse, Dickens' text is fundamentally about the formation of the Victorian imperial ideology that would steer the Empire into an unprecedented period of expansion and conquest.

For a film adaptation to successfully negotiate the colonial trappings of a source text like *Oliver Twist*, it must acknowledge the legacy of the imperial space within which is it working. Yet, defining resistance against the legacies of what Hardt and Negri refer to as 'The power of Eurocentrism' in which 'Even Indians (and Indonesians, Peruvians, and Nigerians too) have to measure themselves to the standard of European identity' is difficult to articulate.[11] If, as Harvey contends, 'place' acts as a localised, oppositional 'other', then the most effective form of resistance lies not in a text in which a self-exiled, Western-educated author or film auteur alone speaks about a nation, but in a text that, though guided by a singular authorial presence, attempts to include the complexities of a particular place against colonial and imperial discourses, in effect, speaking to a larger conversation taking place in the nation of origin that can extend to those from other nations.[12] Such a strategy echoes Hardt and Negri's characterisation of singularity as the most cohesive strategy to oppose a transitional imperialism built on the foundations of Eurocentrism. As Hardt and Negri write:

> This singularity does not mean, however, that the world is merely a collection of incommunicable localities. Once we recognize singularity, the common begins to emerge. Singularities do communicate, and they are able to do so because of the common they share. We share bodies with two eyes, ten fingers, ten toes; we share life on this earth; we share capitalist regimes of production and exploitation; we share common dreams of a better future. Our communication, collaboration, and cooperation, furthermore, not only are based on the common that exists but also in turn produce the common.[13]

Through this process of singularity, a film adaptation of a colonial text indirectly about the imperial project acknowledges the structure at its source while combating it with an inclusive perspective that tries to reconcile the disparate cultural positions within its nation from an industrial position not beholden to a national film industry or monolithic corporation with a global reach. Rather than define and propagate an image of the nation with a global audience in mind, the filmmakers behind such adaptations foreground their material's relationship to place, highlighting multiple perspectives by utilising the collaborative processes of film production.

Considering that Hardt and Negri's primary example of singularity stems from protests over evictions and utility cutoffs in Chatsworth, South Africa, in which Black South Africans and South African Indians mobilised around the chant, 'We are not Indians, we are the poors. We are not Africans, we are the poors',[14] that this study's most prominent example of a singularity-based film adaptation would hail from South Africa attests to the long-term implementation of place-based resistance in the nation. Shifting the novel's setting from London to Cape Town, Greene's film follows the orphan Twist through a South Africa-accented version of Dickens' narrative in which Blacks, 'coloureds', Afrikaners and various Muslim communities perceive identity in the wake of Apartheid. Eschewing national funding or coproduction deals with multinational film studios, Greene financed the film through an unprecedented strategy of standing at intersections and seeking individual investors from a multitude of ethnic origins, which ultimately led to it setting a record as the film with the largest number of coproducers in history, numbering at more than one thousand.[15] Though such financing methods appear unorthodox even to independent filmmakers in places such as the US with no national film board, Greene's methods were revolutionary for South Africa, a nation under, as Ntongela Masilela and Isabel Balseiro write, the near total hegemony of 'an unrepresentative white minority, consisting not only of diehard upholders of the Apartheid system but also of white liberals and progressives as well, in their roles as academics, as critics, as anthologists, as impresarios, as gallery owners and publishers and as consultants of those who own virtually all the means of cultural production.'[16]

Despite a financing concept that won media attention and Greene's stated intent of making the film primarily about Cape Town's 'local sound and colour,' it remained entwined with the complexities of Hollywood's global reach that affects all national cinemas.[17] As Tom O'Regan writes:

> So to be 'wholly local' in a pure form in front of and behind the camera is not the natural condition of a national cinema – even when it looks to be doing precisely that . . . A feature filmmaker's domestic career often hinges on getting their film into and comporting themselves appropriately at the Cannes, New York, Venice, Montreal, Toronto, and London film festivals. In their choice of actors, locations, production personnel, story and dialogue, local producers routinely take into account the requirements of international circulation.[18]

The political resonance of *Oliver Twist* in South Africa aside, Greene's choice to adapt such an internationally recognised book accented by a South African perspective also positions the film as an example of South African national cinema that showcases the nation and its film culture internationally, which the film did when it screened as an official selection at the 2005 Cannes Film Festival in the Tous les Cinémas du Monde sidebar category. Hollywood critics praised the film for its distinct South African take, including Ronnie Scheib who singled out the spaciousness of 'Greene's South African topography' in her review for Hollywood trade magazine *Variety*.[19] Yet, regardless of its novelty, it never received international distribution as Scheib predicted: 'Without a strong hook, theatrical prospects look dodgy, but cable could provide a solid niche.'[20] In a review that praises every aspect of the film from its cinematography to the performances of its non-professional cast, such an assessment seems counterintuitive. However, for Greene, adapting Dickens and cultivating a strong sense of place were not a strong enough hook. In O'Regan's terms, the film was too South African, as a result of its lack of name players and mini-major studio polish, lacking the appeal of the films selected for Cannes' main competition Palm d'Or line-up in 2005 by world cinema luminaries such as Lars von Trier, Michael Haneke, Gus Van Sant, Jim Jarmusch, David Cronenberg, Hou

Hsiao-hsien, Tommy Lee Jones and the Dardenne Bros, all of whom saw their films distributed by Hollywood mini-majors and vie for Academy Award and Independent Spirit Award nominations.

While Greene acted as both writer and director of the film and admittedly belongs to the unrepresentative white minority that Masilela and Balseiro discuss, his sensitivity to South Africa's multiethnic sense of 'place' and active attempt to create a film representative of the nation's diversity marks a shift from the other film adaptations discussed in this book. In fostering a unified sense of place similar to the 'we are the poors movement' that preceded the film's release, Greene ceases to act as authorial spokesperson for his nation while favouring collective production over the Eurocentric, globalised culture industry. Consequently, Greene was able to transcend the problematic racial depictions of other Afrikaner-directed films such as Hood's adaptation of Athol Fugard's novel *Tsotsi* (2005) and Neill Blomkamp's Apartheid allegory *District 9* (2009) that avoided direct discussion of settler colonial cultural dominance.[21] Though never reaching the international audience of his contemporaries, Greene's film is a prime example of a postcolonial revision that complicates its associations to past and present imperialisms while working toward a singularity that represents the local and serves as a global model of resistance.

THE 'SINGULAR' ORPHAN OF *BOY CALLED TWIST*

Considering independent cinema's associations with the margins of popular culture, what is most striking about Greene's adaptation is its utter lack of narrative and stylistic experimentation and absence of overt social and political critique. Greene makes no attempt to either radicalise Dickens' source text or integrate a colonised perspective into a work of Empire literature à la Nair and Kapur. Instead, the film not only transplants *Oliver Twist* into a South African context but also follows a nearly identical structure as David Lean's 1948 film adaptation of the novel, resulting in a film that, apart from its narrative structure, seems wholly removed from global capital's influence.[22] Yet, Greene's seeming fidelity to Dickens and Lean serves as an acknowledgement of the global economy's omnipresent cultural influence over formerly colonised nations, positioning his film as an intervention into strategies of negotiating a coherent, all-inclusive South African identity that situates the nation's colonial past in conjunction with its future. Through his choice to mine Lean's adaptation as a source text as well as the original novel, Greene also references a filmmaker whose early-career adaptations of Dickens' *Oliver Twist* and *Great Expectations* depict a Victorian England inundated with scenes of bright sunlight, a sanitised historical portrait that reveres a society built on the profits of imperialism during the anxiety of the British Empire's fall. Reappropriating

Dickens' source text and engaging with an adaptation made a decade after the Statute of Westminster declared South African independence, Greene executes the adaptation not by writing back to the imperial centre but by writing through the centre of colonial discourse, endowing the film with an aware yet nonabrasive depiction of national identity.

Greene's primary method of situating his nation within and outside of the British Empire is his extension of Dickens' career-long obsession with orphans into the context of a South Africa in which the orphan serves as a vital symbol of the nation's difference from 'the West' and solidification of its status as a developing nation. For Dickens, the orphan acted as a trope that aroused the importance of the hierarchal family structure at the centre of both Victorian society and the areas under the paternalistic dominion of the British Empire.[23] In the case of *Oliver Twist*, Dickens' focus on orphans also allowed him to directly attack the Poor Law Board that served as the book's central target through subverting the status of the orphan. According to Laura Peters, orphans underwent the symbolic role of 'the child of the Poor Law Board' through the Board's emphasis on downtrodden orphans in their rhetoric.[24] Throughout the novel, Dickens defines Oliver's interaction with such forms of social authority almost entirely in the terms of family.[25] Desiring to rid himself of Oliver after the young boy's iconic request for more gruel, Bumble the Beadle plans to unload him onto the nearest tradesman in need of an apprentice. Relating this fate to the trembling orphan, Bumble explains the concept of apprenticeship:

> The kind and blessed gentlemen which is so many parents to you, Oliver, when you have none of your own: are going to 'prentice you: and to set you up in life, and make a man of you: although the expense to the parish is three pound ten! – three pound ten, Oliver! – seventy shillin's – one hundred and forty sixpences! – and all for a naughty little orphan which nobody can't love.[26]

While the concept of becoming a 'prentice' terrifies Oliver and leaves him trembling, Bumble dictates the terms of Oliver's exploitation within the context of the family as a way to position employment as an establishment of a family unit, an association Dickens undercuts when Oliver's apprenticeship to undertaker Mr Sowerberry swiftly ends when Oliver collects 'his whole force into one heavy blow' and attacks the elder apprentice Noah Claypole over his remark that Oliver's mother was 'a regular right-down bad'un.'[27] Despite Bumble's characterisation of apprenticeship as a familial enterprise, it is ultimately Oliver's recognition of an absence of family in his current situation that leads to his resistance and subsequent journey to find a family structure – whether through Fagin as a patriarch, who refers to Oliver as 'my dear', or the surrogate families of Maylies and Brownlows that will reintegrate him into Victorian society.

Through this portrayal of orphans as exploited individuals outside the legitimate framework of Victorian society that Sheila Smith refers to as 'The Other Nation' (a play on Benjamin Disraeli's 1845 novel *Sybil, or The Two Nations*) of the lower classes that Londoners refused to see, Dickens' descriptions of orphan characters such as Oliver also often bear close associations with the slaves that drive the economies of colonised territories such as the West Indies, which are so vital to Monks' social position.[28] As Bumble delivers Oliver to Sowerberry's shop, Dickens writes:

> Mr Sowerberry was closeted with the board for five minutes; and it was arranged that Oliver should go to him that evening 'upon liking,' – a phrase that means, in the case of a parish apprentice, that if the master find, upon a short trial, that he can get enough work out of a boy without putting too much food into him, he shall have him for a term of years, to do what he likes with.
>
> When little Oliver was taken before 'the gentlemen' that evening and informed that he was to go, that night, as general house-lad to a coffin-maker's; and that if he complained of his situation, or ever came back to the parish again, he would be sent to sea: there to be drowned, or knocked on the head, as the case might be . . .[29]

In his characterisation of Oliver in purely economic terms, Dickens provides a clear example of the extensions of domestic policy into colonised territory. As long as Oliver agrees to the wishes of 'the gentlemen', he can maintain a position in servitude that contributes to Sowerberry, Bumble and the board's agency. However, the local board also retains the power to send Oliver to the colonies via the vague otherness of 'the sea', in effect, benefiting from his labour if he survives the journey. While firmly entrenched in the hierarchy in which early Victorian England processes its fringe subjects, the landscape outside the boundaries of the island, as Dickens' description indicates, remain somewhat controlled by the same officials from London despite its status as a mysterious place where the Empire sends its rebels and refuse.

If, as James R. Kincaid contends, Oliver comes from the modern tradition of 'the empty, eroticized, androgynous child' and 'is looked on by everyone', this gaze of authority belonging to those such as Bumble that control Oliver acts in a similar manner to the colonial gaze that Bhabha discusses.[30] Therefore, it is only in the instances when Oliver gazes upon others, when Fagin sees that 'the boy's eyes were fixed on his in mute curiosity; and although the recognition was only for an instant – for the briefest space of time that can possibly be observed – it was enough to show the old man that he had been observed' as 'the Jew' peruses a box of his sacred treasures, and when he gazes 'with his eyelids as wide open as they would possibly go' at the Artful Dodger stealing from Mr Brownlow – that Oliver encounters direct moments of confrontation.[31] Applying Bhabha's discussion of the 'displacing gaze of the disciplinary double' to Dickens' novel, Oliver acts as a figure who, while subjugated by every form of Victorian authority, including the family, uses these moments of gazing to isolate 'some strategic limitation or prohibition *within* the authoritative discourse itself', forcing those who try to erase or overlook his existence as a member of the 'other nation' into a direct acknowledgement of his presence.[32]

Working with a similar concept of a 'colonised' Oliver from the beginning of his film, Greene directly deals both with the continuing influence of imperial policies on South Africa and the role of his nation in the globalised world through his depiction of the orphanage, Weltevreden. After the scene of Twist's mother's death that opens the film, Greene cuts to a low, straight-on angle shot of a group of orphans playing 'Ring a Ring o' Roses' in which only the children's feet are visible. As the camera pans, the feet of an Afrikaner woman in high heels bursts into the frame, disbanding the circle on her way up the stairs to the orphanage's entrance. Upon reaching the door, the woman, Weltevreden's director, Mrs Corlet (Terry Norton), finds a black nurse holding the baby Twist lovingly. With the nurse looking at her boss guiltily, Corlet stoically censures her: 'Have we or have we not discussed mothering the babies? . . . Sorry doesn't help. Just don't do it. God, I wonder why I bother.' In establishing the orphanage, Greene economically situates it as a multifaceted space in which the various imperial powers that have asserted dominion over South Africa merge into one bureaucratic entity. Named after a city in the Netherlands (and a traditional South African house name that means 'well-satisfied'), the orphanage is run by a woman whose lineage is clearly rooted in Britain, a coupling that defines the space entirely through an amalgamation of South Africa's original Dutch and British colonisers.[33] The harsh tone in which Corlet addresses the nurse appears to characterise her as a simplistic and latently racist Afrikaner, yet Greene seeks to humanise her with comments she makes directly after the scolding. Noticing the nurse's humiliation, Corlet responds by saying, 'It's to protect new patients. They die. You can't love them. Some live longer, others not, but they all die. And it will break your heart', before asking the nurse to give the baby some formula and run a PCP, T-cell count, and other blood tests. Though implied, Corlet's futility-tinged comments about the lifespan of orphans is a direct result of the prominence of AIDS in the nation, which dictates that an orphanage – which houses no Afrikaner children – must test baby Twist for the virus and order him clean formula. In addition, Corlet's orphanage is not an affluent NGO entity, a fact Greene makes clear during a meeting between Corlet and the social services agent Mr Bedel (Goliath Davids) in which she reveals that she hires out orphans for farm work because 'Every cent goes into keeping this place open.' In retaining a bureaucratic structure from the legacy of European imperialism, the orphanage is a facility to deal with local challenges of a post-Apartheid South Africa such as the AIDS epidemic. Yet, without the support of the global entities of which Harvey is so critical, Corlet propagates the legacy of exploitation in a seemingly more progressive South Africa in which a black citizen such as the stuttering farmer Boese (Ivan Abrahams) to whom Bedel leases the orphans owns land – a contradiction that demonstrates the influence of a transnational imperialism that coopts local issues to maintain its own hegemony.

While the ramifications of the AIDS epidemic serve as an undercurrent throughout the film, Greene again avoids a simplistic characterisation of his nation by rejecting the idea of the 'global orphan' through structuring his film around an orphan not suffering from the disease. As Twist (Jarrid Geduld) makes his journey from Boese's farm to the funeral parlour of the Afrikaner Mr Brakwater (Johan Malherbe) to the streets of Cape Town, Greene's dialogue makes constant references to Twist's 'HIV Negative' papers, a document that both allows for his mobility and his exploitation by the film's various adults. However, the spectre of childhood AIDS remains apparent throughout the film via Greene's adaptation of scenes from the novel within the AIDS context, not only when Twist enters into the service as a funeral procession leader because, in Brakwater's words, 'we're burying so many children' but also when Twist's only friend at the orphanage, Dickie (Remi Lawrence) reveals that he cannot join Twist on the journey to Cape Town because he's dying and 'had a dream he went to heaven' and 'saw his sister there.'[34] Though he does not suffer from the disease, the lethal virus remains a source of anxiety for Twist so strong that Greene includes a dream sequence soon after his employment with Brakwater in which a coffin crushes Twist as he is digging a grave.

In establishing the proliferation of AIDS orphans and children suffering from AIDS passed onto to them by birth, Greene acknowledges the pervasiveness of the disease within the country. Yet, the film opposes the construct of the 'global orphan' as the primary depiction of South African children in the film. Instead, this Twist is a 'coloured' child character who, while neither possessing the purity of Dickens' Oliver as a result of older age and his experiences with AIDS nor suffering from the disease himself, is able to serve as a link among the disparate demographics of the nation.[35] Greene first alludes to Twist's hybridity during Corlet's naming of him early in the film. After the nurse tells her that the baby has no name, Corlet immediately turns to her bookshelf and moves an index card beside a leather copy of *Oliver Twist*, stating that his name shall be Oliver. When the nurse reminds Corlet that they already have an Ollie, she settles on just calling him Twist. As Greene introduces the other orphans, he reveals that Corlet names orphans by arbitrarily moving the index card through her library shelf and naming the children after the authors and protagonists of the British canon: Mariner, Silas, Middlemarch, Ollie, Gulliver, Emily, and Charlotte live with Dickie and Twist.[36] In addition to recalling Bhabha's characterisation of the 'English Book' discussed in Chapter 5, Corlet's naming of Twist is indicative of the character's hybrid status. He can twist the cultural legacy of British colonialism within South Africa's current social problems while transcending the nation's racial, cultural and class barriers to act as a unifying force. In stark contrast to the 'global orphan' as indicative of South Africa's 'otherness' from the West, Twist's very identity openly flaunts the arbitrariness of British influence while presenting South Africa as a diverse nation with multifaceted local colour that can also be applied to, as Harvey writes, the 'new systems alliance' formed between nations such as India, Brazil, China and South Africa as a force in global politics.[37]

VICTORIAN RACIAL STEREOTYPES AND SINGULAR ETHNICITIES

Employing Twist's hybridity as a method of revealing the complex ethnic makeup of a South Africa largely globally defined by the Apartheid struggles, Greene uses the host of eclectic characters from Dickens' source text to foster an inclusive ethnic space through which Twist travels. As an author who was, as Liora Brosh writes, 'Obsessed with characters who subvert national boundaries', Dickens suits the type of postcolonial revision of central concern to Greene with relative ease.[38] However, through his concern with subverting national boundaries, Dickens often created characters who appeared more stereotype than subversive, such as *Oliver Twist*'s Fagin, 'a very old shriveled Jew, whose villainous looking and repulsive face was obscured by a quantity of matted red hair.'[39] Arguably the best-known Jewish character in English literature (barring Shakespeare's Shylock), Fagin, with his exaggerated nose and red hair, resembles the description of the stage Jew so popular during the rote anti-Semitism of the early Victorian era.[40] In addition, Dickens' Fagin appears as an extremely effeminate character through his 'playful' manner with the male children and pickpocket game in which he places his valuables near his genitals for his charges to retrieve – a sharp contrast to Sikes' rugged masculinity and Monks' shadowy colonial business prowess.[41] Regardless of the enduring critical debate over whether Dickens' depiction of Fagin is a relatively ambivalent sign of the times (which also extends to the Fagin [Alec Guinness] of Lean's film, whose large nose and demeanor bordering on homosexual stereotypes led to severe cuts to the film in the US), the fact remains that the character Dickens refers to as 'The Jew' throughout the majority of the novel is, in the words of Juliet John 'the archetypal passionless villain who experiences no constructive emotional connection with others.'[42]

Fagin's status as the only character in the novel whose ethnicity Dickens explicitly defines provides an ideal site for a postcolonial filmmaker such as Greene to revise Victorian treatments of race as well as realise a space of identification for marginalised groups within his own culture. Taking Jay Clayton's view that, for postcolonial novelists, Dickens fails at consolidating a 'coherent national identity' and instead symbolises 'the madness of contemporary existence' into consideration, Fagin appears as a potent character for connecting the various forms of imperial control that asserted themselves on nations such as South Africa.[43] Diverging from the Dickens and Lean characterisations of Fagin as an effeminate other, the character in Greene's film is a black Rastafarian with dreadlocks, an intimidating presence who towers over the other characters in the film, including Sykes and Monks. Rather than advise Oliver to look to the Artful Dodger because 'he'll be a great man himself, and will make you one too', Greene's Fagin serves as a model of cunning masculinity.[44] Fagin's status as a masculine model is most apparent in his 'mock theft' performance for the boys. Wearing a long trench coat and placing objects throughout his body, not just in the genital region, Fagin dares the boys to trick their leader. Though Fagin does not exert violence against the boys as each approaches, he catches them and looks at them cuttingly, positioning Greene's execution of Dickens' original scene as more similar to a training sequence from a war film than a Victorian stage Jew's comedic performance. In his depiction of Fagin, Greene recalls bell hooks's discussion of the pervasiveness of the violent black male. Discussing Black Panther George Jackson's prison letters, hooks writes that those of African descent who embrace the ethos of violence and criminal activity are not 'defying imperialist white-supremacist capital patriarchy; unwittingly they were expressing their allegiance. By becoming violent they no longer have to feel themselves outside the cultural norms.'[45]

In light of hooks's view, while Greene's Fagin rewrites the ethnic stereotypes of Dickens' Jewish villain that have remained controversial since the narrative's inception, it seems that he may well have displaced the old stereotypes with those so pervasive in the postcolonial world. However, Greene undercuts his unabashed depiction of Fagin as the violent black male that hooks cautions against by situating him into the broader context of South African politics through Fagin's relationship with the film's other criminal personalities. Though Fagin and Sikes have a contentious relationship in Dickens' novel, their interactions are marked by a sense of mutualism in which the two are vital to each other's endeavours despite the latter's insults, including referring to Fagin's hand as a 'withering old claw' that reminds him of being 'nabbed by the devil.'[46] Suffering from a fever that nearly kills him, Sikes lashes out at Fagin for his neglect:

> You've been scheming and plotting away, every hour that I have laid shivering and burning here; and Bill was to do this; and Bill was to do that; and Bill was to do it all, dirt cheap, as soon as he got well: and was quite poor enough for your work. If it hadn't been for the girl, I might have died.[47]

Though the exchange subtly alludes to Fagin's effeminate qualities through implying that Sikes expects him to assume Nancy's role as caretaker, it also demonstrates that the two men are colleagues, associated with each other in both personal and professional bonds. Yet, in Greene's film, Fagin embodies the role of a freelance criminal for the white Sykes (Bart Fouche), who only seeks Fagin's help with small-time pickpocket operations so that he can focus on larger operations such as burglary. Greene sets the meeting between Sykes and Fagin (Lesley Fong) at a tavern where Fagin, on his way to meet with Monks (Peter Butler), encounters a drunken Sykes at a corner table as the all-white patrons glare at him.[48] When Fagin asks to sit down, Sykes bellows: 'of course I fucking mind' and calls him 'old scum'. The two engage in strained conversation (Figure 7.1) until Sykes asks if Fagin is 'interested in a loan out' for Twist. Fagin then sees Monks enter and asks Sykes to use his room for the meeting 'to make a good impression.' Glancing at Monks and needing Twist for his planned burglary, Sykes begrudgingly agrees to Fagin's request with a nod and a 'nothing worth stealing in there anyway.'

Through his changes to Dickens' source text, Greene works within the tradition of Fanon's characterisation of colonialism's effect on the black psyche. As Fanon writes:

> For not only must the black man be black; he must be black in relation to the white man. Some critics will take it upon themselves to remind us that this proposition has a converse. I say this is false. The black man has no ontological resistance in the eyes of the white man. Overnight the Negro has been given two frames of reference within which he has had to place himself. His metaphysics, or, less pretentiously, his customs and the sources on which they were based, were wiped out because they were in conflict with a civilization that he did not know and that imposed itself on him.[49]

Influenced by the lingering ramifications of Apartheid and South Africa's colonial past, Fagin is denied access to a legitimate frame on which to base his identity, left instead to assert his power through assuming a leadership role over black and 'coloured' orphans or associating himself within a hierarchy of the criminal underworld in which Sykes maintains a privileged position.

At the same time, Fagin's side dealings with the Muslim Monks are an

Figure 7.1 Fagin (Lesley Fong) negotiates with Bill Sykes (Bart Fouche).

attempt to form an autonomy outside of the framework imposed upon Fagin by the white minority's hegemony in the nation, an alliance that, albeit criminal in nature, bears a striking resemblance to the 'we are the poors' unity indicative of singularity. Discussing Monks in Dickens' novel, Mr Brownlow characterises him as follows:

> Your mother being dead, I knew that you alone could solve the mystery if anybody could, and as when I had last heard of you were on your own estate in the West Indies – whither, as you well know, you retired upon your mother's death to escape the consequences of vicious courses here – I made the voyage. You had left it, months before, and were supposed to be in London, but no one could tell where. I returned. Your agents had no clue to your residence. You came and went, they said, as strangely as you had ever done: sometimes for days together and sometimes not for months: keeping to all appearance the same low haunts and mingling with the same infamous herd who had been your associates when a fierce ungovernable boy.[50]

Unlike Dickens' Monks who migrates to a colony to transform his 'ungovernable' nature into a for-profit dominance of natives, the Monks of Greene's film has worked to overcome the stigma of an ethnicity that originated in South Africa as a slave class through his successful criminal enterprises.[51] Within this context, Sykes' eventual acquiescence to Fagin's request represents an anxious acknowledgement of the shifting power dynamics of postcolonial South Africa. While, if successful, Monks and Fagin's plan to divest Twist of his inheritance will lead to a legitimate wealth denied to Sykes, such success is only attained through a criminal means suggestive of the still-dominant racial hierarchy existing in the nation.

Though Monks serves as an example of a Muslim character enmeshed in the criminal underworld of South Africa, Greene's most radical break from Dickens' novel is his depiction of Mr Brownlow, not as a middle-class, Victorian gentleman, but as Ebrahim Bassedien (Bill Curry), a wealthy and devout Muslim who lives in Cape Town's Malay Quarter – a neighbourhood of liberal Muslims where miscegenation and tolerance are the norm.[52] While still classified as 'coloured' citizens within South African culture, the Malay Muslims and the more conservative Indian Muslims within the nation have used Islam as a way for, according to Suleman Dangor, 'socially and ethnically marginalised classes' to 'secure status and distinct identity' since the religion was introduced to the region during the period of Dutch colonisation.[53] Because of this distinct identity, Islam in South Africa has served as both a unifying and radical force, opposing Apartheid and creating schools open to children of all ethnicities and religious beliefs, traits that Bassedien exemplifies.[54] Described by Dickens as an 'absent old gentlemen' who speaks '*like* a gentlemen', Brownlow not only refuses to press charges against Oliver but also reserves his considerable class power against the vicious magistrate Fang for the sake of his future young charge: 'Mr Brownlow's indignation was greatly roused; but, reflecting perhaps, that he might only injure the boy by giving vent to it, he suppressed his feelings, and submitted to be sworn in at once.'[55] Though Bassedien retains Brownlow's formidable moral character, he appears just as involuntarily subjected to the Afrikaner judge's ill-treatment as Twist, positioning the courtroom scene as a microcosm of racial injustice in South Africa rather than the heralding of industrial and colonial capitalists such as Brownlow over bureaucratic government entities that is customary of Dickens' work.[56]

Under the guidance of Bassedien, who Greene eventually reveals as Twist's grandfather, the boy adopts traditional Muslim dress and begins to attend school in the Malay Quarter, becoming integrated within a South African community that typifies resistance to imperial control as well as an all-inclusive minority population indicative of what Abdulkader Tayob views as 'the quest for utopia and representation that preoccupies Islamic politics both in South Africa and elsewhere.'[57] Harnessing the political potential of South African Islam, Greene presents it as a viable location for a singular politics in contrast to the failed forms of resistance embodied by Fagin and Monks. As a hybrid figure who traverses the various 'coloured' populations of South Africa, Twist and his constant bouncing between Bassedien and the criminal underworld positions him as teetering between the two ideologies held by these parental models, a factor Greene, like Dickens before him, highlights through Twist's costume changes.[58] When in Bassedien's home, the elder discards Twist's streetclothes while Fagin sells Twist's pristine white robe and cap to a second-hand shop after he recaptures Oliver.

Through this constant allegiance shifting, Twist exemplifies Iqbal Jhazbhay's discussion of Islam's concern with a map of borders:

> . . . it is increasingly not what is inside the texts of Islam that matters but rather it is the map of the borders – the textualisation of reality – that has come to matter most . . . For some critics, this study brings no essentialist Islam; rather, it brings news of the nothingness that lurks outside essentialist Islam.[59]

In the wake of past and present imperial forces, this news of nothingness has clouded methods of resistance in nations such as South Africa. As Greene's depictions of Fagin and Monks indicate, opposition based on the perversion of the laws dictated by the imperial structure remain tied to the very hierarchies against which individuals rebel, allowing such figures to fall into the same trappings that Harvey discusses. However, by embracing the utopian politics of Bassedien's Islam, the marginalised can cultivate a relatively autonomous space such as the Malay Quarter and practice an inclusive politics that advocates a sense of singularity for those hailing from an array of ethnicities and religious positions. While Greene ultimately reveals Twist to belong to the Islamic faith and to assume his role as heir to Bassedien's substantial wealth, the fact remains that without his grandfather's inclusive ideological position that gratefully welcomed the orphan into the fold, his identity would have remained that of a marginalised orphan more akin to the 'global orphan' than an autonomous individual moving toward a singular politics within his nation.

Greene's singular politics reaches its peak in the film's final scenes, which mark a sharp break from both Dickens' novel and Lean's film. After his grotesque murder of Nancy in Dickens' novel, a wracked-with-guilt Sikes attempts to escape by moving to the roof of Fagin's hideout:

> . . . at that very instant the murderer, looking behind him on the roof, threw his arms above his head, and uttered a yell of terror.
>
> 'The eyes again!' he cried in an unearthly screech.
>
> Staggering as if struck by lightning, he lost his balance and tumbled over the parapet. The noose was on his neck. It ran up with his weight, tight as a bow-string, and swift as the arrow it speeds. He fell for five-and-thirty feet. There was a sudden jerk, a terrific convulsion of the limbs; and there he hung, with the open knife clenched in his stiffening hand.
>
> The old chimney quivered with the shock, but stood it bravely. The murderer swung lifeless against the wall; and the boy, thrusting aside the dangling body which obscured his view, called to the people to come and take him out, for God's sake.[60]

While Lean's film preserves Sikes' rooftop death, he refashions the scene as a hostage situation by having Sikes take Oliver captive in an action-packed chase sequence as he evades the police. Though Sikes falls victim to multiple

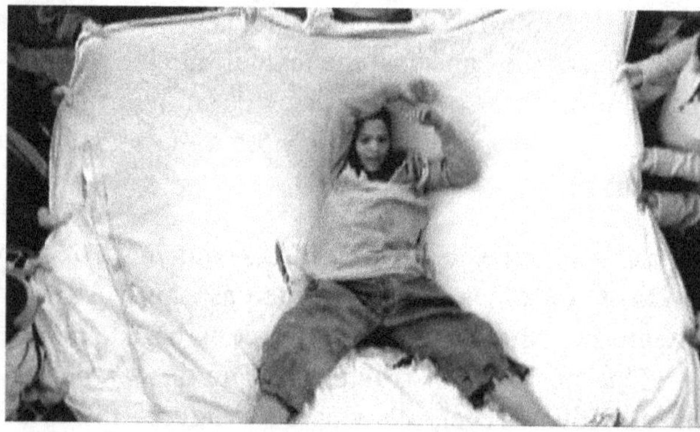

Figure 7.2 Twist (Jarrid Geduld) saved by the diverse multitude.

gunshots, Lean preserves the haunting noose-imagery from the novel, complicating Sikes' character by maintaining his guilty conscience even as he endangers Oliver much more directly. Greene retains Lean's chase sequence, but, when the police dispatch Sykes in a shootout, they indifferently send Twist spiraling to the roof's edge as he becomes entangled in Sykes' rope. Twist hangs on for dear life as Greene cuts to shots of Bassedien and Monks amid the enormous crowd of onlookers. In an act of redemption, Monks yells for Bassedien to take a blanket from the baby of a nearby mother and form a makeshift life net. Several bystanders grab the blanket and Twist falls to safety and into the arms of the citizens of Cape Town (Figure 7.2).

Despite generally positive international reviews, critics such as Joan Dicks took issue with the suspension of disbelief the finale requires, especially as Twist's fall is broken by the blanket 'thoughtfully worn by a female bystander.'[61] While the scene does undermine much of the realism Greene so painstaking establishes, it is a distinctly South African ending that provides an example of post-Apartheid unity reminiscent of 'we are the poors!' rhetoric. Endangered by a trigger-happy police force who ignore Bassedien's pleas, Twist survives because of a multitude of multiethnic citizens working together. Monks' atonement and role as a catalyst for mass action also echo the controversies that erupted in the wake of South Africa's Truth and Reconciliation Commission. While the commission sought to move South Africa away from the traumas of Apartheid, it also faced criticisms that, according to Katherine Mack, 'there may indeed be an 'elective affinity' between the political liberal individualism of human rights as it was translated into the commission's work via the transnational human rights movement and South Africa's adoption of a neoliberal economic agenda.'[62] As a marginalised figure under Apartheid and a budding capitalist who covets Twist's birthright, Monks' transformation serves as a rejection of the opportunity provided by the neoliberal economy. At the same time, it is an embrace of local (albeit melodramatic) action to save Twist and rescue him from the poverty caused by an amalgamation of colonialism, NGO influence, police brutality and a racial hierarchy that benefited individuals as debased as Sykes.

Applying Dickens' social concerns to the orphans of post-Apartheid South Africa and appropriating racialised depictions of characters such as Fagin to represent South Africa's black and Muslim communities, Greene's independent film exposes ties between Victorian Britain's domestic and imperial policies, making parallels to the contemporary dynamic occurring between the globalised world and developing nations. Yet, its lack of international dissemination and marketability call into question the effectiveness of such postcolonial rewritings as they remain of limited interest beyond niche groups such as Dickens scholars and enthusiasts, sidelined by the narrow definition of national cinema within the scope of global Hollywood.

CHAPTER 8

Three-Worlds Theory Chutney: *Oliver Twist*, *Q&A* and the Curious Case of *Slumdog Millionaire*

Following Danny Boyle's *Slumdog Millionaire* sweeping the Golden Globes on a path that would eventually lead the film to win eight Academy Awards and earn $362 million internationally, film critic David Gritten published an editorial in *The Daily Telegraph*, proclaiming the worldwide hit, 'the first film of the Obama era', for its globalised worldview.[1] As Gritten writes:

> The first striking thing about this British-made film is its even-handed, generous spirit of universality. It is set in India and it's about Indians. There is no hint of Merchant Ivory decorum, the predicaments of rich westerners far from home, nor any notion that Boyle and his team were engaged in a David Lean-style imperial adventure in what was once one of the pink regions on the globe.[2]

Yet, despite the article's evisceration of Merchant Ivory's aesthetic and David Lean's imperial undertones, Gritten resoundingly credits *Slumdog Millionaire*'s success to his own nation, imploring his audience not to forget that the film is, in fact, 'a British triumph'.[3] For Gritten, the film's status as an adaptation by British screenwriter Simon Beaufoy of Indian author Vikas Swarup's 2005 novel *Q&A* goes as uninterrogated as his editorial's neocolonial undertones, leading to his positioning of Swarup's source text as merely the rudimentary outline for the film's unprecedented brilliance:

> Screenwriter Beaufoy profoundly altered his source material, Indian author Vikas Swarup's agreeable, amusing novel *Q&A*. Swarup's hero was called Ram Mohammed Thomas, a name with Hindu, Muslim and Christian connotations, suggesting an Indian everyman. Beaufoy deliberately plumped for a specifically Muslim hero.[4]

Notwithstanding drastic changes to Swarup's novel during the adaptation process, discussion about the film's relationship to the source text was conspicuously absent from the film's criticism as the press opted to focus on coverage of its child stars' living conditions and accusations that Boyle's representation of India exploited poverty.[5] While Boyle's representation of Mumbai and the film's production practices certainly deserve critical attention, the near-total dilution of Swarup's imperial and neocolonial critique and the lack of media commentary on the alterations indicate a much keener insight into Western media depictions of postcolonial nations than even the most vocal charges of 'poverty porn' aimed at the film. Though *Slumdog Millionaire* has attracted, according to Jonathan J. Cavallero, more academic attention than any film in recent memory because, 'its release came at a time when scholarly interest groups, academic conferences, and special journal issues turned their focus to the transnational phenomenon', discussions of it within the context of adaptation studies have been rare.[6] More importantly, scholars such as Cavallero and Nathalie Vanfasse who have examined the film as an adaptation have opted not to focus on Boyle's film as an adaptation of a novel that is itself a sustained rewriting of *Oliver Twist*, either making cursory references to Dickens or, in the case of Vanfasse, highlighting an impressive list of the film's 'Dickensian overtones' that range from nods to *Twist* to the novel's fading film star Neelema Kumari resembling Ms Havisham to the savant Shankar as Smike from *Nicholas Nickleby*.[7]

Sharing the narrative structure of *Slumdog Millionaire*, Swarup's novel uses Ram's appearance on *Who Will Win a Billion?* as a site to negotiate the relationship between India and a globalised entertainment industry in which the Indian version of a game show with multiple international iterations becomes integral to the nation's culture. However, while the novel directly depicts the rise of transnational corporate imperialism, it also employs a similar strategy as postcolonial authors such as Rhys and Carey of rewriting a canonical text of colonial discourse complete with the Faginesque gangster Maman, who blinds children for use in his street-begging con operations, and a Victorian twist ending that allows Swarup to examine the lingering ramifications of British colonialism on an Indian culture now firmly entrenched in the globalised world. Yet, rather than adapt Swarup's nuanced critique of postcolonial India's interactions with the globalised world, Boyle's 'British triumph' appears as a primer on contemporary India for a global audience, in the words of Ana Cristina Mendes, an example of 'armchair tourism' more akin to the late-Victorian adventure tales of the Kipling and Mason variety than a cinematic extension of Swarup's political concerns.[8]

For postcolonial writers such as Swarup, the problems of resistance become compounded when considering the relationship between author and representation of the homeland. Though born in Allahaband to a middle-class family of lawyers, Swarup has spent most of his adult life abroad, acting as minister and high commissioner of India in a variety of nations, including Britain, Pakistan, and South Africa. Telling the press, 'I'm no Arundhati Roy' (who would later criticise the film in the press), in the wake of *Q&A* and *Slumdog Millionaire*'s success, Swarup explained his intent behind a novel he wrote primarily in London as a thriller that places Major Charles Ingram's real-life quiz show scandal into an Indian context, making it a novel that 'isn't a social critique'.[9]

Regardless of his stated intent, Swarup's novel still acts as a devastating social critique of past and present imperialism in his homeland, applying his diplomatic insight to a depiction of India marred by religious violence that stems from colonial influence and reeling from the corruption of national film and television industries hoping to situate themselves within a profitable position in globalised media. Yet, in his dismissal of *Q&A*'s social significance, Swarup concisely alludes to the structure that made the seamless integration of his novel into a Hollywood coproduction so easy. In his discussion of Rushdie's contributions to the 'Third World' novel, Aijaz Ahmad distinguishes between the postcolonial writer in exile – whose readership is 'materially absent from the immediate conditions of their production' and 'more vividly and excruciatingly present in the writer's imagination because their actuality is deeply intertwined with the existential suffering of the exile' – and the writer in self-exile, who 'has no such irrevocable bond' and 'is free to choose the degree of elasticity in that bonding'.[10] While Swarup's diplomatic responsibilities allow him a closer bond with his homeland than a migrant author such as Rushdie who willingly moves from home, they also account for conditions of production and a readership more global in scope and removed from national concerns, which may contribute to Swarup's reticence to join the ranks of Roy and Rushdie and acknowledge the political undercurrents of his fiction.[11]

Working from a position both within and outside of a national culture, a self-exile such as Swarup serves as a mediator between his homeland and its role within the globalised world. Though such a relationship appears ripe with potential for a global solidarity of colonised nations, it also runs the risk of aiding in the transition from 19th-century colonialism to the rise of transnational imperialism that governs the worlds of both *Q&A* and *Slumdog Millionaire.* As Ahmad writes:

> This idea of the availability of *all* cultures of the world for consumption by an individual consciousness was, of course, a much older European idea, growing in tandem with the history of colonialism as such, but the perfection and extended use of it in the very fabrication of modernism . . . signaled a real shift, from the age of old colonialism *per se* to the age of modern imperialism proper, which was reflected also in the daily

> lives of the metropolitan consumers in a new kind of shopping: the supermarket.[12]

Entrenched in the already established colonial discourse foundational to *Oliver Twist*'s narrative from the perspective of a cosmopolitan self-exile writing the majority of his novel in London, Swarup – despite *Q&A*'s resistant strains – exists within a context steeped in past and present imperialisms that allows his depiction of India to be reintegrated into the global order with relative ease and adapted into a film coproduction between Warner Bros., French company Pathé, and the British film industry. As a result, Swarup's distinctly Indian perspective is coopted into a global economy where a film like *Slumdog Millionaire* seemingly embraces the globalised worldview of the Obama era as DVD copies of the film are available at checkout aisles and vending machines in supermarkets around the globe a few feet away from ethnic foods aisles in which instant chai and frozen curry share shelf space with variations of other international cuisines. As Jigna Desai writes of the film, 'With its transnational production, it may in fact to (*sic*) be said not only to perpetuate Orientalism and re-Orientalism, but also to simultaneously create and feed a desire for or consumption of the same.'[13]

With the cultural and ideological differences between *Q&A* and *Slumdog Millionaire* so glaring, one could easily dismiss Boyle and screenwriter Beaufoy's fraught representation as well as critics' lack of attention to the film's erasure of Swarup's critique of imperialism as systematic of an unconscious embroilment within the very corporate-owned media entities so vital to the circulation of contemporary imperial politics. Despite the film's controversies, Boyle was extremely aware of his Westerner status, hiring a predominately Indian crew, including codirector Loveleen Tandan because, as he notes, 'That kind of Western superiority complex, however wrong, is innate. And if you're surrounded by the comfort zone of your own people, you'll never lose it.'[14] Consequently, such criticism overlooks not only the overarching narrative similarity of the two texts but also the continuing influence of British colonialism on the cultures of its former colonies.

In his discussion of the constructions of 'space' and 'place' central to current understandings of geography discussed in the previous chapter, Harvey cautions that postcolonial critiques are often 'secretly imprisoned within a cartographic image of India bequeathed by British imperial rule, all the while trying to stuff it full, as it were, with hefty doses of Heideggerian mythology.'[15] Defining space as the territory conquered by imperialism and place as a local, oppositional 'other', Harvey writes:

> How Indian nationalists took all of this apparatus to construct their own sense of national identity is a major study in Indian colonial and

> postcolonial history. They could not and indeed would not abandon the map they were inheriting and refill it with a meaning that was distinctly their own, even as it replicated part of that 'structure of feeling' that the British legacy imparted. Herein lay the origins of a powerful constructed myth of Indian statehood, a myth that to this day has enormous power in the Indian political consciousness.[16]

While Harvey's contention deals specifically with overt political actions and government policy, one can also extend his critique to the influence of colonial literature on postcolonial writers' efforts at writing back to the imperial centre. Building upon Fredric Jameson's oft-debated conception of Third-World novels as national allegories, Brian Larkin positions *Slumdog Millionaire* and its controversy as central to understanding how 'the allegorical capacity of texts to stand in for the nation stems not just from authorial intention but from the movement that looses them from original contexts of production and reception and opens them up to different publics that do not share the same contexts or understanding.'[17] If, as Larkin posits, texts such as Swarup's novel and Boyle's films go beyond intent and into the realm of a text to different publics that often fail at properly contextualising, then postcolonial rewritings of British texts such as *Oliver Twist* remain as, if not more, imprisoned within the cultural confines of global capital, calling their effectiveness into question.

In discussing the networks of control stemming from the legacies of British colonialism and the rise of global imperialism, my aim is not to dismiss the critical interventions of Swarup's novel or Boyle's film adaptation. Despite its complex associations with imperial discourses, Swarup's text retains a keen insight into India's role in the globalised world. Likewise, apart from its problematic representations of India and skirting of Britain's role in the nation's contemporary political situation, *Slumdog Millionaire* expresses an extremely relevant, albeit often compromised, postmodern critique of globalisation and constructions of a 'flat' world. Instead, my aim is to grapple with a question of interfidelity: how a film adaptation of a Victorian novel such as *Oliver Twist* that does not directly deal with a specific imperial context to which it can write back in a manner such as Thackeray's India, Mason's Sudan, or even Greene's South Africa can interrogate the legacy of colonial discourse without remaining tied to the imperial structure that Harvey cautions against and *Slumdog Millionaire* typifies.

In contrast to Greene's 'singular' adaptation of *Oliver Twist*, I argue that with the release of *Slumdog Millionaire*, the use of adaptation as a form of resistance for postcolonial filmmakers was usurped by the globalised imperial presence of the transnational media corporation. Diluting its source text's subversive rewriting of *Oliver Twist* and gestures toward national allegory, Boyle's film streamlines the narrative into Hollywood genres accented with Bollywood conventions while presenting India as a nation of others, far removed from the ramifications of British imperialism and benefiting from the structures of the globalised world such as the transnational quiz show that fuels Jamal's rise from the slums. Through my examinations of Swarup's novel and Boyle's film in this concluding chapter, I demonstrate the importance of the interfidelity approach in navigating the influence of positionality on the adaptation process, especially as Hollywood and other national film industries embark on a globalised business model that not only controls representations of postcolonial nations but also has begun to appropriate the concept of 'writing back to the imperial centre' for its own purposes.

THE GLOBAL SPECTACLE OF *SLUMDOG MILLIONAIRE*

As the critical and commercial success of Boyle's *Slumdog Millionaire* indicates, Hollywood's adaptation of postcolonial texts without proper regard for the source material's politics has increased with the rise of transnational corporations consolidating national film industries over the past decade. Swarup's *Q&A* is a hybrid text that interrogates the cultural commodities of British imperialism and transnational corporate Empire. In addition to the aforementioned Faginesque gangster Maman – who is 'no angel' but gives his pickpocket gang 'two square meals a day' – and a Dickensian twist-ending, *Q&A* positions Ram Mohammad Thomas – a character whose name directly addresses the hybrid nature of India – as an often passive spectator (and occasional avenging angel) who relates stories of individuals destroyed by the intersections of India's colonial legacy and Empire's mass media influence as he justifies his grand-prize winnings on *Who Will Win a Billion?*[18] In the profound alterations to Swarup's novel during the adaptation process, *Slumdog Millionaire* substitutes a topical and universal politics for Swarup's presentation of India's hybrid status in the wake of British influence and its effect on the Post-Independence religious clashes that Ram Mohammad Thomas's name addresses.

However, Beaufoy's renaming of Ram Mohammad Thomas to Jamal in the film is merely the most obvious of the radical thematic and political alternations that occurred during the adaptation process. In usurping the conventions of the Victorian novel – a cultural product with a narrative form that mirrors, according to Said, 'the complex ideological configuration underlying the tendency to imperialism' – Swarup examines the lingering ramifications of British colonialism on an Indian culture now ingrained in the globalised world.[19] Setting the novel during the 1990s in the wake of India's 1991 shift from one state-run television station to a wave of satellite channels with international programming geared toward the middle class, Swarup captures a cultural moment that, according to Desai, 'went hand in hand with the shifts in the political economy of the larger nation-state and the rise of neoliberalism.'[20] Within this context, Swarup uses the novel's quiz show structure to present *Who Will Win a Billion?* host Prem Kumar as the film's primary antagonist, an Indian character whose corruption by the machinations of the globalised entertainment industry manifests itself in his serial beating and burning of sexual partners with cigarettes, including the prostitute Nita with whom Ram falls in love. Negotiating both the impact of British colonialism and the imperial endeavours of the globalised corporate Empire to consolidate power, Swarup's *Q&A* subverts the cultural formations of Empires past and present, creating a potential model for resistance and preservation of identity for a culture long suppressed by imperial force.

Slumdog Millionaire streamlines Swarup's narrative, positioning it within the conventions of the melodrama and gangster genres common to Hollywood and – as discussed in Chapter 4 – the increasingly Hollywood-influenced Hindi film industry. Boyle does allude to the 1970s 'Angry Young Man' Bollywood films of Amitabh Bachchan with protagonists who, notes Cavallero, 'tended to come from working-class backgrounds, endured a traumatic event in their childhood, and as adults, often confronted the corrupt individuals and practices that led to their childhood traumas.'[21] However, despite the depth of Boyle's international cinema knowledge, the case of *Slumdog Millionaire* demonstrates a pivotal, if not the first, instance of a globalised Hollywood transforming its former strategy of opposition in the studio system days of *Gunga Din* into a form of cultural imperialism.

Boyle indirectly alludes to this synergy between the two national film industries in Amy Raphael's career-spanning book of interviews written in the days after the adaptation's Oscar domination: 'I think the business side of Hollywood realises that Bollywood may well prove to be their saving grace, their chance to be reborn. The Indian film industry may well be their way out of the maze. They are all over there already, trying to set up companies.'[22] What results is an accented global Hollywood that merges national industries and conventions to trade in multicultural images and, in the words of Anjana Mudambi, 'superimposes a positive sentiment of common humanity onto these representations, shifting the focus from the 'other' to '(an)other,' an Oriental object of sameness and difference that functions for the benefit of the Western audience.'[23] While Boyle and Beaufoy somewhat retain Swarup's structuring of the narrative as an extended quiz show with flashbacks, the adaptation excises Swarup's central concerns with India's relationship to imperial forces, largely through the dilution of the narrative's revisions to Dickens' novel. Beaufoy expands Nita's role from a prostitute Swarup introduces near the end of the novel who alludes directly to *Oliver Twist*'s Nancy into the character Latika (Freida Pinto), Jamal's childhood true love and motivation for his

Figure 8.1 The illustrated copy of *The Three Musketeers* at Jamal and Salim's school.

quest to appear on the game show. Incidentally, he also adds a motif of three characters as 'The Three Musketeers' (Figure 8.1), a proclamation Jamal makes after recalling seeing the book when he and Salim were briefly enrolled in school before they are orphaned – and a change Boyle had reservations was 'old colonial' until he realised the story's popularity in India after travelling for the production.[24] Maman still retains his Faginesque qualities, but he serves an anecdotal presence, primarily included in the narrative for his assassination by Jamal's now brother Salim to serve as an introduction to Mumbai's criminal underworld. Beaufoy erases references to British colonialism to such an extent that Hindu-Muslim clashes such as the one that claims the life of Jamal and Salim's mother act as devices to propel the story forward, slices of life in a dangerous foreign country that its inhabitants must cope with daily. Similarly, the film positions Jamal's game show appearance on the Prem Kumar-hosted *Who Wants to be a Millionaire?* not only as a way of escaping poverty but also as a force that will forever unite him and Latika, a shift Mudambi views as global culture and economic capital 'saving' him.[25] In its universality so championed by Gritten, *Slumdog Millionaire* annihilates Swarup's political intentions, curtailing his interrogation of Indian identity in the wake of British colonialism and Empire and presenting India as a nation of others, insular and far removed from the imperial foundations and structures of the globalised world.

However, though Boyle's film warrants criticism over its problematic depiction of India and its people, an outright dismissal of *Slumdog Millionaire* as a neocolonial or even racist film overlooks its merits and provides little insight into either its motivation or the relative dearth of critical focus on its alterations to the source text. Produced within a society marked by globalisation and cultural fusion, Boyle's film operates under the presumption that, the world is, indeed flat, allowing for an unmitigated sense of cultural borrowing and diffusion in which British, American and Indian cultural attributes can traverse boundaries and become part of the same international mélange. Consequently, Boyle articulates a critique of the ramifications of globalised capital, mirroring Debord's concept of the spectacle of a transnational economic system, a mechanism of control that is 'at once united and divided'.[26] According to Debord:

> Just as the development of the most advanced economies involves clashes between different agendas, so totalitarian economic management by a state bureaucracy and the condition of those countries living under colonialism or semi-colonialism are likewise highly differentiated with respect to modes of production and power. By pointing up these great differences, while appealing to criteria of quite a different order, the spectacle is able to portray them as markers of radically distinct social systems. But from the standpoint of their actual reality as mere *sectors*, it is clear that the specificity of each is subsumed under a universal system as functions of a single tendency that has taken the planet for its field of operations. That tendency is capitalism.[27]

For a film steeped in quick cuts, warm colours and a general music-video aesthetic set to a soundtrack by Indian superstar A. R. Rahman and British-Sri Lankan rapper M.I.A., *Slumdog Millionaire* appears the perfect embodiment of the spectacle, showcasing India's difference under the guise of the sleek aesthetic of a global Hollywood. Yet, within this sense of difference, Boyle seeks to demonstrate the far-reaching and all-encompassing scope of global capital.

From the opening shots of the film, Boyle calls attention to the dissemination power of global capital using an Indian boy wearing a T-shirt bearing the title of his film (in English) as the opening credit. Similar to the logo shirts featuring sports teams, musical acts and other pop-culture symbols, Boyle establishes the pervasiveness of global capital, positioning the film not merely as an Orientalist depiction of a strange land, but as an examination of the sheer scope of the type of transnational corporate dominance executed by multinational entities such as NewsCorp, which owns the film's distributor, Fox Searchlight.[28] Though represented as a land of difference, India remains under the same capitalistic influences as the other 'Western' nations in which the film achieved its greatest popularity. Such an interest in depicting global capital's reach also extends to Boyle's choice to change the game show at the centre of the narrative from Swarup's fictional *Who Will Win a Billion?* to *Who Wants to be a Millionaire?*, a programme that originated in Britain, became a late-1990s cultural fad in America, and exists in numerous iterations across the globe. Boyle and Beaufoy's desire for this change was so strong that they negotiated with Celador, the owners of *Who Wants to be a Millionaire?*, and – in a sign of the pervasiveness of global media entities – co-financiers of their film to include its title, stage and theme music, agreeing to further villainise Prem Kumar rather than associate any corrupt activity with the conglomerate.[29] In the novel, the quiz show is run by an 'Indian subsidiary of NewAge Telemedia' for which Ram's win becomes a problem because such shows, as Neil Johnson, a representative of the company tells a police commissioner, 'have to follow a script. And according to our script, a winner was not due for at least eight months, by which time we would have recouped most of our investment through ad revenues.'[30] While Swarup's depiction of NewAge Telemedia calls attention to the influence of global capital, the subsidiary structure and exploitation of Mumbai's natives such as 'penniless waiter' Ram demonstrate a form of global capital modeled directly after the structure of British colonialism.[31] Seemingly less innocuous, Boyle's situation of the quiz show within the context of a media property that, despite existing in various iterations across the globe, remains a brand owned by one media entity exposes the tendencies of global capital that Debord discusses.[32] Though Kumar functions as the film's villain, he, like Jamal, is caught up in the machinations of those capital forces beyond his control, an Indian iteration of a game-show host performing the role of Anglo-American TV personality in order to attain some semblance of autonomy in a postcolonial India fully integrated into the globalised economy.

In what is perhaps the most drastic change from novel to film, Jamal (Dev Patel) works not as a waiter at the vaguely named 'Jimmy's Grill and Bar' but as a chaiwallah for the employees of a global telecommunications firm whose customer service line operates out of Mumbai. As Boyle details Jamal's time in the workplace, he largely focuses on the employees' efforts to seem like they are located 'right down the street' from the Scottish clients they service, holding group meetings to learn about Scotland's geography, history and contemporary culture. When Jamal sneaks onto a computer to find Latika's phone number as his superiors abandon their stations, he mistakenly takes a customer call. Awkwardly trying to pass himself off as a customer-service representative, he tells the Scottish woman on the other line that he lives near the 'Loch Big Ben', before hanging up on her and fleeing the call centre. Swarup often undertakes a similar view of globalisation, but his critiques remain rooted within the context of British colonialism such as the scene in which Ram, working at the home of an Australian diplomat inquires to the cook about a bra from Victoria's Secret:

> 'Who is Victoria?' I ask him.
> 'Victoria. I don't know any Victoria.'
> 'This bra belongs to Victoria. It even has her name. Where did you get it from?'[33]

Though discussing the international popularity of an American commodity, Swarup ties it to the lingering influence of the Queen (and the body of the Queen) who ascended the throne the same year Dickens published his novel, creating a markedly Indian discussion of the confluence of colonial and transnational corporate imperial endeavours. Through his focus on the reiteration potential of international commodities, the film differs from Swarup's depiction of global capital, more in line with Jameson's criticism of pastiche – 'the imitation of a peculiar or unique, idiosyncratic style, the wearing of a linguistic mask.'[34]

However, through undertaking a line of criticism more postmodern than embroiled within a complex web of postcolonial concerns, Boyle and Beaufoy ultimately rely on the same power dynamics (the focus on difference that Debord mentions) through their neglect of the singular manner in which British colonialism influences India's contemporary position within the globalised world. Such abandonment of Indian context and focus on global concerns explains the film's near absence of Dickens' source text. If, as Jean-François Lyotard contends, 'Narratives allow the society in which they are told, on the one hand to define its criteria of competence, and, on the other, to evaluate according to those criteria what is performed and can be performed within it', such an abandonment of colonial discourse's influence over the national narratives of countries such as India undercuts a description of the nation's individual concerns and contexts, leaving its representation to rely on relatively shallow depictions of various cultural attributes.[35]

In the case of *Slumdog Millionaire*, such decontenxtualisation is most apparent in the stark contrast between the novel and film's depictions of the Bollywood film industry. For Swarup, Bollywood acts more as a national film industry than a national cinema, a distinction, according to Desai, in which 'the latter is thought to represent the nation, which increasingly is seen as threatened from the inside (minorities) and from the outside by the hegemony of Hollywood . . .' and 'the former may be considered a commercial, profit-seeking enterprise that often is protected as a national industry against other international producers of similar commodities.'[36] Yet, as this book has discussed, Bollywood and Hollywood have increasingly embarked on coproductions relying on transnational corporate funds, a factor foundational to Swarup's depiction of the film industry. As a result of this concern with globalised media's reach on individual nations, Swarup's novel depicts Bollywood within the context of molestation to critique transnational influence on the film industry. As the novel's first chapter begins, Ram and his best friend Salim ready themselves to watch the latest film starring Armaan Ali at a movie palace, an activity that Ram speaks of with reverence:

> The third bell has sounded. The purple velvet curtain is about to be raised. The lights are progressively dimming, till only the red signs

> showing EXIT remain, glowing like embers in a darkened hall. Popcorn sellers and cold-drinks vendors begin to leave. Salim and I settle down in our seats.[37]

As they watch the film, a bearded man sits next to Salim, intermittently brushing his leg against the boy. However, Ram notices that the older man's advances soon become more direct:

> I see that the bearded man's left hand has moved. It is now placed in Salim's lap and rests there gently. Salim is so engrossed in the death scene that he doesn't register it. The old man is emboldened. He rubs his palm against Salim's jeans. As Armaan takes his last breaths, the man increases pressure on Salim's crotch, til he is almost gripping it.[38]

When Salim attacks the man and pulls off his fake beard, he escapes into the darkness of the theatre, leaving Salim in shock:

> . . . in that split second Salim and I have seen a flash of hazel-green eyes. A chiseled nose. A cleft chin.
>
> As the credits begin to roll over the screen, Salim is left holding a mass of tangled gray hair smelling vaguely of cologne and spirit gum. This time he does not see the names of the publicity designer and the PRO, the light men and the spot boys, the fight director and the cameraman. He is weeping.
>
> Armaan Ali, his hero, has died.[39]

Through this presentation of molestation, Swarup explodes the myth of the culture industry's unity, indicating how its corruption taints the lives of the icons so central to its function as well as those who passively consume it. As the novel's first association with Bollywood cinema, the molestation scene establishes Swarup's opposition to the totality of the culture industry that will eventually consume all of his characters.

Despite this traumatic experience, Salim and Ram eventually become immersed in the film industry. Salim never shakes his 'celluloid dreams of life in Mumbai' and works as a day player until Ram uses his quiz show winnings to launch Salim's acting career.[40] Ram works for fading Bollywood icon Neelima Kumari, witnessing her desperation, abusive relationship with Kumar, and eventual suicide while clutching her 'National Award for Best Actress. Awarded to Ms. Neelima Kumari for her role in *Mumtaz, Mahal*, 1985.'[41] Integrating Bollywood into his narrative in this context, Swarup undercuts his seemingly Neo-Victorian happy ending, positing that regardless of Ram's newfound wealth and opportunity for Salim, he and his friend remain entrenched in the network of an India contending with globalised economic imperialism.[42]

Excising Swarup's focus on Indian national film industries and revisionary Victorian ending, *Slumdog Millionaire* only directly references Bollywood twice: during the game show's opening question and during the film's end credit dance sequence in which the entire cast dances to Rahman's 'Jai Ho' in a train station.[43] In the first instance, Swarup's loaded molestation sequence is replaced by a dubious comedic flashback in which young Salim locks Jamal in a stall after losing a customer at a pay toilet. Hearing that Bollywood actor Amitabh Bachchan is approaching in a helicopter, Jamal jumps into the excrement pit and runs toward the mob of fans covered in faeces. Seemingly as arbitrary but much less offensive, the Bollywood item number in the wake of Jamal winning the quiz show and uniting with Latika serves as a final accent to the narrative, which, as Ajay Gehlawat writes, streamlines conceptions of the 'real India':

> Bollywood (as its moniker suggests) simultaneously references a multiplicity of identities and repudiates any one, essentialized form other than, paradoxically, one of impersonation. With *Slumdog*, then, we see popular Indian cinema which, in turn, impersonates popular Indian cinema, which, in turn, impersonates popular Western cinema.[44]

Instead of employing Bollywood convention's impersonation capabilities to directly represent repression of native cultures à la Nair's Bollywood item number in *Vanity Fair*, the sequence in Boyle's film serves merely as a surface presentation of the film's setting – demonstrating no connection to the narrative and existing as an example of global pastiche in a film otherwise concerned with exposing such tendencies.

While the Bollywood inspired closing sequence is the film's most obvious direct engagement with Indian culture, the most problematic aspect of the film, which Gehlawat refers to as 'an essentially British operation with the superficial veneer of hybridity' is its graphic depiction of Mumbai's slum neighbourhoods.[45] With his on-location shooting and the assistance of Indian codirector, Loveleen Tandan – who, incidentally, was largely unacknowledged by award nominations boards during the deluge of accolades Boyle received – *Slumdog Millionaire* cannot be accused of creating an entirely fabricated depiction of life in the slums. As Boyle said of Tandan and his first assistant director Raj Acharya, 'I'd have made so many mistakes [without them]. It has nothing to do with skill and everything to do with understanding the country.'[46] Boyle's reliance on his local crew aside, the film's greatest flaws lie in its evasion of contemporary and historical contexts, factors especially problematic considering the web of colonialism and global corporations present in Swarup's novel.

Despite the film's depiction of Mumbai's Dharavi slums as a space one can only escape through the salvation of a television quiz show, the neighbourhood is, as A. J. Sebastian writes, 'known for its vibrancy with entrepreneurial activities' that have recently led NGOs and state policy makers to 'acknowledge the residents of the slums as future taxpayers and property holders.'[47] Situating himself between Boyle's decontextualised imagery and Sebastian's revisionary optimism, Swarup presents the slums in a much less decisive manner, opting instead to focus on the network of various influences that have contributed to their existence. As the novel begins, the Indian producer of *Who Will Win a Billion?*, Billy Nanda, nervously remarks on the police's rough interrogation of Ram: 'I've enough problems on my plate already without having to be sued by a bloody civil rights NGO.'[48] In addition, before Maman's underling Sethji takes Ram and Salim from a juvenile home 'for training', Ram speaks of a field trip sponsored by 'An international NGO'.[49] For Swarup, NGOs serve a very similar function as the workhouses in *Oliver Twist*, meant to protect and create autonomous individuals, or 'future taxpayers', but easily corrupted because they operate under the same mechanisms that govern the controlling forces they seek to counteract – a critique Greene also presents through his depiction of the orphanage in *Boy Called Twist*.

Revelling in local colour yet marketed internationally, *Slumdog Millionaire* largely ignores the encroachment of neocolonial presences such as NGOs and global capital except for a scene in which an American couple respond to Jamal's satirical remark, 'You wanted to see a bit of the real India, here it is' after a recently robbed cabbie beats him. Outraged, the wife says to Jamal, 'Well, here is a bit of the real America, son' before her husband gives him a $100 bill. The scene coyly, although rather blatantly, calls into question the arbitrary pumping of money by American citizens into NGOs or institutions such as the IMF and, as Alpana Sharma, writes, 'the US's inflated self image as the richest, most powerful country in the world'.[50] But, it sacrifices a sustained critique of globalisation for a throwaway gag, differing sharply from Ram's asides in the novel such as, 'The smartly attired waiters at McDonald's look at me suspiciously but don't shoo me away. They can't turn back a customer in Levi's jeans, however scruffy he may be', and 'I shake and twist my wrist, hoping the others, particularly the girl, will notice that I am wearing a brand-new Kasio digital watch, made in Japan, with day and date, which cost me a whopping two hundred rupees in Palika Bazaar.'[51] Working from a perspective inside India, Swarup provides insight into how individual nations react to transnational influence while still contending with their colonial legacies, an aspect of the globalised world vastly simplified in *Slumdog Millionaire*.

Though one could attribute much of the glossing over of cultural nuance in *Slumdog Millionaire* to Boyle's Irish/British positionality, the most regressive aspects of the film occur through its focus on global India at the cost of sacrificing a detailed depiction of the British legacy in the nation, a factor that makes Boyle's gloss of the issue appear a lot more nefarious than he likely intended. As Swarup said repeatedly during interviews, *Q&A*, at least superficially, is an engrossing thriller that does not obviously showcase the wordplay and literary theory allusions of a writer like Rushdie. However, *Q&A* also relies heavily on the contexts of domestic religious clashes and wars between India and Pakistan stemming from the post-Independence dividing of the nation in 1947, references that Swarup does not explain to an audience unfamiliar with the nation's history. Detailing his first encounter with Salim, Ram reveals how his friend became an orphan:

> Last week in the cold and frosty month of January, an incident took place in the village's Hanuman temple. Someone broke into the sanctum sanctorum at night and desecrated the idol of the monkey god. The temple's priest claimed he saw some Muslim youths lurking near the grounds. *Bas*, that was it! The moment the Hindus heard this they went on a rampage. Armed with machetes and pickaxes, sticks and torches, they raided the homes of all the Muslim families . . . Before his very eyes they set fire to the hut. He heard his mother's shrieks, his father's cries, his brother's wails, but the mob would not allow anyone to escape. His whole family was burned to death in the inferno.[52]

Because of his childhood trauma, Salim expresses a deep hatred of all Hindus throughout the novel, leaving Ram to refer to himself as Mohammad when in the presence of his friend. Similarly, as Ram is holed up in an apartment basement with a Sikh military officer, Balwat Singh, who served in the 1971 war, he waits out the bombings of the 1999 Kargil War as the former soldier entertains his audience with stories of past battles: 'You see, we had heard that these Pakistanis, if they found the dead bodies of any Indian soldiers, would never return them to us, Instead they would deliberately bury them according to Muslim tradition, even if the Indian soldiers were Hindu.'[53] Throughout the anecdotal snapshots of Ram's life that the quiz show interrogation frames, Swarup presents the intricacies of the nation's tumultuous post-Independence history. Employing Ram's hybrid identity, Swarup allows his protagonist to not only transcend the nation's religious clashes and provide insight into often conflicting groups but also embrace a multifaceted, allegorical India evoking Jameson's national allegory and Harvey's cautions concerning imperial structures.

These religious clashes play an important role in Boyle's film, serving as the catalyst for the orphanhood of Ram and Salim (brothers in the film) as a Hindu mob bludgeons their mother to death in what Mudambi views as an allusion to 'the destruction of the Babri Masjid in Ayodhya in December 1992'.[54] Regardless, the violence comes suddenly and out of context, a two-minute chase sequence shot in the sun's glare that removes any British culpability for the religious conflicts and portrays India as a blistering nation of arbitrary violence – equivalent to the showdowns of the American western. Through the lack of attention Boyle pays to the historical context of the scene, the film recalls Jameson's discussion of historicity in the postmodern era. As Jameson writes, historicity is:

> . . . neither a representation of the past nor a representation of the future (although its various forms use such representations): it can first and foremost be defined as a perception of the present as history; that is, as a relationship to the present which somehow defamiliarizes it and allows us that distance from immediacy which is at length characterized as a historical perspective.[55]

In the case of period films such as Robert Altman's *M*A*S*H* (1971), David Lynch's *Blue Velvet* (1986), Robert Zemeckis' *Forrest Gump* (1994), Greta Gerwig's *Lady Bird* (2017), or even Paul Greengrass' *Bloody Sunday* (2002), history becomes collapsed into a reflection of the present, exposing the myths behind nostalgia and the enduring underbelly of the economic and social systems that remain largely unaffected by time. For a radical American filmmaker or even a British sympathiser for the Irish, such films can serve as potent commentaries on founding myths and fissures in nationalism. However, in the case of a film like *Slumdog Millionaire*, such a defamiliarisation with history only serves to perpetuate the structure of a colonial discourse relying on the timelessness of the Orient, the innate violence of the East, and, especially in the post-9/11 era, the enduring savagery of 'others' in a film that appears to be taking place in a contemporary setting largely because it includes virtually no historical or sociopolitical context.

Such a depiction of religious violence indicates the film's desire to utilise the postmodern and disregard the postcolonial, a symptom of what one could also attribute to Boyle and Beaufoy's tendency to, according to Sharma, 'reproduce the global perspective in how they efface their own perspectivising operation in the supposed unmediated production of *a street child's world from the street child's own point of view*.'[56] However, the disparity between Swarup and Boyle's depiction of India comes to fruition through the presence of one of Indian literature's most common tropes: the train. While Swarup neither directly mentions the importance of the railway to the British colonial imagination nor the mass executions aboard trains between India and Pakistan in the wake of Partition, his novel includes numerous scenes aboard trains, almost exclusively associated with acts of violence. Recalling the story behind his answer to the question 'Who invented the revolver?' Ram says: 'Train journeys are about possibilities. They denote a change in state. When you

Figure 8.2 Jamal (Tanay Chheda) and Salim (Ashutosh Lobo Gajiwala) ride the train to the sounds of M.I.A.'s 'Paper Planes'.

arrive, you are no longer the same person who departed.'[57] Intertwining individual autonomy with the quite literal changes in state through Ram's comment, Swarup alludes to the enduring legacy of the train murders during the Indo-Pakistan post-Independence migration, which Louise Harrington notes, 'became the medium through which the religious and ethnic violence could take form', a legacy of violence continued in Swarup's novel through scenes as various as Ram shooting a robber aboard the Western Express and Salim encountering a suicide bomber there.[58]

Yet, in adapting the novel, Boyle and Beaufoy reject the historical legacy of the train in India, instead employing it as the setting for the orphaned Jamal and Salim to escape from Maman's control and expand their financial ingenuity. Depressed over abandoning Latika after fleeing from Maman, Jamal stares into the horizon while sitting atop the train's roof. Consoling his brother, Salim tells Jamal 'Got to let it go' before telling him to 'Come on.' Jamal asks where, and Salim responds, 'I'm starving.' As the opening beats of M.I.A.'s 'Paper Planes' begin, Boyle cuts to an extreme long shot of the boys on the train's roof (Figure 8.2) before moving to a montage of them selling fruit on various trains and collecting money. For Boyle, the train appears as his protagonists' salvation as well as a primary method of including the shots of the Indian landscape that were the hallmarks of empire cinema filmmakers such as Lean and Korda. Removed from history and rooted in a globalised worldview, the film dilutes one of the most potent symbols of Britain's lingering colonial influence over India, bridging its Indian setting with an all-inclusive and transnational view as much a part of the ideology it appears to resist.[59]

Though *Slumdog Millionaire* and its source text may seem to have little in common with Greene's revision of Dickens in *Boy Called Twist*, the two films are indicative of vastly different methods of postcolonial representation and resistance at a time in film history when the concept of independent film is quickly changing. Regardless of Greene's piecemeal fundraising and Boyle's partial financing from several international production companies, the two films broadly fall into the category of independent cinema. While a film such as *Boy Called Twist* emphasises the local and attempts to actively engage a diverse population through a space of singularity, *Slumdog Millionaire* seeks to capitalise on an international audience by masking both its debt to colonial discourse and Hollywood convention through an overarching representation of a culture largely absent from Hollywood cinema, but of such appeal that official slum tours for Westerners became a niche industry in Mumbai after the film's release.[60] As a result of the complexities of transnational distribution, source text revisions and genre play no longer seem adequate methods of resistance, especially after their appropriation by global Hollywood. Yet, through viewing the singularity *Slumdog* feigns and *Twist* imagines through the lens of interfidelity, one can work toward methods to address the appropriation of the multicultural within transnational corporate discourse while asserting the singularity so foundational to contending with the colonial past and preserving national identity in the globalised world.

CONCLUSION

Streaming Interfidelities and Post-Recession Adaptation

Three months before *Slumdog Millionaire* began its awards-season journey, former Miramax and Warner Independent president Mark Gill gave his infamous 'Yes, The Sky Really is Falling' speech at the L.A. Film Festival's Financing Conference. Setting a tone that would prove eerily prophetic in the wake of the global recession to come a few weeks later, Gill lamented the gutting of the indie film industry that began earlier that winter with the dissolving of several specialty divisions of the major studios, including Paramount Vantage, New Line Cinema and his own Warner Independent. Given Paramount Vantage's success with 2008 Academy Award winners *There Will Be Blood* and *No Country for Old Men* and New Line Cinema's versatility as a studio that could reach art house audiences with Terrence Malick and David Cronenberg films, open blockbusters such as *Rush Hour 3* (2007), and bridge commercial and critical success with Jackson's *The Lord of the Rings*, such a trend demonstrated the dire situation of the industry. Two years after releasing the hit documentary *March of the Penguins* (2005) and George Clooney's *Good Night, and Good Luck* (2005), Gill found himself speaking to an audience of independent film producers with *Slumdog Millionaire* slated to go direct to DVD via Warner Bros. rather than on the books as his division's most successful release (it eventually sold to Fox Searchlight). Though Gill was not entirely apocalyptic – he correctly foresaw Netflix's role in niche entertainment and heralded a growing market interest in specialty films from Baby Boomers – he succinctly outlined the state of the industry: 'We're entering an era where the only films with any chance for success will be the $100 million-plus tentpoles, and reasonably priced films of some perceived quality.'[1]

As Gill predicted, that era is here and has significant implications for postcolonial filmmakers and the interfidelity approach. With the obvious exception of *Gunga Din*, the films under discussion in this project were all released between 1996 and 2008, a period that spans the rise of the global indie in film culture and the heyday of mini major and specialty division studios whose last gasp was the accidental blockbuster release of *Slumdog*. In a film industry experiencing the level of disruption Gill discusses in addition to the global recession's aftermath, Hollywood has all but halted the risk of politically intriguing misfires that do not connect with critics and fail to translate the name recognition of their source texts into box-office success. Such is especially true considering that 2008 also marked the sudden collapse of the DVD market that throughout the early 2000s all but guaranteed any film that was not a high-budget failure like Kapur's *The Four Feathers* would eventually turn a profit.[2] As a result of consolidation, recession and declining home-video revenues, Hollywood studios have shifted focus, providing fewer opportunities for such types of adaptation. By 2014, the situation had deteriorated to such an extent that journalist Jason Bailey proclaimed the midbudget movie dead and Hollywood in an era in which indie icons like John Waters, Steven Soderbergh, Spike Lee, and David Lynch could no longer get a studio movie financed, adrift in an industry with an average cost of over $107 million per picture, $50 million of which is typically dedicated to promotion and advertising.[3]

Adaptations of Victorian literature did not die in this climate; they merely conformed to market demands. The last decade has seen a reduced, though largely well-received, series of 19th-century-set stories and literature adaptations: Campion's *Bright Star*, Tim Burton's *Alice in Wonderland* (2010) and its James Bobin-directed sequel *Alice through the Looking Glass* (2016), Cary Joji Fukunaga's *Jane Eyre* (2011), Andrea Arnold's *Wuthering Heights* (2011), Mike Newell's *Great Expectations* (2012), Thomas Vinterberg's *Far from the Madding Crowd* (2015), Jon Favreau's *The Jungle Book* (2016), Nalluri's *The Man Who Invented Christmas*, and – though historical biopics – Stephen Frears' *Victoria & Abdul* (2017), and *The Young Victoria* (2009), which was written by Julian Fellowes (screenwriter of *Vanity Fair*) and directed by Jean-Marc Vallée. Most are modest coproductions primarily financed by British companies. They are also helmed either by well-established international auteurs such as Campion, Frears, Newell and Vinterberg or recent Sundance/Cannes/Toronto sensations Fukunaga, Arnold and Vallée following up their breakout films.

The exceptions are the three Disney-financed tentpoles that are also live-action remakes of the studio's classic animated properties. *Alice in Wonderland* and *The Jungle Book* grossed close to $1 billion each at the international box-office. Despite underperforming, *Through the Looking Glass* still made $300 million worldwide. All three films generated two-thirds of their revenue outside the US.[4] In contrast, *Jane Eyre*, which shares its lead with the *Alice* films in Australian actress Mia Wasikowska, grossed $34 million internationally, making it the most financially successful non-Disney adaptation listed. This is a higher take than the works discussed in this book apart from Jackson's *King Kong* and *Dracula 2000*, but for a film made on a significantly lower budget. Likewise, barring Judi Dench's supporting role as Mrs Fairfax, *Jane Eyre* featured no major stars to rival the name recognition of Kidman, Witherspoon, Hawke or Paltrow, which tabloids underscored when 'little-known' Wasikowsa became the highest-grossing movie star of 2010 on the strength of *Alice*'s success.[5] Although she has sustained a dynamic career working with Jim Jarmusch, Guillermo del Toro, Cronenberg, Chan-Wook Park, and Mia Hansen-Løve, Wasikowska and her career exemplify post-recession Hollywood: an acclaimed transnational performer ultimately subservient to blockbuster spectacle designed for global appeal and the endless future iterations firmly rooted in Murray's industrial centric model of adaptation.

As opposed to subversively adapting for the purposes of postcolonial resistance and revision, the blockbusters in the last decade's wave of Victorian adaptations operate under a strategy that, as Thomas Elsaesser writes, is 'all about connecting the past with the future' as a means to synergise commodities within the global service economy.[6] Given Disney's absorption of Marvel Studios, Pixar, LucasFilm and, as of late 2017, Fox Studios, it has successfully created a profitable postmodern through line from canonical texts to computer-generated narrative that, while significantly raising the bar for blockbuster quality, also serves as a cogent example of Hardt and Negri's conception of global imperialism. Apart from Campion, Nalluri and the French-Canadian Vallée, none of these adaptations' directors hail from postcolonial nations. Consequently, imperial critique is relatively absent in these adaptations, replaced by general narrative faithfulness, a focus on style and period authenticity and, in the case of Arnold's *Wuthering Heights* and Vinterberg's *Far from the Madding Crowd*, an enhancement of the source texts' feminist undercurrents. In contrast to the works under discussion in this study, these post-recession adaptations all met with positive critical reception with the exception of the *Alice* films, a testament both to the endurance of fidelity as a critical criterion and the comfort of the canon as a way of, to paraphrase McFarlane, letting the light back in on the Empire of late capital.

Despite this dearth of postcolonial perspectives behind the camera, the success of *Slumdog Millionaire* led to an increased focus on India for the remaining mini-majors as several adaptations (which less-than-coincidentally feature *Slumdog*'s Dev Patel) became modest hits and awards contenders. Fox Searchlight released *The Best Exotic Marigold Hotel* (2012) and its sequel, *The Second Best Exotic Marigold Hotel* (2015), based on British writer Deborah Moggach's 2004 novel *These Foolish Things* to a combined $210 million international gross, tapping into the 'grey pound, grey dollar' demographic for prestige releases.[7] Yet, the film, which follows a group of pensioners migrating from England to India to live their golden years in exotic surroundings, is awash with uninterrogated Orientalist representations that reinforce what Claudia Bell calls a 'collective imperial imagination'.[8] Also featuring Patel, Australian filmmaker Garth Davis' *Lion* (2016) proved a box-office hit with a $141 million worldwide gross and the last Best Picture Academy Award nomination for The Weinstein Company before the actions of its co-founder, Harvey Weinstein, ignited an international movement to combat sexual harassment in the entertainment industry. Based on the memoir by Indian-Australian Saroo Brierley, the film centres on a hotel management student adopted by an Australian couple (Nicole Kidman and David Wenham) who searches for his birth family in India after he was accidentally separated from them two decades earlier. Largely evading the criticisms that met *Slumdog* and *Marigold* due to its transnational scope, the film is perhaps the closest descendant of the works under discussion here, an adaptation with studio backing that, notwithstanding its universalism and humanist bent, makes gestures toward a global postcolonial identity.

Given the increased focus on blockbusters and the general upheaval of the film industry, the intersections of Victorian and postcolonial adaptation were much more prevalent on television, where the rise of Internet streaming services ushered in the 'Peak TV' landscape. Following *The Young Victoria*, Fellowes achieved the pinnacle of his success with the ITV Long Victorian drama *Downton Abbey* (2010–15), which enjoyed global success only arguably rivaled by the BBC's latest adaptation of *Sherlock* (2010–), starring Benedict Cumberbatch. As *Downton Abbey* ended its run, the BBC further mined colonial nostalgia for *Poldark* (2015–), its adaptation of Winston Graham's 18th-century-set historical novels and *Dickensian* (2015–16), a limited series based on the works of Dickens. ITV followed with *Victoria* (2016–), a series treading the same period as Fellowes' feature biopic. While these *Masterpiece* productions proved successful international exports, they, like their feature film counterparts, owe more to David Lean and Merchant Ivory than Mira Nair. Yet, television has also proven fruitful for postcolonial content as Campion and *Lion* director Davis shifted to serial drama for *Top of the Lake* (2013) and *Top of the Lake: China Girl* (2017), procedurals set in New Zealand and Sydney that openly examine Pacific Rim racial tensions and settler identity with financing from the BBC. Likewise, Canadian author Margaret Atwood has become a cottage industry – on streaming networks with Hulu's adaptation of *The Handmaid's Tale* (2017) and Netflix's miniseries of *Alias Grace* (2017). Both series were shot on location in Canada and, though the former was adapted and directed by Americans Bruce Miller and Reed Morano, *Alias Grace* is a collaboration between Canadian filmmakers Sarah Polley (*Away from Her* [2007], *Stories We Tell* [2013]) and Mary Harron [*I Shot Andy Warhol* [1996], *American Psycho* [2000]). As the lead in both *Top of the Lake* and *The Handmaid's Tale*, American actress Elisabeth Moss adds a transnational settler dynamic to both series that serves as an example and implicit critique of Hollywood's continuing global presence even in a time of industry disruption.

The rise of online streaming platforms has the potential to provide both additional avenues for postcolonial filmmakers to distribute their work and a demand for content that could prove a viable substitute for studio financing of the midbudget film. In the last few years, Amazon Studios and Netflix have stepped in to finance auteur-driven films from indie staples like Noah Baumbach, Todd Solondz, and Kenneth Lonergan and have provided some opportunity for postcolonial voices, including Amazon's release of *The Dressmaker* (2015), an adaptation of Australian writer Rosalie Ham's 2000 novel directed by the Sydney-based Jocelyn Moorhouse and starring Kate Winslet. However, such arrangements are precarious and may not be as stable as those that governed indie financing and distribution before 2008. As Chuck Tryon writes,

> Although a number of niche films have found an audience online, the persistent availability of movies through different VOD services has altered their value, often with the result that consumers have felt less urgency to own copies of individual films, taking away one of the primary sources of income for moviemakers.[9]

Almost a decade after the recession that dismantled Hollywood's business as usual, the postcolonial filmmaker working within the realm of the prestige adaptation has an untenable access to the platform.

Within this context, interfidelity's holistic approach and negotiation of specific relationships between texts as well as the production and industrial contexts in which films are produced is all the more vital. In bridging a contrapuntal reading of Victorian works with recent advances in adaptation studies, interfidelity fosters a space in which fidelity is a fundamental tool in tracing the development of Empire from colonial discourse to global capital's post-recession evolution and its effect on Hollywood production. Though best illustrated by direct application to films that share the context of those discussed in this study, interfidelity is applicable to the host of current adaptation situations that result from Victorian texts' continuing appeal and Hollywood's increasingly transnational make-up. In a field of often rigid boundaries between approaches, it serves as a universal adapter, dedicated to the politics of adaptation while foregrounding the transnational implications of the postcolonial filmmaker working in Hollywood.

Notes

Introduction

1. 1982: 8.
2. Scorsese 1995.
3. 2005: 153.
4. UNESCO PRESS 2009.
5. Ibid.
6. 1993: 291.
7. Desai 2004: 204–205.
8. Adesokan 2009: 602.
9. 2000: 300.
10. Okiche 2017.
11. McClintock and Galloway 2017.
12. 2014.
13. 2011: 4.
14. 2011: 30.
15. See Pamela Church Gibson's 'Otherness, Transgression, and the Postcolonial Perspective: Patricia Rozema's *Mansfield Park*.' *Janespotting and Beyond: British Heritage Retrovisions since the Mid-90s*. Eckart Voigts-Virchow (ed.), Tübingen: Gunter Narr Verlag, 2004. 51–64.
16. 2014: 112.
17. 1996: 8.
18. 1988: 89.
19. 2011: 215.
20. 2008: 14
21. Beyond superhero films, post-recession Hollywood has relied largely on franchise reboots and self-referential properties steeped in nostalgia such as *Jurassic Park/World, Star Wars* and *Power Rangers* as well as films like David Robert Mitchell's *It Follows* (2015) and the Netflix series *Stranger Things* (2017–). See Myke Bartlett's 'Rose-Colored Rear-View: *Stranger Things* and The Lure of a False Past', *Screen Education* 85 (2017): 16–25.
22. Leitch 2007:13.
23. 1988: 23.

24. 2015: 156.
25. 2006: 117.
26. 1968: 30.
27. 1998: 23.
28. 1988: 209.
29. 2001: 6.
30. 2008:187.
31. 2005: 355.
32. 2002: 63.
33. 2014: 125–129.
34. 1996: 111.
35. Crofts 1996: 27–28.
36. 2011:10.
37. I discuss Maddin's *Dracula* adaptation at length in 'Hybrid Empires: Hollywood Convention and the Settler Colony in Guy Maddin's *Dracula: Pages from a Virgin's Diary*', *Settler Colonial Studies*, 7.1 (Fall 2016): 94–110.
38. Limbrick 2010: 37–38.
39. Childs 1999: 188.
40. 2012: 135.
41. Jordan Vogt-Roberts' *Kong: Skull Island* (2017), the first film in the Warner Brothers reboot of the franchise, is even more intertextual in its postcolonial critique, making nods not only to the long cinematic history of Kong but also Francis Ford Coppola's *Apocalypse Now* (1979) as a loose adaptation of *Heart of Darkness*. Set in 1973, the film follows James Conrad (Tom Hiddleston) as US government agent Bill Randa (John Goodman) hires him to explore Skull Island at the end of the Vietnam War. After Kong attacks the expedition for dropping seismic mapping explosives, Lieutenant Colonel Preston Packard (Samuel L. Jackson) instigates an attack on the island to avenge the death of the men killed during the altercation. Conrad and pacifist photojournalist Mason Weaver (Brie Larson) must navigate the island's dangers and Packard's Kurtz-like madness with the help of castaway Hank Marlow (John C. Reilly), who has been stranded on the island since World War II.
42. (100% Pure New Zealand: 2005).

Chapter 1

1. Although *Gone with the Wind* would ultimately become and remains the most popular film in the history of American cinema, its December release led to its box-office dominance of 1940. *The Wizard of Oz* also later outgrossed *Gunga Din*.
2. van Wœrkens 2002: 285.
3. 1985: 75.
4. A fictionalised biography of the American outlaw, Henry King's *Jesse James* is a competent western also released in 1939 that was overshadowed by John Ford's convention-bending and stylistically inventive work in *Stagecoach* later that year.
5. Schatz 1981: 64–67.
6. Jaher and Kling 2008: 42.
7. 1973: 2–4.
8. Mast and Kawin 2003: 100–101.
9. 2015: 29.
10. RKO also released an adaptation of William Makepeace Thackeray's *Vanity Fair* titled

Becky Sharp in 1935. However, the Rouben Mamoulian-helmed project focused almost entirely on the war elements of the text, placing it much more in line with *Gunga Din* than with *Wuthering Heights*. The film was renowned for its use of Technicolor, but was otherwise a commercial and critical disappointment.

11. 2010: 2.
12. Jaher and Kling 2008: 37.
13. Mast and Kawin 2003: 242.
14. Moss 2004: 60. The film cost $2 million to make and, despite its box-office success, took years to turn a profit.
15. 2002: 90.
16. Stevens and Cronin 2004: 6.
17. 2005: 8.
18. The screenplay is by Joel Sayre and Fred Guiol, story by Ben Hecht and Charles MacArthur. William Faulkner also wrote an early, unused draft of the film.
19. Chowdhry 2000: 182.
20. 2008: 33.
21. 1890: lines 7–12.
22. 2010, 47.
23. 1993: 133–134.
24. 2002: 166.
25. 1890: lines 1–6.
26. 2008: 36.
27. Jaher and Kling 2008: 38.
28. Ray 1985: 58.
29. David O. Russell's Desert Storm drama *Three Kings* (1999) shares many similarities to Stevens' *Gunga Din* adaptation. It features a trio of American soldiers (George Clooney, Ice Cube, Mark Wahlberg) and their lower-ranked, comic-relief sidekick (Spike Jonze) searching the desert for Saddam Hussein's gold after finding a map in the waning days of the conflict. Though O. Russell's film is much more overtly political and sensitive in its representations of ethnicity, its concerns with American hegemony and status as a disguised western demonstrate the lingering influence of Stevens' film.
30. Jaher and Kling make a convincing case that the Guru bears strong associations to Benito Mussolini, a factor that taps into America's anxieties about participation in World War II.
31. With his Cockney accent, Cutter may also be the British character with the lowest social standing in the film.
32. Such is a common motif in Kipling, perhaps most prevalent in his 1889 poem 'The Ballad of East and West'.
33. 1985: 141.
34. 1981: 152.
35. Schatz 1981: 164.
36. Moss 2004: 57.
37. 1985: 67.
38. 1973: 167.
39. Jaher and Kling 2008: 37.
40. 2002: 87.
41. McDaniel 2004: 27.
42. Moss 2004: 60.
43. 1994: 142.
44. 1986: 67.

45. 2012: 25.
46. 1890: line 65.
47. Ibid., lines 75–85.
48. Dillingham 2005: 45–46.

Chapter 2

1. Joslin 2017: 3.
2. Williamson 2005: 5.
3. Martin 2012: 524.
4. Skall 2004: 98.
5. Weaver and Brunas 1990: 39.
6. The Hammer Dracula sequels are *The Brides of Dracula* (1960), *Dracula: Prince of Darkness* (1966), *Dracula Has Risen From the Grave* (1968), *Taste the Blood of Dracula* (1970), *Scars of Dracula* (1970), *Dracula A.D. 1972* (1972), *The Satanic Rites of Dracula* (1973), *The Legend of the 7 Golden Vampires* (1974).
7. Ascher-Walsh 2000.
8. Ibid.
9. White: 6.
10. Heidt 2011: 195.
11. Benjamin Svetkey, 'Monsters, Inc.', *Entertainment Weekly*, 26 March, 2004: 22.
12. *Dracula Untold* was an international success with a $217 million gross. It ignores Stoker completely, opting to focus on the mythological turn of Vlad the Impaler into the Count.
13. The film ultimately spawned only two tie-ins, an eponymous 2004 video game, and the animated prequel *Van Helsing: The London Assignment* (Sharon Bridgeman, US, 2004), which details Van Helsing's tracking of Mr Hyde that begins Sommers' film.
14. See Donald Wilson, 'Over There', *Film Comment* 25, no. 2 (January 2010): 52. While the standard ratio of domestic to international box-office grosses has been 1:1.5 for years, international receipts have steadily made up the majority of grosses of major studio films over the past half decade. Wilson cites domestic blockbusters such as *Avatar* (James Cameron, US, 2009) nearly tripling its record-breaking domestic gross internationally and *Harry Potter and the Half-Blood Prince* (David Yates, US/UK, 2009) earning double its domestic total as indicative of studios needing to 'rely even more heavily on simultaneous or near-simultaneous world-wide releases and their international receipts to recoup'. The article also discusses how Hollywood's domestic hits in 2009 such as Carlos Saldanha and Mike Thurmeier's *Ice Age: Dawn of the Dinosaurs* ($196 million domestic) and Roland Emmerich's *2012* ($165 million domestic) became enormous blockbusters for their studios ($688 million and $603 million respectively) and how even underperformers such as *Angels and Demons* (Ron Howard, US, 2009) and *Terminator Salvation* (McG, US, 2009) become solid hits when international grosses were factored in. 2004 was a landmark year for international grosses in Hollywood as underperformers and outright failures like *Troy* (Wolfgang Peterson, US), *The Day After Tomorrow* (Roland Emmerich, US), *King Arthur* (Antoine Fuqua, US) and *The Chronicles of Riddick* (Dave Twohy, US) broke even or turned a modest profit only after international release. Like the previously mentioned underperformers, *Van Helsing* was far less successful domestically than 2004 films such as *Spiderman 2* (Sam Raimi, US), *The Bourne Supremacy* (Paul Greengrass, US), and *Harry Potter and the Prisoner of Azkaban* (Alfonso Cuarón, UK/US), but it still ended the year as one of the highest-grossing films in the world. Wilson's article does not discuss home-video revenues.

15. Arata 1990: 623.
16. Ibid: 637.
17. Craft 1988: 169.
18. Stoker 1897: 106.
19. Ibid.
20. Wood 2015: 396.
21. 2005: 2.
22. 1983: 181–182.
23. *Dracula 2000* DVD commentary with Patrick Lussier and John Soisson 2001.
24. 1897: 325.
25. 2015: 71.
26. 2005: 32.
27. Holden: 2000.
28. 2007: 13.
29. 2004: 138.
30. Dyer 2014: 89.
31. 1835: 130.
32. 1986: 237, 245.
33. Houston 2005: 119.
34. 2002: 68.
35. 2012, 201–203.
36. Ibid. 211
37. 2003: 21.
38. 1897: 282.
39. 2011: 221.
40. 2006: 126.
41. Tomkins 2009: 72.
42. 1988: 69.
43. 1897: 60.
44. 1997: 101.
45. 1897: 168.
46. This is likely a reference to Langella's Count in *Dracula* (1979), who utters the line 'I don't drink . . . wine.'
47. 1897: 89.
48. 1897: 42–43.
49. Wood 2015: 395.
50. Leach 2011: 83.
51. Vatnsdal 2004: 121.
52. 2002: 9–10.
53. 2006: 149, 153.
54. 1990: 157.
55. Ibid. 51.
56. 2015: 52.

Chapter 3

1. 1996: 87.
2. Collins and Davis 2004: 22.

3. Danks, Gaunson, Kunze 2018: 2.
4. Ibid. 10.
5. Mayer and Beattie 2006: 3.
6. 2004: 26.
7. Gulpilil began his career in Nicolas Roeg's outback-set *Walkabout* (1971) and has appeared in most of Australian cinema's most iconic films, including Peter Weir's *The Last Wave* (1977), *Crocodile Dundee*, Phillip Noyce's *Rabbit-Proof Fence* (2002), John Hillcoat's *The Proposition* (2005) and *Australia*.
8. 2006: 22.
9. Eaton 2000: 158.
10. Ayan and Çubukcu 2009: 53.
11. Sanner 2005: 149.
12. 1989: 15.
13. *The Piano* is also a Victorian era-set film.
14. O'Regan 1996: 72.
15. Hughes 2006: 5 and Simmons 2006: 150.
16. The film won Academy Awards for Best Original Screenplay, Best Actress (Holly Hunter), and Best Supporting Actress (Anna Paquin). It was also nominated for Best Director as well as for its editing, score, costume design and cinematography.
17. 2009: 14.
18. Tinter 1991: 2–3.
19. Ibid. 3.
20. Ibid. 4–5.
21. 1881: 33.
22. Ibid. 183.
23. 2005: 149.
24. 1881: 104.
25. Ibid. 21.
26. Ibid. 247.
27. Ibid. 349.
28. Ibid. 68.
29. Ibid. 367.
30. Ibid. 106.
31. 2005: 6.
32. 1881: 106.
33. Ibid. 141.
34. Jöttkandt 2005: 19.
35. 1881: 197.
36. Ibid. 214.
37. Ibid. 153.
38. Ibid. 224.
39. Ibid. 219.
40. Ibid. 275.
41. Ibid. 238.
42. Ibid. 298.
186 Ibid. 376.
44. 2005: 53.
45. 1881. 83.
46. Ibid. 43.

47. Ibid. 160.
48. Ibid. 114.
49. Ibid. 245.
50. Ibid. 251.
51. Ibid. 409.
52. Ibid. 85.
53. Ibid. 109.
54. 2013: 172–173.
55. 1957: 50.
56. 2000: 163.
57. 2000: 179.
58. Ibid. 178.
59. 1997: 188.
60. 1996: 250–251.
61. 1998: 70.
62. 2004: 79.
63. 2006: 149.
64. 2009: 147.
65. 2013: 75.
66. 1881: 274.
67. 2006: 124.
68. 1987: 15.

Chapter 4

1. 2006: 152 and 2007: 1–2.
2. 2011: 49.
3. 2011:44.
4. Muir 2006: 207.
5. *Salaam Bombay!* ignited a storm of controversy during its international release largely because of its alleged exploitation of poor children, a similar criticism that faced Boyle's *Slumdog Millionaire*. See Gordon Collier's *Us/Them: Translation, Transcription and Identity in Post-Colonial Literary Cultures*. Atlanta: Rodopi, 1992.
6. 2001: 70.
7. Lowenstein 2000: 247.
8. 1980: 171.
9. 2007: 180. Perhaps the nadir of Nair's embrace of 'Hollywood style budgets' occurred in 2009 with the release of her Amelia Earhart biopic *Amelia* starring Hilary Swank. The film was such a critical and commercial failure with its $14 million gross that her career has not fully recovered.
10. 2001: 2201.
11. The only other female Indian filmmaker who has achieved similar success as Nair is Kenyan-born Gurinder Chadha, director of *Bhaji on the Beach* (1993), *What's Cooking?* (2000), *Bend it Like Beckham* (2002), *Bride and Prejudice* (2004) and *Angus, Thongs and Perfect Snogging* (2008). However, unlike Nair, Chadha's American success has been relegated to imported British films rather than a formidable Hollywood career.
12. Stevenson 1947: 7–8.

13. Stevenson 1947: 75.
14. Said 1993: 63.
15. 1993: 68.
16. 2006: 208.
17. Said 1978: 128.
18. 2004: 437.
19. 1994: 142.
20. Rao 2007: 58.
21. Ganti 2012: 343.
22. Rao 2007: 70; *Kites* was released in the US in 2010 as *Kites: The Remix*, a version of the film edited by Hollywood filmmaker Brett Ratner.
23. 2012: 350; *Lagaan* lost the Academy Award to Serbia's *No Man's Land* (2001) directed by Danis Tanović.
24. Rao 2007: 70–71.
25. Nair 2004: 12.
26. Shillingsburg 2001: 66–69.
27. 1848: 326.
28. 1848: 329, 362.
29. 1990: 143.
30. 1990: 143.
31. 2008: 42.
32. 2008: 42.
33. 2004: 76.
34. 1848: 578.
35. 1848: 430.
36. Nair 2004: 12.
37. 1848: 184.
38. 1848: 263.
39. 2010: 222; The Zulu conflicts were the subject of Cy Endfield's touchtone of Empire cinema *Zulu* (UK, 1964), starring Michael Caine.
40. 1848: 25.
41. 1848: 53.
42. 1848: 208–209.
43. Said 1978: 190.
44. 2011: 49.
45. 1848: 551.
46. 2010: 81.
47. Clarke 2008: 47.
48. 2010: 82.
49. 2002: 570.
50. Boehmer 2005: 44.
51. 1997: 240.
52. 1848: 22.
53. 2004: 418.
54. 1848: 685.
55. Clarke 2008: 53. Clarke talks at length in his article about the now-rare illustrations Thackeray included with the initial publication of *Vanity Fair*, which complicate the adaptation process. At the end of the novel, Thackeray included a sketch of Sedley on his knees begging Dobbin to save him as Becky hides behind a curtain with a dagger. Labeled,

'Becky's second appearance as Clytemnestra', it, according to Clarke, reintroduces Becky as Iphigenia's avenger (2008: 52–53).
56. 1848: 16.
57. 1848: 462.
58. Nair 2004: 47.
59. Lane 2004: 87.
60. Moya 2010: 74.
61. 2004: 73.
62. 2010: 42.
63. Roy 43.

Chapter 5

1. Rastegar 2015: 63.
2. 2002.
3. 2002: 49.
4. 2006: 94.
5. Tibbetts 2003: 311. A similar fate befell Sam Mendes' 2005 adaptation of Anthony Swafford's Operation Desert Storm memoir *Jarhead*. Reviews tended to eschew discussion of the film, instead criticising it for refusing to make ties to the ongoing War on Terror policy in Iraq.
6. Jensen and Karger 2002: 30.
7. 2005: 30.
8. Barthorp 1984: 47.
9. Steele 1983: 4–5.
10. Barthorp 1984: 84. Gordon also served during the Second Opium War in China, where he earned his nickname.
11. Warburg 1992: 127.
12. 2002: 168–169.
13. 1973: 3. The other five adaptations are as follows: J. Searle Dawley's silent *Four Feathers* (1915), René Plaissetty's British silent film from 1921, Cooper's 1929 Hollywood adaptation, Korda's remake of his own film *Storm over the Nile* (1955), and the 1977 British television movie that directly lifts scenes from Korda's film.
14. The Imperial Trilogy is comprised of *Sanders of the River* (1935), the story of a British officer in Nigeria and *Drums* (1938), an adaptation of Mason's India-set novel *The Drum* (1937).
15. Smyth 2004: 6.
16. 2004: 11.
17. Lowenstein 2008: 131.
18. Mason's novel was out of print for decades until Penguin reissued a new edition in 2001 after production on Kapur's adaptation was underway.
19. 2006: 8.
20. Wilkinson-Latham 1976: 36. Many uniforms during the campaign detailed in Kapur's film were a khaki colour. All were khaki-coloured during the time period of Korda's film, making the featured uniforms historically inaccurate. See Robert Wilkinson-Latham and Michael Roffe's *The Sudan Campaigns 1881–98*. London: Osprey, 1976.
21. 1978: 63.
22. 1902: 153.

23. 1994: 160.
24. 1902: 97.
25. 1902: 97.
26. 2004: 199.
27. 1902: 109.
28. 1902: 284.
29. 1994: 149.
30. 2005: 67.
31. 2015: 63.
32. 1994: 5.
33. 1973: 279.
34. 1994: 68.
35. 1985: 159.
36. Ibid.
37. 2003: 7.
38. 1902: 12.
39. 1902: 28.
40. 2009: 423.
41. 1902: 52.
42. 2003: 13.
43. 1902: 130.
44. 1902: 282.
45. Given the tumultuous production history of the film and 130-minute running time, this scene could easily have been cut by the studio.
46. 2005: 341–342.
47. Kapur directly addresses the issue of the other in the sequence in which Harry stops a French human trafficker and guide's beating of a slave prostitute. After an intense scene of voyeurism in which Harry watches her have sex with another slave, the prostitute bludgeons the trafficker to death with a rock, but stops her partner from killing Harry.
48. 2002: 176.
49. 2006: 46.
50. 1902: 87.
51. 2006: 21.
52. 1992: 12. It is important to note that Žižek's discussion of the purloined letter is taken from his analysis of Charlie Chaplin's *City Lights* (1931), a film that hinges on the tropes of blindness and recognition in a very similar way to all versions of *The Four Feathers*.
53. 1993: 159.
54. 1902: 61.
55. 2008: 38.
56. 2005: 40.
57. While Harry's muteness serves as a play on the 'mute native' discussed in the previous chapter, the fact that the muteness under discussion in Korda's film stems from the Mahdi's torture of other tribes complicates the dynamic.
58. 2002: 44.
59. 1902: 61.
60. 2010: 21.
61. 2008: 21.

Chapter 6

1. Pointer 1996: 3.

2. Petrie 2017: 185.

3. Pointer 1996: 3–7.

4. Christol 2015: 2. *Scrooged* screenwriter Mitch Glazer also wrote Cuarón's *Great Expectations*.

5. 2003: 10.

16. 1949: 206. Eisenstein also notes that one of D. W. Griffith's earliest films was an adaptation of Dickens' *The Cricket on the Hearth* (1909).

7. 1998.

18 8. 2003: 99. Ebert offered lavish praise for the film's style and performances, but, like Cuarón, cited fundamental script problems that hindered the film from being great. His archived review is here: https://www.rogerebert.com/reviews/great-expectations-1998 (last accessed 6 January 2018).

9. 2007:71.

10. 2013: 173.

11. 2006: 300.

12. Shaw, 2013: 121.

13. Lubezki has shot all of Cuarón's films as well as films for the Coen Brothers, Terrence Malick, and Cuarón's friend Alejandro G. Iñárritu. He won three consecutive Academy Awards for *Gravity*, Iñárritu's *Birdman, or The Unexplained Virtue of Ignorance* (2014) and *The Revenant* (2015).

14. Cuarón, Iñárritu, and Guillermo del Toro (*Pan's Labyrinth* [2006], the *Hellboy* franchise [2004, 2008], *Crimson Peak* [2015], *The Shape of Water* [2017]) have been dubbed the 'three amigos' in the US press since they dominated the international awards season in 2006 with *Children of Men*, *Babel* and *Pan's Labyrinth*.

15. 2013: 167–168.

16. 2014: 232.

17. 2004: 171.

18. Lucas: 1992, 126–127.

19. Romero 1995: 797.

20. Nericcio 2007: 59.

21. Katz 2003: 95–96.

22. 2014: 68.

23. 2015: 235.

24. 1995: 798.

25. 2013: 89.

26. 2014: 1040.

27. Antinucci 2006: 317.

28. 1983: 11–12.

29. Hixson 2013: 88.

30. 2004: 454.

31. 2004: 447.

32. 2011: 411.

33. 1973: 39–40.

34. 2000: 64.

35. 1861: 57.

36. 1861: 59.

37. Ibid. 71.
38. Ibid. 91.
39. Ibid. 91.
40. Ibid.
41. Ibid. 308.
42. 1989: 217.
43. 1861: 329.
44. Ibid. 334.
45. 1993: xvi.
46. 1861: 482.
47. Ibid. 478.
48. Ibid. 479.
49. Bertellini 2005: 210–211.
50. 1997: 10.
51. 2006: 102.
52. Ibid. 105.
53. 1987: 292.
54. 2000: 192.
55. Katz: 2003: 99.
56. 2005: 88.
57. 1973: 163–164.
58. 2005: 69.
59. 2006: 307.
60. Boehmer 2005: 100.
61. 2005: 102.
62. 2008: 182.

Chapter 7

1. 2006: 408.
2. Cluver and Orkin 2009: 1191.
3. Meintjes and Giese 2006: 421.
4. Van der Heijden and Swartz 2010: 46.
5. Harvey 2006: 51–52.
6. Brown 2016: 170.
7. 2013: 45.
8. 1837: 290.
9. 1998: 8.
10. 1837: 18.
11. 2004: 128.
12. 2006: 49.
13. 2004: 128.
14. Hardt and Negri 2004: 135.
15. Dicks 2007: 69.
16. 2003: 2.
17. *Proudly South African* 2004.
18. 1996: 103–104.
19. 2006: 36.

20. Ibid.
21. Hood's film often stereotypes Black South Africans as innately violent as it revels in the impoverished communities in which it is set. Likewise, though *District 9* allegorises Apartheid through human engagements with aliens located in camps by the government, it retains racist depictions of blacks, most notably in its characterisation of Nigerians as gangs of cannibals. In addition, it makes no reference to the lingering aspects of Apartheid as its white and black characters are united in their prejudices against the aliens.
22. Lean's film differs from the novel primarily through excising Rose Maylie and, by consequence, endowing Mr Brownlow with a larger role in the narrative in which he never leaves for the West Indies to search for Monks.
23. Ashcroft 2000: 190.
24. Peters 2000: 8.
25. Peters 2000: 43.
26. 1837: 33.
27. 1837: 52.
28. 1980: 3.
29. 1837: 39.
30. 2000: 36.
31. 1837: 67–68, 73.
32. 1994: 123.
33. Dicks 2006: 68.
34. Dickie and Oliver's final exchange almost exactly mirrors the one between Oliver and Dick in the novel: 'I hope so,' replied the child. 'After I am dead, but not before. I know the doctor must be right, Oliver, because I dream so much of Heaven, and Angels, and kind faces that I never see when I am awake. Kiss me,' said the child, climbing up the low gate, and flinging his little arms round Oliver's neck. 'Good-b'ye, dear! God bless you!' (p. 59).
35. Dickens' Oliver is nine at the beginning of the novel whereas Twist is eleven.
36. Though Dickie is an orphan friend of Oliver in the novel, the name may also allude to Lord Mountbatten, last Viceroy of India, who also went by the nickname 'Dickie'. See Stanley Wolpert's *Shameful Flight: The Last Years of the British Empire in India*. Oxford: Oxford University Press, 2006.
37. Harvey 2006: 41. See Harvey's discussion of the Cancun Conference in *Spaces of Global Capitalism*. New York: Verso, 2006.
38. 2008: 94.
39. 1837: 65.
40. Stone 1993: 450.
41. Brosh 2008: 90.
42. 2001:118. Guinness' prosthetic nose caused a huge public outcry in Britain and the US that was again revisited when the stage and film adaptation of *Oliver!* gained popularity in the 1960s. See Michael Sragow's liner notes for the Criterion Collection release of *Oliver Twist*.
43. 2003: 159.
44. 1837: 69.
45. 2004: 50. hooks' comments could also apply to the problematic depictions of Nigerians in Blomkamp's *District 9*, though their status as cannibals is much more racially problematic than Greene's Fagin and his gang.
46. 1837: 297.
47. Ibid. 259.
48. The bar scene is appropriated from Lean's film adaptation. Similar to Greene's adaptation,

Sikes is disgusted by Fagin's presence at the tavern and exhibits an open anti-Semitism throughout the film.
49. 1967: 110.
50. 1837: 329.
51. Mason 2002: 7.
52. Mandivenga 2000: 351.
53. 1997: 141.
54. Dangor 1997: 144.
55. 1837: 76–78. It is worth mentioning that Dickens sarcastically refers to Fang as 'the presiding Genii' during Oliver's trial scene, an example of the inherent Orientalist stereotypes embedded within colonial discourse that Said discusses (80).
56. Clayton 2003: 148.
57. 2008: 583.
58. Achmat Dangor's South African novel *Bitter Fruit* (2001) shares a similar movement between family life and criminals for its protagonist.
59. 2002: 225.
60. 1837: 340.
61. 2007: 69.
62. 2011:153.

Chapter 8

1. 2009.
2. Ibid.
3. Ibid.
4. Ibid.
5. Gehlawat 2009: 7–8.
6. 2017: 836.
7. 2012: 10.
8. 2010: 475.
9. Jeffries 2009. Aside from *Slumdog Millionaire*'s depiction of a Hindu massacre of Muslims, Swarup had few objections to Boyle and Beaufoy's alterations to his source text, even supporting the film's use of 'slumdog' and the changing of Ram's name and religious affiliation.
10. 1992: 131.
11. Like Roy, Rushdie also publicly criticised Boyle's film in 2009, both in a lecture at Emory University and in an editorial for *The Guardian* entitled 'A Fine Pickle'.
12. 1992: 128.
13. 2011: 73.
14. Raphael 2011: 292.
15. 2006: 49.
16. 2006: 49.
17. 2013: 5.
18. 2005: 91.
19. 1993: 70.
20. 2011: 80.
21. 2017: 839.
22. 2011: 292.

23. 2013: 280–281.
24. Raphael 2011: 291.
25. 2013: 283.
26. 1967: 36–37.
27. Ibid.
28. Fox Searchlight is the specialty division of 20th Century Fox, which specialises in art-house releases with mass audience appeal such as Mark Webb's *(500) Days of Summer* (US, 2009), Jason Reitman's *Juno* (US, 2007), Nair's *The Namesake* (US/India, 2007), Jonathan Dayton and Valerie Faris's *Little Miss Sunshine* (US, 2006), and Alexander Payne's *Sideways* (US, 2004) in addition to all of Boyle's films since 2003.
29. Cavallero 2017: 843–844.
30. 2005: 7.
31. 2005: 1.
32. Over the past few years, Boyle has exhibited an increased concern with globalisation in his films from his examination of the fall of British nationalism in the age of the Euro in *Millions* (UK, 2004) to the corrupt corporation allegory of his science-fiction film *Sunshine* (US/UK, 2007) to the juxtaposition of landscape shots and television commercials in *127 Hours* (US, 2010).
33. 2005: 115.
34. 1991: 17.
35. 1984: 20.
36. 2004: 54.
37. 2005: 19.
38. Ibid. 30.
39. Ibid. 31
40. Ibid. 85.
41. Ibid. 232. The scene is also an allusion to Rushdie's *Midnight's Children* (1981).
42. I discuss the relationship between molestation and cinema in postcolonial Indian literature at length in the essay, 'Imperial Gazes, Hollywood Predators: A Cinema of Molestation in Postcolonial Indian Literature', in David Gallagher (ed.) *World Cinema and the Visual Arts* (New York: Anthem, 2012).
43. The song shares its name with the non-profit organisation The Jai Ho Trust, which provided a home and financial support for the film's child stars (Raphael 2011: 315–317).
44. 2009: 5.
45. Ibid. 8.
46. Raphael 2011: 284.
47. 2009: 901–902.
48. 2005: 11.
49. Ibid. 83.
50. 2012: 200.
51. 2005: 299, 151.
52. Ibid. 77.
53. Ibid. 173.
54. 2013: 281.
55. 1991: 284.
56. 2012: 203.
57. 2005: 153.
58. 2007: 299.

59. Trains also serve as a central trope in Wes Anderson's 2007 film *The Darjeeling Limited* (US), which uses them to satirise the enduring legacy of Orientalist thought among the educated upper-classes of American society.
60. Mendes 2010: 248.

Conclusion

1. Gill 2008.
2. Tyron 2013: 8.
3. Bailey 2014.
4. All numbers are from Boxofficemojo.com
5. Bull and Thompson 2010.
6. 2012: 279.
7. 2016: 1983.
8. Ibid. 1980.
9. 2013: 3

Bibliography

Abbott, Stacey (2006), 'Embracing the Metropolis: Urban Vampires in the American Cinema of the 1980s and 90s', in Peter Day (ed.), *Vampires: Myths and Metaphors of Enduring Evil,* Amsterdam: Rodopi, pp. 125–142.

Adesokan, Akin (2009), 'Practising "Democracy" in Nigerian Films', *African Affairs* 108.433, pp. 599–619.

Agger, Michael (2004), 'Vanity Fair, Bright Future', review of *Vanity Fair*, director Mira Nair, *Film Comment*, September/October, pp. 72–73.

Ahmad, Aalya (2015), 'Blood in the Bush Garden: Indigenization, Gender, and Unsettling Horror', in Gina Freitag and André Louiselle (eds), *The Canadian Horror Film: Terror of the Soul,* Toronto: University of Toronto Press.

Ahmad, Aijaz (1992), *In Theory: Classes, Nations, Literatures*, New York: Verso.

Andrew, Dudley (2011), 'The Economies of Adaptation', in Colin MacCabe, Rick Warner, Kathleen Murray (eds), *True to the Spirit: Film Adaptation and the Question of Fidelity* Oxford: Oxford University Press, pp. 27–40.

Anesko, Michael (2000), 'The Consciousness on the Cutting Room Floor: Jane Campion's *The Portrait of a Lady*', in John R. Bradley (ed.), *Henry James on Stage and Screen,* New York: Palgrave, pp. 178–189.

Antinucci, Raffaella (2006),'Alfonso Cuarón's "Late Experimentations": Dickens and Post-modernism', in Francesco Marroni (ed.), *Great Expectations nel laboratorio di Charles Dickens*, Rome: Aracne, pp. 293–317.

Appadurai, Arjun (2004), 'Commodities and the Politics of Value', in Bill Ashcroft, Gareth Griffiths, and Helen Tiffin (eds) *The Postcolonial Studies Reader* 2nd edition, London: Routledge, pp. 417–420.

Arata, Stephen D. (1990), 'The Occidental Tourist: *Dracula* and the Anxiety of Reverse Colonization', *Victorian Studies*, 33, no. 4, pp. 621–645.

Ascher-Walsh, Rebecca and Scott Brown (2000), 'Neck & Neck,' *Entertainment Weekly*, 17 November, Issue 569.

Ashcroft, Bill (2000), 'Primitive and Wingless: The Colonial Subject as Child', in Wendy S. Jacobson (ed.), *Dickens and the Children of Empire*, New York: Palgrave, pp. 184–202.

Ashcroft, Bill, Gareth Griffiths, and Helen Tiffin (1989), *The Empire Writes Back: Theory and Practice in Post-Colonial Literature,* London: Routledge.

Ayan, Meryem and Feryal Çubukcu (2009), 'Adapting Americas in Novels Adapted for Films', *Buletinul* 56.2, pp. 51–60.

Bailey, Jason (2014), 'How the Death of Mid-Budget Cinema Left a Generation of Iconic Filmmakers MIA', *Flavorwire* 9 December, <http://flavorwire.com/492985/how-the-death-of-mid-budget-cinema-left-a-generation-of-iconic-filmmakers-mia/2> (last accessed 3 January 2018).

Barthorp, Michael (1984), *War on the Nile: Britain, Egypt and the Sudan 1882–1898*, Poole: Blandford Press.

Bell, Claudia (2016), '*The Best Exotic Marigold Hotel*: International Retirement Migration on Film', *Ageing & Society*, 37: 1975–1986.

Bertellini, Giorgio (2005), 'Black Hands and White Hearts: Southern Italian Immigrants, Crime, and Race in Early American Cinema', in Lee Grieveson, Esther Sonnet, and Peter Stanfield (eds), *Mob Culture: Hidden Histories of the American Gangster Film*, New Brunswick, NJ: Rutgers University Press, pp. 207–237.

Bhabha, Homi (1994), *The Location of Culture*, London: Routledge.

Black, Jeremy (2010), *The Battle of Waterloo*, New York: Random House.

Bluestone, George (1957), *Novels into Film*, Baltimore: Johns Hopkins University Press.

Boddy, Janice (2005), 'Purity and Conquest in the Anglo-Egyptian Sudan', in Adeline Marie Masquelier (ed.), *Dirt, Undress, and Difference*, Bloomington: Indiana University Press, pp. 168–188.

Boehmer, Elleke (2005), *Colonial and Postcolonial Literature: Migrant Metaphors,* 2nd edition, London: Oxford University Press.

Boy Called Twist (2004), film, directed by Tim Greene, South Africa: Peace Arch Trinity.

Breakfast on Pluto (2005), film, directed by Neil Jordan, UK/USA: Sony Pictures Classics.

Brinded, Nicolas (2014), 'Exceptionalist Discourse and The Colonization of Sublime Spaces: Alfonso Cuarón's *Gravity*, Ridley Scott's *Prometheus* and Thomas Cole's *The Oxbow*', *European Journal of American Culture* 33: 3, pp. 223–236.

Brosh, Liora (2008), *Screening Novel Women: From British Domestic Fiction to Film*, New York: Palgrave.

Brown, Julian (2016), *The Road to Soweto: Resistance and the Uprising of 16 June 1976*, Woodbridge: James Currey.

Brown, Mark (2002), 'Crime, Governance and the Company Raj: The Discovery of Thugee', *British Journal of Criminology*, 42.1, pp.77–95.

Bull, Sarah and Paul Thompson (2010), 'Little-Known Actress Mia Wasikowska Beats Robert Downey Jr. and Daniel Radcliffe in list of Highest Grossing Actors', *The Daily Mail,* 22 December <http://www.dailymail.co.uk/tvshowbiz/article-1340919/Mia-Wasikowska-beats-Robert-Downey-Jr-Daniel-Radcliffe-Forbes-list-highest-grossing-actors.html#ixzz553txPNTL> (last accessed 20 November 2017).

Byrd, Jodi A. (2011), *The Transit of Empire: Indigenous Critiques of Colonialism,* Minnesota University Press.

Carroll, Nöel (1988), *Mystifying Movies: Fads and Fallacies in Contemporary Film Theory,* New York: Columbia University Press.

Cavallero, Jonathan J. (2017), 'Transnational Adaptation: *Q&A*, *Slumdog Millionaire*, and Aesthetic and Economic Relationships Between Bollywood and Hollywood', *The Journal of Popular Culture* 50.4, Fall 2017, pp. 835–854.

Chatman, Seymour (1990), *Coming to Terms: The Rhetoric of Narrative in Fiction and Film*, Ithaca: Cornell University Press.

Chérif, Mustapha and Teresa Lavender Fagan (trans) (2008), *Islam & the West: A Conversation with Jacques Derrida*, Chicago: University of Chicago Press.

Childs, Peter (1999), 'Introduction', in Peter Childs (ed.), *Post-Colonial Theory and English Literature: A Reader*, Edinburgh: Edinburgh University Press, pp. 1–20.

Chowdhry, Prem (2000), *Colonial India and the Making of Empire Cinema: Image, Ideology and Identity*, Manchester: Manchester University Press.

Christensen, Tim (2012), 'The Unbearable Whiteness of Being: Misrecognition, Pleasure, and White Identity in Kipling's *Kim*', *College Literature*, 39.2, pp. 9–30.

Christol, Florent (2015), 'Screening *A Christmas Carol* (Dickens, 1843): Adaptation as Completion', *Cahiers victoriens et édouardiens*, 82, pp. 2–12.

Clarke, Micael M (2008), 'Celluloid Satire, or the Moviemaker as Moralist: Mira Nair's Adaptation of Thackeray's *Vanity Fair*', in David L. Kranz and Nancy C. Mellerski (eds), *In/Fidelity: Essays on Film Adaptation*, Cambridge: Cambridge Scholars Publishing, pp. 38–59.

Clayton, Jay (2003), *Charles Dickens in Cyberspace: The Afterlife of the Nineteenth Century Postmodern Culture*, London: Oxford University Press.

Clover, Carol (1992), *Men, Women, and Chainsaws: Gender in the Modern Horror Film*, Princeton: Princeton University Press.

Cluver, Lucie and Mark Orkin (2009), 'Cumulative Risk and AIDS-Orphanhood: Interactions of Stigma, Bullying, and Poverty on Child Mental Health in South Africa', *Social Science and Medicine* 69, pp. 1186–1193.

Collins, Felicity and Therese Davis (2004), *Australian Cinema after Mabo*, Cambridge: Cambridge University Press.

Crofts, Stephen (1996), 'Reconceptualizing National Cinema/s', in Alan Williams (ed.), *Film and Nationalism*, New Brunswick, NJ: Rutgers University Press, pp. 25–51.

Dangor, Suleman (1997), 'The Expression of Islam in South Africa', *Journal of Muslim Minority Affairs*, 17.1, pp. 141–152.

Danks, Adrian (2018), Stephen Gaunson, and Peter C. Kunze, 'Where I'm Calling From: An Australian-American Cinema?', in Adrian Danks, Stephen Gaunson and Peter C. Kunze (eds), *American-Australian Cinema: Transnational Perspectives*, New York: Palgrave Macmillan, pp. 1–19.

Davis, Thadious M. (2012), *Southscapes: Geographies of Race Religion and Literature*, Chapel Hill, University of North Carolina Press.

Desai, Jigna (2004), *Beyond Bollywood: The Cultural Politics of South Asian Diasporic Film*, London: Routledge.

Desai, Jigna (2011), 'Pulp Frictions', in Lisa Lau and Ana Cristina Mendes (eds), *Re-orientalism and South Asian Identity Politics: The Oriental Other Within*, London: Routledge, pp. 72–88.

Despotopoulou, Anna (2006), 'Girls on Film: Postmodern Renderings of Jane Austen and Henry James', *Yearbook of English Studies*, 31.6, pp.115–130.

Dever, Carolyn (1998), *Death and the Mother from Dickens to Freud: Victorian Fiction and the Anxiety of Origins*, Cambridge: Cambridge University Press.

Dickens, Charles [1861] (1993), *Great Expectations*, Oxford: Oxford University Press.

Dickens, Charles [1837–8] (1993), *Oliver Twist*, New York: Norton.

Dicks, Joan (2007), review of *A Boy Called Twist*, *Dickensian* 103.471, pp. 67–70.

Dillingham, William B. (2005), *Rudyard Kipling: Hell and Heroism*, New York: Palgrave.

Dracula 2000 (2000), film, directed by Patrick Lussier, US: Miramax/Dimension, 2000.

Dracula: Pages from a Virgin's Diary (2004), film, directed by Guy Maddin, CA: Tartan.

Dyer, Keith (2014), 'The Empire of God, the Postcolonial Jesus, and Postapocalyptic Mark', in Mark Brett and Jione Havea (eds), *Colonial Contexts and Postcolonial Theologies Storyweaving in the Asia-Pacific*, New York: Palgrave, pp. 81–97.

Eaton, Mark (2000), 'Henry James Films as Middlebrow Culture', in John R. Bradley (ed.), *Henry James on Stage and Screen*, New York: Palgrave, pp. 157–176.

Eisenstein, Sergei [1949] (1977), *Film Form: Essays in Film Theory*, Orlando: Harcourt, Brace, Jovanovich.

Elsaesser, Thomas (2012), *The Persistence of Hollywood,* London: Routledge.

Fanon, Frantz, Constance Farrington (trans) (1993), *The Wretched of the Earth*, New York: Grove.

Fish, Stanley (1980), *Is There a Text in This Class?: The Authority of Interpretive Communities*, Cambridge, MA: Harvard University Press.

'Following *King Kong* in New Zealand' (2005), *100% Pure New* Zealand, 11 December, <http://media.newzealand.com/en/story-ideas/following-king-kong-in-new-zealand/> (last accessed 10 October 2017).

The Four Feathers (1939), film, directed by Zoltan Korda, UK: MGM.

The Four Feathers (2002), film, directed by Shekhar Kapur, UK/USA: Paramount.

Fox, Alistair (2011), *Jane Campion: Auteurship and Personal Cinema,* Bloomington: University of Indiana Press.

Freedgood, Elaine (2006), *The Ideas in Things: Fugitive Meaning in the Victorian Novel*, Chicago: University of Chicago Press.

Friedman, Stanley (1989), 'Ridley's *Tales of the Genii* and Dickens's *Great Expectations. Nineteenth-Century Literature*, 44.2, pp. 215–218.

Ganti, Tejaswini (2012), 'No Longer a Frivolous Singing and Dancing Nation of Movie-Makers: The Hindi Film Industry and Its Quest for Global Distinction', *Visual Anthropology*, 25, pp. 340–365.

Gasher, Mike (2002), *Hollywood North: The Feature Film Industry in British Columbia,* Vancouver: University of British Columbia Press.

Gehlawat, Ajay (2009), 'Slumdog Comprador: Coming to Terms With the *Slumdog* Phenomenon', *CineAction*, 78, pp. 2–9.

Gill, Mark (2008), 'Yes, The Sky Really is Falling', *Indiewire,* 22, <http://www.indiewire.com/2008/06/mark-gill-yes-the-sky-really-is-falling-72174/> (last accessed 7 September 2017).

Gilmour, David (2002), *The Long Recessional: The Imperial Life of Rudyard Kipling*, New York: Farrar, Straus, and Giroux.

Gilroy, Paul (2005), *Postcolonial Melancholia*, New York: Colombia University Press.

Gleiberman, Owen (2002), review of *The Four Feathers*, *Entertainment Weekly,* 15 September.

Gleiberman, Owen (1998), review of *Great Expectations*, *Entertainment Weekly,* 30 January.

Goldsberry, Kirk (2014), 'All the World's a Stage: How International Box Office Is Changing the American Blockbuster Economy', *Grantland,* 25 April, <http://grantland.com/hollywood-prospectus/all-the-worlds-a-stage-how-international-box-office-is-changing-the-american-blockbuster-economy/> (last accessed 1 July 2017).

Gordon, Rebecca M. (2003), 'Portraits Perversely Framed: Jane Campion and Henry James', *Film Quarterly*, 56.2, pp. 14–24.

Great Expectations [1946] (1998), film, directed by David Lean, UK: Criterion Collection.

Great Expectations [1998] (1999), film, directed by Alfonso Cuarón, US: 20nd Century Fox.

Gritten, David (2009), '*Slumdog Millionaire*: The First Film of the Obama Era', *The Daily Telegraph,* 12 January, <https://www.telegraph.co.uk/culture/film/4224827/Slumdog-Millionaire-the-first-film-of-the-Obama-era.html> (last accessed 5 April 2018).

Grossman, Jonathan H. (2015), 'Living the Global Transport Network in *Great Expectations*', *Victorian Studies*, 57.2, pp. 225–250, <http://www.jstor.org/stable/10.2979/victorianstudies.57.2>.225 (last accessed 1 November 2015).

Gubar, Susan (1997), *Racechanges: White Skin, Black Face in American Culture*, Oxford: Oxford University Press.

Gunga Din [1939] (2004), film, directed by George Stevens, USA: Warner Bros.

Hall, Donald E. (1994), 'Introduction', in Donald E. Hall (ed.), *Muscular Christianity: Embodying the Victorian Age*, Cambridge: Cambridge University Press, pp. 3–16.

Hall, Stuart (1997), 'The Spectacle of the 'Other'', in Stuart Hall (ed.), *Representation: Cultural Representations and Signifying Practices*, London: Sage, pp. 223–290, 435–438.

Hall, Stuart (2004), 'Cultural Identity and Diaspora', in Bill Ashcroft, Gareth Griffiths, and Helen Tiffin (eds), *The Postcolonial Studies Reader*, 2nd edition, London: Routledge, pp. 417–420.

Hardt, Michael and Antonio Negri (2000), *Empire*, Cambridge, MA: Harvard University Press.

Hardt, Michael and Antonio Negri (2004), *Multitude: War and Democracy in the Age of Empire*, New York: Penguin.

Harrington, Louise (2007), 'The Train Nation: the Railway as a Leitmotif in South Asian Literature', in Michèle Lurdos and Judith Misrahi-Barak (eds), *Transport(s) in the British Empire and the Commonwealth*, Montpellier: Presses universitaires de la Méditerranée, pp. 289–307.

Harvey, David (2009), *Cosmopolitanism and the Geographies of Freedom*, New York: Columbia University Press.

Harvey, David (2009), *Spaces of Global Capital: A Theory of Uneven Geographical Development*, London: Verso.

Heidt, Sarah J. (2011), 'Teaching Stoker's *Dracula* with Multiple Film Versions: *Nosferatu*, *Dracula*, and *Pages from a Virgin's Diary*', in Abigail Burnham Bloom and Mary Sanders Pollock (eds), *Victorian Literature and Film Adaptation*, Amherst: Cambria, pp.183–204.

Hermansson, Casie (2015), 'Flogging Fidelity: In Defense of the (Un)Dead Horse', *Adaptation*, 8.2, pp. 147–160.

Hixson, Walter L. (2013), *American Settler Colonialism: A History*, New York: Palgrave Macmillan.

Hobson, Fred (1983), *Tell About the South: The Southern Rage to Explain*, Baton Rouge: Louisiana State University Press.

Holden, Stephen (2000), 'Film Review; Those Wacky, Drooling, Foaming, Biting Undead', *The New York Times*, 23 December <http://www.nytimes.com/2000/12/23/movies/film-review-those-wacky-drooling-foaming-biting-undead.html> (last accessed 5 January 2018).

Holt, Shari Hodges (2007), 'Dickens from a Postmodern Perspective: Alfonso Cuarón's *Great Expectations* for Generation X', *Dickens Studies Annual*, 38, pp. 69–92.

hooks, bell (2004), *We Real Cool: Black Men and Masculinity*, New York: Routledge.

Houston, Gail Turley (2005), *From Dickens to* Dracula*: Gothic, Economics, and Victorian Fiction*, Cambridge, Cambridge University Press.

Hurst, Rochelle (2008), 'Adaptation as an Undecidable: Fidelity and Binarity from Bluestone to Derrida', in David Kranz and Nancy C. Mellerski (eds), *In/Fidelity: Essays on Film Adaptation*, Newcastle: Cambridge Scholars Press, pp. 172–196.

Hutcheon, Linda (2006), *A Theory of Adaptation*, London: Routledge.

Jaher, Frederic Cople and Blair B. Kling (2008), 'Hollywood's India: The Meaning of RKO's *Gunga Din*', *Film and History*, 38.2, pp. 33–44.

James, Henry [1881] (1995), *The Portrait of a Lady*, New York: Norton.

Jameson, Fredric (1991), *Postmodernism or, the Cultural Logic of Late Capitalism*, Durham, NC: Duke University Press.

Jameson, Fredric (2011), 'Afterward: Adaptation as a Philosophical Problem', in Colin MacCabe, Rick Warner, Kathleen Murray (eds), *True to the Spirit: Film Adaptation and the Question of Fidelity*, Oxford: Oxford University press, pp. 215–234.

Jeffrey, Keith (2006), 'Crown, Communication and the Colonial Post: Stamps, the Monarchy and the British Empire', *The Journal of Imperial and Commonwealth History*, 34.1, pp. 45–70.

Jeffries, Stuart (2009), 'I'm the Luckiest Novelist in the World', *The Guardian*, 16 January, Web, 27 November 2010, <http://www.guardian.co.uk/books/2009/jan/16/danny- boyle-india> (last accessed 7 September 2017).

Jensen, Jeff and Dave Karger (2002), 'Desert Storm', *Entertainment Weekly*, 27 September, pp. 30–31.

Jhazbhay, Iqbal (2002), 'South African Political Islam: A Preliminary Approach towards Tracing the Call of Islam's Discourse(s) of Struggle', *Journal of Muslim Minority Affairs*, 22.1, pp. 225–231.

John, Juliet (2001), *Dickens's Villains: Melodrama, Character, Popular Culture*, London: Oxford University Press.

Johnson, Michael K. (2005), 'Not Telling the Story the Way It Happened: Alfonso Cuarón's *Great Expectations*', *Literature Film Quarterly*, 33.1, pp. 62–78.

Johnston, Susan (2004), 'Historical Picturesque: Adapting *Great Expectations* and *Sense and Sensibility*', *Mosaic*, 37.1, pp. 166–183.

Joslin, Lyndon W. (2017), *Count Dracula Goes to the Movies: Stoker's Novel Adapted*, 3rd edition, Jefferson, NC: McFarland.

Jöttkandt, Sigi (2005), *Acting Beautifully: Henry James and the Ethical Aesthetic*, Albany: State University of New York Press.

Katz, Pamela (2003), 'Directing Dickens: Alfonso Cuarón's *Great Expectations*', in John Glavin (ed.), *Dickens on Screen*, Cambridge: Cambridge University Press, pp. 95–103.

Keohane, Robert O. (1984), *After Hegemony: Cooperation and Discord in the World Political Economy*, Princeton: Princeton University Press.

Kincaid, James R. (2000), 'Dickens and the Construction of the Child', in Wendy S. Jacobson (ed.), *Dickens and the Children of Empire*, New York: Palgrave, pp. 29–41.

Kipling, Rudyard [1890] (1989), 'Gunga Din', *Complete Verse*, New York: Anchor, p. 404.

Lacan, Jacques, Bruce Fink (trans) [1966] (2006), *Écrits*, New York: Norton.

Lane, Anthony (2004), 'Power Plays', *The New Yorker*, 6 September, p. 87.

Larkin, Brian (2013), 'National Allegory', in Ajay Gehlawat (ed.), *The Slumdog Phenomenon: A Critical Anthology*, London: Anthem, pp. 3–8.

Lawrence, Kathleen Anne (2005), 'Osmond's Complaint: Gilbert Osmond's Mother and the Cultural Context of James's *The Portrait of a Lady*', *The Henry James Review* 26.1, pp. 52–67.

Leach, Jim (2011), *Film in Canada*, 2nd edition, Oxford: Oxford University Press.

Ledger, Sally (1997), *The New Woman: Fiction and Feminism at the Fin de Siècle*, Manchester: Manchester University Press.

Lee, Carol (2013), *A Child Called Freedom*, London: Thistle Publishing.

Lee, Klaudia Hiu Yen (2014), 'Rethinking "Global Dickens": The Case of the Cross-Cultural Transfer of *David Copperfield*', *Journal of Victorian Culture*, 19.1, pp. 63–78.

Leitch, Thomas (2007), *Film Adaptation and Its Discontents: From* Gone with the Wind *to* The Passion of the Christ, Baltimore: Johns Hopkins University Press.

Leitch, Thomas (2011), 'Introduction: Reframing the Victorians', in Burnham Bloom and Mary Sanders Pollock (eds), *Victorian Literature and Film Adaptation*, Abigail Amherst, New York: Cambria Press, pp. 1–24.

Lewis, Glenn (1987), *Australian Movies and the American Dream*, New York: Praeger.

Limbrick, Peter (2010), *Making Settler Cinemas: Film and Colonial Encounters in the United States, Australia, and New Zealand*, New York: Palgrave Macmillan.

Linder, Christoph (2002), 'Thackeray's Gourmet: Carnivals of Consumption in *Vanity Fair*', *Modern Philology*, 99.4, pp. 564–581.

López, Alfred J (2011), 'The Plantation as Archive: Images of "the South" in the Postcolonial World', *Comparative Literature*, 63:4, pp. 402–422.

Lowenstein, Stephen (2000), *My First Movie: 20 Celebrated Directors Talk about Their First Film*, New York: Penguin.

Lowenstein, Stephen (2008), *My First Movie Take Two: Ten Celebrated Directors Talk about Their First Films*, New York: Vintage.

Lucas, John (1992), *Charles Dickens: The Major Novels*, New York: Penguin.

Lyotard, Jean-François, Geoff Bennington and Brian Massumi (trans) (1984), *The Postmodern Condition: A Report on Knowledge*, Minneapolis: University of Minnesota Press.

McBratney, John (2002), *Imperial Subjects, Imperial Spaces, Rudyard Kipling's Fiction of the Native Born*, Columbus: Ohio University Press.

McClintock Pamela and Stephen Galloway (2017), 'Matt Damon's "The Great Wall" to Lose $75 Million; Future U.S.-China Productions in Doubt', *The Hollywood Reporter*, 2 March 2017, <https://www.hollywoodreporter.com/news/what-great-walls-box-office-flop-will-cost-studios-981602> (last accessed 11 November 2017).

McDaniel, June (2004), *Offering Flowers, Feeding Skulls: Popular Goddess Worship in West Bengal*, London: Oxford University Press.

McFarlane, Brian (1996), *Novel to Film: An Introduction to the Theory of Adaptation*, Oxford: Oxford University Press.

Macaulay, Thomas (2005), 'Minute on Indian Education (1835)', in Gaurav Desai and Supriya Nair (eds), *Postcolonialisms: An Anthology*, New Brunswick, NJ: Rutgers University Press, pp. 121–131.

Maccoby, Hyam (1986), 'The Wandering Jew as Sacred Executioner', in Galit Hasan-Rokem and Alan Dundes (eds), *The Wandering Jew: Essays in the Interpretation of a Christian Legend*, Bloomington: University of Indiana Press, pp. 236–260.

Machalias, Helen (2011), 'Enraptured with Every Scent and Flavor of the East?: Mira Nair's *Vanity Fair* as a Contrapuntal Film Adaptation', in Jane Stadler, Peta Mitchell, Adam Atkinson, Tricia Hopton (eds), *Pockets of Change: Adaptation and Cultural Transition*, New York: Lexington Books, pp. 43–56.

Mack, Katherine (2011), 'Remembering Winnie: Public Memory and the Truth and Reconciliation Commission of South Africa', in Kendall R. Phillips and G. Mitchell Reyes (eds), *Global Memoryscapes: Contesting Remembrance in a Transnational Age*, Tuscaloosa: University of Alabama Press, pp. 133–158.

Mandivenga, Ephraim C. (2000), 'The Cape Muslims and the Indian Muslims of South Africa: A Comprehensive Analysis', *Journal of Muslim Minority Affairs*, 20.2, pp. 347–352.

Manlove, Clifford T. (2012), '"An Image of Africa"': Representations of Modern Colonialism in Africa in Peter Jackson's *King Kong*', in *Hollywood's Africa after 1994*, (ed.) MaryEllen Higgins, Athens, OH: Ohio University Press 125–141.

Martin, Daniel (2012), 'Some Trick of The Moonlight: Seduction and The Moving Image in Bram Stoker's *Dracula*', *Victorian Literature and Culture*, 40, pp. 523–547.

Masilela, Ntongela and Isabel Balseiro (2003), 'Introduction', in Ntongela Masilela and Isabel Balseiro (eds), *To Change Reels: Film and Culture in South Africa*, Detroit: Wayne State University Press, pp. 1–14.

Mason, A. E. W. [1902] (2001), *The Four Feathers*, New York: Penguin.

Mason, John Edwin (2002), '"A Faith for Ourselves": Slavery, Sufism, and Conversion to Islam at the Cape', *South African Historical Journal*, 46, pp. 3–24.

Mast, Gerald and Bruce F. Kawin (2003), *A Short History of the Movies*, 8th edition, New York: Longman.

Mayer, Geoff and Keith Beattie (2006), 'Introduction', in Geoff Mayer and Keith Beattie (eds), *The Cinema of Australia and New Zealand*, New York: Wallflower, pp. 1–10.

Meintjes, Helen and Sonja Giese (2006), 'Spinning the Epidemic: The Making of Mythologies of Orphanhood in the Context of AIDS', *Childhood*, 13, pp. 407–430.

Mendes, Ana Cristina (2010), 'Showcasing India Unshining: Film Tourism in Danny Boyle's *Slumdog Millionaire*', *Third Text*, 24.4, pp. 471–479.

Michie, Elsie B. (2009), 'Rich Woman, Poor Woman: Toward Anthropology of the Nineteenth-Century Marriage Plot', PMLA, 124.2, pp. 421–436.

Mohl, Raymond A. (2005), 'The *Nuevo* New South', in James C. Cobb and William Stueck (eds), *Globalization and the American South*, Athens, GA: University of Georgia Press, pp. 66–99.

Moore, Stephen D. (2004), 'Mark and Empire: "Zealot" and "Postcolonial" Readings', in Catherine Keller, Michael Nausner and Mayra Rivera (eds), *Postcolonial Theologies: Divinity and Empire,* St Louis: Chalice Press, pp. 134–148.

Moore-Gilbert, B. J. (1986), *Kipling and Orientalism*, London: Croom Helm.

Moss, Marilyn Ann (2004), *Giant: George Stevens a Life on Film*, Madison: University of Wisconsin Press.

Moya, Ana (2010), 'The Politics of Re-presenting *Vanity Fair*: Mira Nair's Becky Sharp', *ATLANTIS, Journal of the Spanish Association of Anglo-American Studies*, 32.2, pp. 73–87.

Moya, Ana and Gemma López (2008), '"I'm a Wild Success": Postmodern Dickens/Victorian Cuarón', *Dickens Quarterly*, 25.3, pp. 172–189.

Mudambi, Anjana (2013), 'Another Look at Orientalism: (An)Othering in *Slumdog Millionaire*', *The Howard Journal of Communications*, 24, pp. 275–292.

Muir, John Kenneth (2006), *Mercy in Her Eyes: The Films of Mira Nair*, New York: Applause Theatre & Cinema Books.

Mulvey, Laura [1975] (2000), 'Visual Pleasure and Narrative Cinema', in Ann Kaplan (ed.), *Feminism and Film*, Oxford: Oxford University Press, pp. 35–47.

Murray, Simone (2008), 'Materializing Adaptation Theory: The Adaptation Industry', *Literature Film Quarterly*, 36.1, pp. 4–20.

Naficy, Hamid (2001), *An Accented Cinema: Exilic and Diasporic Filmmaking*, Princeton: Princeton University Press.

Nair, Mira (2004), *Vanity Fair: Bringing Thackeray's Timeless Novel to the Screen*, New York: Newmarket Press.

Nealon, Jeffrey T. (1998), *Alterity Politics: Ethics and Performative Subjectivity,* Durham, NC: Duke University Press.

Nericcio, William Anthony (2007), *Tex(t)-Mex: Seductive Hallucinations of the 'Mexican' in America*, Austin: University of Texas Press.

Newman, Michael Z. (2011), *Indie: An American Film Culture*, New York: Columbia University Press.

Nunokawa, Jeff (2003), *The Afterlife of Property: Domestic Security and the Victorian Novel*, Princeton: Princeton University Press.

Okiche, Wilfred (2017), 'From Figurine to Fifty: How Omoni Oboli Became Nollywood's Box Office Queen', *YNaija*, https://ynaija.com/figurine-fifty-omoni-oboli-became-nollywoods-box-office-queen/ (last accessed 14 May 2017).

Oliver Twist [1948] (1998), film, directed by David Lean, UK: Criterion Collection.

O'Regan (1996), Tom, 'Australian Cinema as a National Cinema', in Alan Williams (ed.), *Film and Nationalism*, New Brunswick, NJ: Rutgers University Press, pp. 89–136.

O'Regan Tom (1996), *Australian National Cinema,* London: Routledge.

O'Sullivan, John (2002), 'New Myths for Old: The Case of *The Four Feathers*', *National Review*, *EBSCO*, 5 November.

Oyêwùmí, Oyèrónké (2005), 'Colonizing Bodies and Minds: Gender and Colonialism', in

Gaurav Desai and Supriya Nair (eds), *Postcolonialisms: An Anthology*, New Brunswick, NJ: Rutgers University Press, pp. 339–361.

A Personal Journey with Martin Scorsese through American Movies (1995), film, Directed by Martin Scorsese and Michael Henry Wilson, UK: Miramax.

Peters, Laura (2000), *Orphan Texts: Victorian Orphans, Culture and Empire*, Manchester: Manchester University Press.

Petrakis, John (2002), 'Period Piece', *Christian Century*, 119.20: p. 49.

Petrie, Graham (2017), 'Dickens in Denmark: Four Danish Variations of His Novels', in John Glavin (ed.), *Adapting Dickens*, London: Routledge, pp. 185–193.

Plotz, Judith (2010), 'How "The White Man's Burden" Lost Its Scare-Quotes; or Kipling and the New American Empire', in Caroline Rooney and Kaori Nagai (eds), *Kipling and Beyond: Patriotism, Globalisation, and Postcolonialism*, London: Palgrave Macmillan, pp. 37–57.

Pointer, Michael (1996), *Charles Dickens on the Screen: The Film, Television, and Video Adaptations*, Lanham, MD: Scarecrow Press.

Ponzanesi, Sandra (2014), *The Postcolonial Culture Industry: Icons, Markets, Mythologies*, New York: Palgrave Macmillan.

The Portrait of a Lady (1996), film, directed by Jane Campion, US/UK: Focus Features.

Proudly South African: A Boy Called Twist (2010), 25 November, <http://www.writingstudio.co.za/page693.html>, last accessed 6 July 2017.

Rao, Shakuntala (2007), 'The Globalization of Bollywood: An Ethnography of Non-EliteAudiences in India', *The Communication Review*, 10, pp. 57–76.

Rastegar, Kamran (2015), *Surviving Images: Cinema, War, and Cultural Memory in the Middle East*, Oxford: Oxford University Press.

Ray, Robert (1985), *A Certain Tendency of the Hollywood Cinema*, Princeton: Princeton University Press.

Retamar, Roberto Fernández (2005), 'Caliban: Notes towards a Discussion of Culture in Our America', in Gaurav Desai and Supriya Nair (eds), *Postcolonialisms: An Anthology*, New Brunswick, NJ: Rutgers University Press, pp. 65–70.

Richards, Jeffrey (1973), *Visions of Yesterday*, London: Routledge.

Rivera, John-Michael (2004), 'Embodying Greater Mexico: Maria Amparo Ruiz de Burton and the Reconstruction of the Mexican Question', in Jon Smith and Deborah Cohn (eds), *Look Away! The U.S. South in New World Studies*, Durham, NC: Duke University Press, pp. 451–470.

Romero, Lora (1995), 'Nationalism and Internationalism: Domestic Differences in a Postcolonial World', *American Literature*, 67.4, pp. 795–800.

Roy, Anjali Gera (2010). 'Is Everyone Saying "Shava Shava" to Bollywood Bhangra?', in Rini Bhattacharya Metha and Rajeshwari Pandharipande (eds), *Bollywood and Globalization: Indian Popular Cinema, Nation, and Diaspora*, New York: Anthem, pp. 35–50.

Rushdie, Salman (1982), 'The Empire Writes Back with a Vengeance', *The Times*, (UK) 3 July, p. 8.

Said, Edward W. (1993), *Culture and Imperialism*, New York: Vintage Books.

Said, Edward W. (1978), *Orientalism*, New York: Vintage Books.

Samuel, Simon (2007), *A Postcolonial Reading of Mark's Story of Jesus*, London: T. & T. Clark.

Sánchez, Rosara and Beatrice Pita (2014), 'Rethinking Settler Colonialism', *American Quarterly*, 66.4, pp. 1039–1055.

Sanders, Julie (2006), *Adaptation and Appropriation*, London: Routledge.

Sanner, Kristin (2005), 'Missing Mothers, Feminized Fathers in *The Portrait of a Lady*', *The Henry James Review*, 26.2, pp. 147–167.

Sarris, Andrew (1968), *The American Cinema: Directors and Directions*, New York: Da Capo Press.

Schatz, Thomas (1981), *Hollywood Genres: Formulas, Filmmaking, and the Studio System*, New York: McGraw Hill.

Scheib, Ronnie (2006), review of *A Boy Called Twist*, *Variety*, 23 January, 401.10, pp. 35–36.

Sebastian, A. J. (2009), 'Voicing Slum-subaltern in *Slumdog Millionaire*', *Journal of Alternative Perspectives in the Social Sciences*, 1.3, pp. 897–920.

Sedgwick, Eve Kosofsky (1985), *Between Men: English Literature and Male Homosocial Desire*, New York: Columbia University Press.

Skal, David J. (2004), *Hollywood Gothic: The Tangled Web of Dracula from Novel to Stage to Screen*, New York: Faber and Faber.

Sharma, Alpana (2007), 'Body Matters: The Politics of Provocation in Mira Nair's Films', in Julie F. Codell (ed.), *Genre, Gender, Race, and World Cinema*, Oxford: Blackwell, pp. 180–194.

Sharma, Alpana (2012), '*Slumdog Millionaire*: The Film, the Reception, the Book, the Global,' *Literature Film Quarterly*, 40.3, pp.197–215.

Shillingsburg, Peter (2001), *William Makepeace Thackeray: A Literary Life*, New York: Palgrave.

Simmons, Rochelle (2006), '*The Piano*', in Geoff Mayer and Keith Beattie (eds), *The Cinema of Australia and New Zealand,* New York: Wallflower, pp. 149–156.

Slumdog Millionaire (2008), film, directors. Danny Boyle and Loveleen Tandan, UK: Fox Searchlight.

Smith, Andrew (2003), 'Demonising the Americans: Bram Stoker's Postcolonial Gothic', *Gothic Studies*, 5.2, pp. 20–31

Smith, Grahame (2003), *Dickens and the Dream of Cinema*, Manchester: Manchester University Press.

Smith, Jon and Deborah Cohn (2004), 'From Plantation to Hacienda: Greater Mexico and the U.S. South', in Jon Smith and Deborah Cohn, *Look Away! The U.S. South in New World Studies*, Durham, NC: Duke University Press, pp. 447–449.

Smith, Sheila A. (1980), *The Other Nation: The Poor in English Novels of the 1840s and 1850s*, Oxford: Oxford University Press.

Smyth, J. E. (2004), 'The Three Ages of Imperial Cinema: From the Death of Gordon to *The Return of the King*', in Janet Brennan Croft (ed.), Essays on Peter Jackson's *The Lord of the Rings*, Albuquerque: Mythopoeic Press, pp. 20–46.

Spivak, Gayatri Chakravorty (2001), 'A Critique of Post Colonial Reason [Can the Subaltern Speak?]', in Vincent B. Leitch (ed.), *The Norton Anthology of Theory and Criticism*, New York: Norton, pp. 2197–2208.

Spivak, Gayatri Chakravorty (1987), 'Subaltern Studies: Deconstructing Historiography', in *Other Worlds: Essays in Cultural Politics*, New York: Routledge, pp. 197–221.

Steele, David (1983), 'Britain and Egypt 1882–1914: The Containment of Islamic Nationalism', in Keith M. Wilson (ed.), *Imperialism and Nationalism in the Middle East: The Anglo-Egyptian Experience 1882–1982*, London: Mansell Publishing, pp. 1–25.

Stevens, George and Paul Cronin (2004), *George Stevens: Interviews*, Jackson: University Press of Mississippi.

Stevenson, Lionel (1947), *The Showman of Vanity Fair: The Life of William Makepeace Thackeray*, New York: Scribner's.

Stoker, Bram [1897] (1997), *Dracula*, New York: Norton.

Stone, Harry (1993), 'Dickens and the Jews', in Fred Kaplan (ed.), *Oliver Twist*, New York: Norton, pp. 448–453.

Sullivan, Sharon (2004), 'The Unconscious Life of Race: Freudian Resources for Critical Race

Theory', in John Mills (ed.), *Rereading Freud: Psychoanalysis through Philosophy*, Albany: State University of New York Press, pp. 195–218.

Svetkey, Benjamin (2004), 'Monsters, Inc', *Entertainment Weekly* 757, 26 March.

Swarup, Vikas (2005), *Q&A*, New York: Scribner's.

Tayob, Abdulkader (2008), 'Islamic Politics and South Africa: Between Identity and Utopia', *South African Historical Journal*, 60.4, pp. 583–599.

Thackeray, William Makepeace [1847] (1994), *Vanity Fair: A Novel Without a Hero*, New York: Norton.

Tibbetts, John C (2003), review of *The Four Feathers*, *American Historical Review*, Feburary, pp. 310–311.

Tincknell, Estella (2013), *Jane Campion and Adaptation: Angels, Demons and Unsettling Voices*, New York: Palgrave Macmillan.

Tinter, Adeline R. (1991), *The Cosmopolitan World of Henry James: An Intertextual Study*, Baton Rouge: Louisiana State University Press.

Tompkins, Joseph (2009), 'What's the Deal with Soundtrack Albums? Metal Music and the Customized Aesthetics of Contemporary Horror', *Cinema Journal*, 49.1, pp. 65–81.

Tryon, Chuck (2013), *On-Demand Culture: Digital Delivery and the Future of Movies*, New Brunswick, NJ. Rutgers University Press.

UNESCO Press (2009), 'Nollywood Rivals Bollywood in Film/Video Production', UNESCO 20 May.

Vanfasse, Nathalie (2012), 'Dickens in Twenty-First Century India: A Study of the Novel *Q&A* by Vikas Swarup and its Film Adaptation by Danny Boyle', in Alain Jumeau and Sara Thornton (eds), *Persistent Dickens*, *Etudes anglaises*, 65.1, January–March, pp. 7–18.

Vanity Fair (2004), film, directed by Mira Nair, UK/USA: Focus Features.

Van der Heijden and Sharlene Swartz (2010), 'Bereavement, Silence and Culture within a Peer-Led HIV/AIDS-Prevention Strategy for Vulnerable Children in South Africa', *African Journal of AIDS* Research 9.1, pp. 41–50.

Van Helsing (2004) film, directed by Stephen Sommers, US: Universal.

Van Wœrkens, Martine, Catherine Tihanyi (trans) [1995] (2002), *The Strangled Traveler: Colonial Imaginings and the Thugs of India*, Chicago: University of Chicago Press.

Vatnsdal, Caclum (2004), *They Came from Within: A History of Canadian Horror Cinema*, Winnipeg: Arbeiter Ring Publishing.

Veracini, Lorenzo (2015), *The Settler Colonial Present*, New York: Palgrave Macmillan.

Verhoven, Deb (2009), *Jane Campion*, London: Routledge.

Voeltz, Richard A. (2010), 'Images and Representations of British Imperialism: Cinematic Adaptations of A. E. W. Mason's *The Four Feathers*', *Interdisciplinary Humanities* 27.1, pp.12–27.

Walker, Casey M. (2013), 'Intimate Cities: *The Portrait of a Lady* and the Poetics of Metropolitan Space', *Studies in the Novel*, volume 45, number 2, pp. 161–177.

Walton, Priscilla L. (1997), 'Jane and James Go to the Movies: Post-Colonial Portraits of a Lady', *Henry James Review*, 18:2, pp.187–190.

Warburg, Gabriel R (1992), *Historical Discord in the Nile Valley*, Evanston: Northwestern University Press.

Weaver, Tom, Michael Brunas, and John Brunas (2007), *Universal Horrors: The Studio's Classic Films, 1931–1946*, 2nd edition, Jefferson, NC and London: McFarland & Company.

Wee, C. J. W-L (1994), 'Christian Manliness and National Identity: The Problematic Constructions of a Racially "Pure" Nation', in Donald E. Hall (ed.), *Muscular Christianity: Embodying the Victorian Age*, Cambridge: Cambridge University Press, pp. 3–16.

Weissman, Judith (1988), 'Women and Vampires: *Dracula* as a Victorian Novel', in Margaret

L. Carter (ed.), *Dracula: The Vampire and the Critics*, Ann Arbor: University of Michigan Press.

White, Jerry (2006), 'Introduction', in *The Cinema of Canada*, New York: Wallflower, pp. 1–13.

Wilkinson-Latham, Robert (1976), *The Sudan Campaigns: 1881–98*, Oxford: Osprey Press.

Williams, Raymond (1973), *The Country and the City*, Oxford: Oxford University Press.

Williamson, Milly (2005), *The Lure of the Vampire: Gender, Fiction, and Fandom from Bram Stoker to Buffy*, London: Wallflower.

Wood, Ellen Meiksins (2005), *Empire of Capital*, New York: Verso.

Wood, Robin (2015), 'Burying the Undead: The Use and Obsolescence of Count Dracula', in Barry Keith Grant (ed.), *The Dread of Difference: Gender and the Horror Film* 2nd edition, Austin: University of Texas Press, pp. 388–402.

Wood, Robin (1998), *Sexual Politics and Narrative Film*, New York: Columbia University Press.

Yu, Eric Kwan-Wai (2006), 'Productive Fear: Labor, Sexuality, and Mimicry in Bram Stoker's *Dracula*', *Texas Studies in Literature and Language*, 48.2 (2006): 145–170.

Žižek, Slavoj (1992), *Enjoy Your Symptom!: Jacques Lacan in Hollywood and Out*, New York: Routledge.

Index

CPSIA information can be obtained
at www.ICGtesting.com
Printed in the USA
JSHW050446090920
7725JS00002B/49

9 781474 429955